The Personal Weblog

Language and Text Studies

Edited by
Alexander Brock and Annette Schiller

Volume 14

PETER LANG
EDITION

Peter Schildhauer

The Personal Weblog

A Linguistic History

PETER LANG
EDITION

Bibliographic Information published by the Deutsche Nationalbibliothek
The Deutsche Nationalbibliothek lists this publication in the Deutsche Nationalbibliografie; detailed bibliographic data is available in the internet at http://dnb.d-nb.de.

Library of Congress Cataloging-in-Publication Data
Names: Schildhauer, Peter, 1986- author.
Title: The personal weblog : a linguistic history / Peter Schildhauer.
Description: Frankfurt am Main ; New York : Peter Lang, [2016] | Series: Hallesche Sprach- und Textforschung. Language and Text Studies. Recherches linguistiques et textuelles; Band 14 | Thesis (Ph.D) — Halle (Saale), Universitäts- und Landesbibliothek Sachsen-Anhalt, 2014. | Originally published as: "Textsorten im Internet zwischen Wandel und Konstanz", 2014. | Includes bibliographical references.
Identifiers: LCCN 2015040979| ISBN 9783631662748 (Print) | ISBN 9783653054408 (E-Book)
Subjects: LCSH: Schildhauer, Peter, 1986—Blogs. | Historical linguistics—Blogs. | Linguistics—Blogs. | Internet. | Online authorship | Corpora (Linguistics)—Technological innovations. Classification: LCC P140 .S29 2016 | DDC 302.23/14—dc23 LC record available at http://lccn.loc.gov/2015040979

ISSN 0941-4134
ISBN 978-3-631-66274-8 (Print)
E-ISBN 978-3-653-05440-8 (E-Book)
DOI 10.3726/978-3-653-05440-8

Peter Lang Edition is an Imprint of Peter Lang GmbH.

Peter Lang – Frankfurt am Main · Bern · Bruxelles · New York · Oxford · Warszawa · Wien

This publication has been peer reviewed.

www.peterlang.com

Acknowledgements

This book is based on my PhD thesis *Textsorten im Internet zwischen Wandel und Konstanz: Eine diachrone Studie der Textsorte Personal Weblog*, which I defended at the English Department of Martin Luther University Halle-Wittenberg University in summer 2014. Part of this thesis was funded by the graduate scholarship of Saxony-Anhalt. In autumn 2014, the proposal of this book won Peter Lang's award for young academics. I am very grateful for this reward as it enabled me to transform a bulky thesis into what I hope is a concise and readable genre history.

I would particularly like to thank Alexander Brock, who not only supervised my PhD but has become a mentor and role model for me outside academia. My colleague and friend Jana Pflaeging contributed with sharp thoughts, critical questions and her unique way of visualising linguistic theory invaluable parts to this book. I would like to thank her, Rebecca Didt, Jennifer Hahn and Hannah Stiehler for their excellent proof-reading. Of course, any inaccuracies – both content- and language-wise – are utterly in my responsibility.

Usually, projects turn out to be more complicated and challenging than expected. The same is true for the present book, which has become more than just a shortened translation of my thesis. Additionally, I wrote most parts of it during a very difficult phase of my life. I would therefore like to thank those who have helped me through this time, most importantly my father Karl-Frieder Grube, Robert Deutschmann, Hannah Stiehler and, of course, Jana Pflaeging. Finally, I would like to thank my sons for being – just the way they are. Karl and Finn, this book is dedicated to you.

Contents Overview

Table of Contents

0 Introduction

0.1 The Right Time for a History of the Personal Weblog

In 1995, blogging pioneer Dave Winer states:

> Imagine being able to find out what's *really* going on in anyone's life. What if everyone wrote about their issues. We could all learn from each other. Friendship would mean a lot more. We could grow more quickly, accomplish more in our lives, live more richly, have more fun. (Dave Winer 1995 in Rosenberg 2009: 53)

No one in Winer's personal environment could believe back then that this vision might turn into reality only a couple of years later. At that time, it was simply impossible to imagine that millions of Internet users worldwide would keep their own websites in order to make their thoughts and experiences public and exchange their views with others. After all, the World Wide Web (WWW) of 1995 – only initiated a couple of years before by Tim Berners-Lee – was mainly a playground for enthusiasts who were excited about new developments and informed each other whenever they found something new. And there was something new literally every day – more and more users got involved in investigating the exhilarating potentials of the WWW. Eventually an abundance of new forms of communication emerged: Chats, discussion forums, personal and corporate websites, FAQ-sites – and *blogs.*

Example 1: Flutterby *(1998) - Weblog of the 1990s*

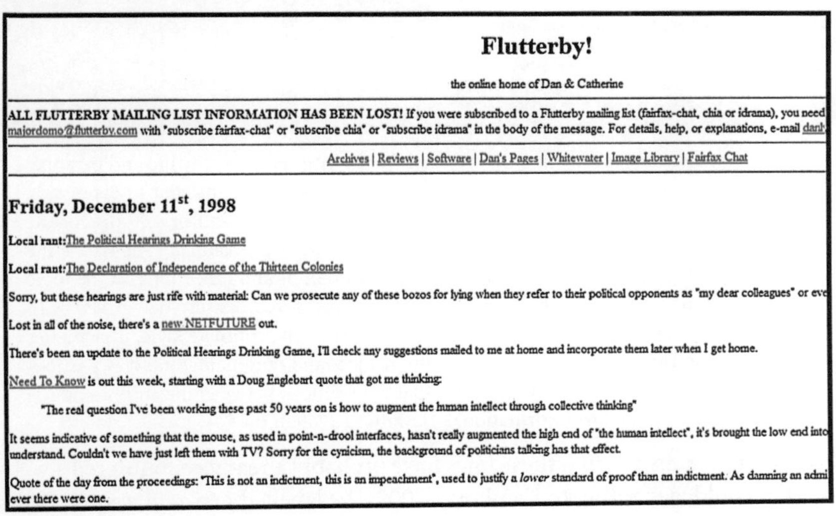

Flutterby!

the online home of Dan & Catherine

ALL FLUTTERBY MAILING LIST INFORMATION HAS BEEN LOST! If you were subscribed to a Flutterby mailing list (fairfax-chat, chia or idrama), you need
majordomo@flutterby.com with "subscribe fairfax-chat" or "subscribe chia" or "subscribe idrama" in the body of the message. For details, help, or explanations, e-mail dan

Archives | Reviews | Software | Dan's Pages | Whitewater | Image Library | Fairfax Chat

Friday, December 11st, 1998

Local rant: The Political Hearings Drinking Game

Local rant: The Declaration of Independence of the Thirteen Colonies

Sorry, but these hearings are just rife with material: Can we prosecute any of these bozos for lying when they refer to their political opponents as "my dear colleagues" or eve

Lost in all of the noise, there's a new NETFUTURE out.

There's been an update to the Political Hearings Drinking Game, I'll check any suggestions mailed to me at home and incorporate them later when I get home.

Need To Know is out this week, starting with a Doug Englebart quote that got me thinking:

> "The real question I've been working these past 50 years on is how to augment the human intellect through collective thinking"

It seems indicative of something that the mouse, as used in point-n-drool interfaces, hasn't really augmented the high end of "the human intellect", it's brought the low end into
understand. Couldn't we have just left them with TV? Sorry for the cynicism, the background of politicians talking has that effect.

Quote of the day from the proceedings: "This is not an indictment, this is an impeachment", used to justify a *lower* standard of proof than an indictment. As damning an admi
ever there were one.

Blogs, still called *weblogs* back then, emerged in the second half of the 1990s. A typical weblog of these early days is shown in Example 1. However, what comes to mind first when reading the term *personal weblog* is probably more similar to Example 2. This example shows a *personal weblog* and therefore a form of blogging that developed several years after the first weblogs of the mid-to-late 1990s. The personal weblog is probably "the best known, perhaps the prototypical representative of the species [blog, P.S.] in public awareness" (Mauranen 2013a: 7) and can be defined as follows:

Example 2: Cheré Takes on the World (2008) – *Personal Weblog*

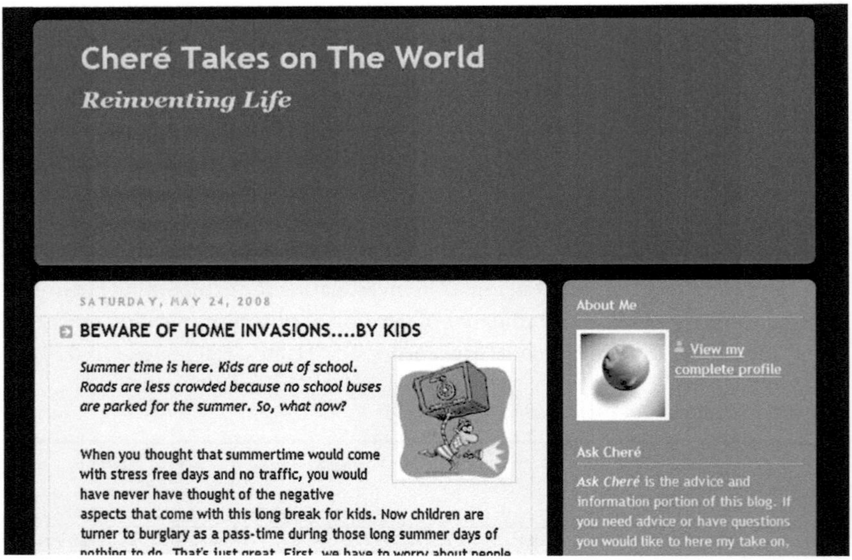

> The personal weblog is a weblog that typically deals with the everyday life and personal matters of the author. It can also be about a specific hobby or dedicated to expressing the author's opinion, if this entails an element of self-reference and/or self-disclosure. Further, the personal weblog has an intimate, sometimes confessional, style where the author provides the readers with subjective representations and reflections on the topic discussed. Finally, the personal weblog can be more or less densely networked with other weblogs, and through the author's self-disclosure and intimate style, it facilitates rather symmetrical communication with the readers and commentators. It is particularly supportive of strong ties in the sense that the relations between the author and the readers are more than just informational. (Lomborg 2009: n.p.)

The fact that many reading these lines have probably already encountered a website that could, according to Lomborg (2009), be labelled *personal weblog* shows that this genre has had significant impact on the genre landscape of the WWW. In addition, the personal weblog looks back on a history of roughly 15 years at the time of writing this book – even close to 20 if the weblog-beginnings of the mid-to-late 1990s are also counted. On the web, this is a very long time. Personal weblogs have seen many developments come and go, they were *Web 2.0* before the concept even existed (Schildhauer 2015: 194) and later, most importantly, have successfully competed with rivals such as Facebook and Twitter. What makes the genre even more interesting are its manifold relations to other established genres: The diary, which has been proposed as *the* ancestor of the personal weblog,[1] is, in fact only one of many – both on- and offline. This turns the personal weblog into an interesting subject for everyone affiliated to research in genre, genre relations and genre change. Most intriguingly, the personal weblog provides us with the rare opportunity of documenting not only genre change but also genre birth.

Of course, there are numerous studies which investigate blogs (and personal weblogs in particular) from various angles. However, since Herring et al. (2006), there have been no linguistic studies on the history of blogs. If blogging history is mentioned (e.g., by Miller & Shepherd 2009; Mauranen 2013a: 13), it's usually the history as told by bloggers themselves (e.g., Blood 2000). While this *view from within* is certainly important, and is also taken into account in the present book, we should not neglect the actual blogs themselves, investigating *what* bloggers do on personal weblogs, *in what way* and *how this changes, or doesn't change, over time*. Certainly a lot has changed as far as Examples 1 and 2 are concerned – but much also remained stable and is not apparent at first glance.

After 15 (or 20) years of blogging, then, this is the right time for a *linguistic* history of the personal weblog. The genre has many interesting stories to tell and this book would like to share at least some of them – from a media linguistic point of view.

0.2 Outline of the Book

This book is based on my PhD thesis, which I defended in summer 2014 at Martin-Luther University Halle-Wittenberg (Schildhauer 2014). However, I planned the present book not only as a translation of that thesis but also saw it also as an opportunity to provide a more readable, concise, revised and updated account of the history of the personal weblog. With this in mind, I took several

1 For a critical view, see Bündgens-Kosten (forthc.: 4.2.1).

shortcuts and also left aside much of the methodological argument provided in my PhD thesis; this was aimed at satisfying the requirements of a committee, not the curiosity of a reader merely intrigued by the subject. Where appropriate, I will reference relevant passages in Schildhauer (2014) for those interested in a more elaborate argument.

This book is divided into three parts. Part A introduces the background of the study presented here and gives an outline of its theoretical framework, method and research corpus. Chapter 1 approaches the concept *genre* from several angles. As genres are complex phenomena, this chapter introduces the descriptive dimensions *communication form*, *situation*, *function* and *multimodal structure,* which will be used later to describe several aspects of the personal weblog in a structured way. This chapter also develops a model suitable to describe genre change and introduces several *types* or *patterns* of genre change as necessary tools for the linguistic history of the personal weblog. Many of the considerations in chapter 1 are illustrated with examples from the research corpus this book is based on. This corpus is called DIABLOC (*diachronic blog corpus*) and is described in detail in chapter 2. Chapter 3 closes part A with some general remarks concerning methodology. This chapter is rather short as I provide only an outline of the *general* methodology here. Each chapter of the main part is introduced by a section entitled *What I Did | What I Read*, which reviews research relevant to the topical section and methods leading to the results presented in the respective chapter.

Part B addresses each of the descriptive dimensions introduced in chapter 1 in turn. It opens in chapter 4 with an account of the blog communication form (that is, technology and software which blogs are based on). Chapter 5 addresses several parameters of the communicative situation of personal weblogs such as authorship (5.5 and 5.6), the bloggers' ideas about their audience (5.7), communicative maxims guiding the production and reception of blog posts (5.8) and others. Chapter 6 then turns to structural concerns, for instance layout and design (6.3.1), language use (6.4.2), image types (6.4.3) and language-image links (6.4.4). The results from chapters 4 to 6 are fused in chapter 7, which deals with the purposes of blogging. This chapter first describes several types of blog posts (7.2 to 7.5) and then moves on to investigate their frequencies (7.6).

Part C provides a synthesis of the results from two different perspectives. Chapter 8 draws on the previous chapters to provide a concise history of the personal weblog, including the weblog as its online-ancestor. While the chapters 4 to 7 are, in fact, separate histories of several related aspects of the personal weblog, these are brought together for a coherent account in chapter 8. Chapter 9 addresses issues of more theoretical concern. 9.1 turns to the question of *why* genres change and shows how Keller's (1990) *Invisible Hand Theory* can be applied to some phenomena of the history of the personal weblog. Chapter 9.2 broadens the view to stability and change of web-based genres in general and situates the present book in the respective research landscape. Chapter 10 closes this book with a summary and questions for further research, as much remains to be done both regarding the personal weblog and the history of web-based genres in general.

Part A: Background

1 The Dynamics of Genre

The question of what *constitutes* a personal weblog is only seemingly straightforward. Indeed, there are several perspectives which could be and have been taken into account, for instance:

- Is a personal weblog about its set-up as a dynamic web page with new entries appearing on top first (Schlobinski & Siever 2005a: 9)?
- Is a personal weblog characterised by a special relationship between blog authors and their readers, forming micro-communities of shared interest (Mauranen 2013a: 13)?
- Is it a diary-like practice of sharing personal experiences (Schildhauer 2013)?

In the course of this book, it will become obvious that the personal weblog is all of this at once and more (see, for example, Lomborg 2009 cited above). Without anticipating too much of what will be dealt with in the following chapters, we can draw a preliminary conclusion: the personal weblog is a complex subject which has to be approached from various angles.

The concept of *genre*, which "has made remarkable ascent in linguistic theory in the past 20 years" (Heyd 2008: 191), provides an appropriate lens through which this complex subject can be studied. Genres are, in fact, a fusion of all aspects addressed by the questions above: structure (for example, arrangement of entries on a blog-page), situation (for instance, authors and their readers) and the function of a particular and recurrent kind of language[2] use such as sharing personal experiences (Devitt 2009: 30). In what follows, I will highlight important facets and current trends in the discussion of the genre concept. In order to do so I will draw on several strands of research:

- The "New Rhetoric" tradition following Miller's (1984) seminal article *Genre as Social Action*: Genre researchers who can be subsumed under this label (e.g., Bazerman 1994; Berkenkotter & Huckin 1993, 1995; Swales 1990 and others) are convinced that genres are essentially social and cultural phenomena (see also Luginbühl 2014b: 25).
- German text linguistics, where '*Textsorte*' has become a central concept: Adamzik (1995: 14–21) points out that the term '*Textsorte*' has gained two

2 Below, I'll argue for a multimodal view of texts and genres, with language being only *one* sign system employed in a specific situation for particular purposes (others being, e.g., *image, layout* and *typography*).

rather distinct readings over the years. Studies applying a *specific reading* such as Brinker (2010), Heinemann (2000a, 2000b), Heinemann & Heinemann (2002) as well as Heinemann & Viehweger (1991) seek to develop systems of classification in which 'Textsorten' are defined by a rigid set of features. Following an *unspecific* reading of the term, 'Textsorten' are rather seen as groups of texts which, to a varying extent, share features on a number of heterogeneous dimensions. This approach, taken, for example, by Luginbühl (2014) and Schildhauer (2014), does not aim at rigid and homogeneous typologies but at *describing* 'Textsorten'/genres with a flexible apparatus tailored to the needs of the respective subject under investigation. The unspecific reading is the one that this book is based on and which is implied when I use the term *genre*.

- Media linguistics (e.g., Burger & Luginbühl 2014; Luginbühl 2015) does not only contribute a focus on mass media, but also on aspects such as communication forms and the relationships between language and other sign systems, or *modes*, employed in a text. For instance, *image* as a mode and language-image-links have been researched extensively over the past years (see, e.g., the volume Klemm & Stöckl 2011).

In this chapter, I'll highlight those aspects of these strands of research that are necessary to pave the way for the remainder of this book.[3]

1.1 Genres as Categories of Everyday Life

1.1.1 Genres and Communities

I use the term *genre* here to denote categories of everyday life, i.e. ethnocategories, which group texts according to certain similarities. These categories acquire labels in the community which makes use of them. For instance, genres such as cooking recipe and weather forecast are part of a wider community of English speakers than, say, conference panel proposals, which are, predominantly, more familiar to members of academia. This ethnographic view of genres was proposed first by Miller (1984) in her influential article "Genre as Social Action". Other members of the *Rhetorical School* follow her focus on ethnocategories and the communicative function of genres (see, e.g., Swales 1990; Askehave & Swales 2001).

In her studies on blogs, Miller & Shepherd extend Miller's earlier approach, stating that "when a type of discourse or communicative action acquires a common

3 For a more detailed account, please see Luginbühl (2014b: esp. chapters 2 and 4) as well as Schildhauer (2014: chapters 2 and 3).

name within a given context or community, that's a good sign it's functioning as a genre" (Miller & Sheperd 2004: 1). The current study, too, takes the community's labels as a starting point for genre analysis. In chapter 3, the question of *how* this was put into practice is addressed. For now, let us turn to another related question.

1.1.2 What Is the Blogging Community?

While Miller's basic assumptions appear intuitively plausible, they also entail a central problem: genres can never be adequately described without referring to their community (Miller 1994: 72–74). This approach works well for relatively clearly defined communities such as academia or institutional discourse (Bazerman 1994; Berkenkotter & Huckin 1995; Schryer 1993; Swales 1990). The blogging community, however, appears to be a highly dynamic, diverse and huge construct, with millions of blogs registered in 2013. Mauranen (2013a: 12) and Puschmann (Puschmann 2010: 24–25; 63) therefore plausibly ask: what is the blogging community and how can we define it? Mauranen (2013a: 12–13) suggests thinking of it as the circle of regular readers which forms around an individual blog. She states that it is not communities which cause the emergence of genres but genres which cause the emergence of communities.

I'd like, however, to distinguish between two notions: Firstly, we need to take the *audience* of a specific blog into account. In chapter 5, I'll show that this audience may, among other readers, comprise a group of regulars who gather around a specific blog. However, this audience, or rather, the countless audiences of innumerable blogs *alone*, neither fully account for the emergence of genre conventions nor genre change processes. Conventions also arise when genre users orient towards what they perceive to be some kind of common usage; in other words, when they do what other authors of personal weblogs do.

Secondly, therefore, I'd like to define the blog community as "Community of Practice" (Mauranen 2013a: 12; see also Bergs 2006) in the sense that its members are not only readers but also, and more importantly, *authors* of blogs. It is the members of the blogging community who repeatedly instantiate blogging genres. They share a common practice (blogging, or more specifically, personal blogging) and also *perceive themselves* as members of a wider community. This is most notable in the early years of blogging when a strong sense of belonging arises from several weblog authors discovering that they keep very similar websites (see 2.2.1). Other indicators of such a sense of community are registration on a blog directory (see 2.2.3) as well as imitation of other blogs, as reflected on in the following example:

Example 3: Imitating Others' Blogging Practices

Arrrgh, why am I always so restless with my web design? Not more than a week ago that I got my new layouts to a standard that pleased (and surprised) me, and now I'm looking at other people site's and asking "Why don't I do that, or mebbe this... or even that! Them's really neat tricks.

(*across a roaring hill* 14, II.A)

Regarding the imitation of others' practices, Hendrick & Efimova (2004) state that "reading other weblogs often results in observing and 'stealing' practices of others [...], for example, use of specific plug-ins or particular style of quoting others." By recognising and imitating what others do, blog authors perceive themselves as members of the blogging community and contribute to spreading innovations, thereby continuously developing their community's shared practice of blogging.

The example above supports the assumption that blog authors are often blog readers as well. Naturally, this doesn't mean that all blog readers are also authors perceiving themselves as members of a community.

1.1.3 The Reciprocity of Genres and Communities

In the light of these considerations, it's important to qualify Mauranen's (2013a: 12–13) proposal that genres produce communities, not vice versa: Indeed, the first blogging community emerged only *because* of a common practice (2.2.1) and, also in later years, new authors continued to join the community at the moment they started blogging and perceiving themselves as bloggers.

Figure 1: Reciprocity of Genre and Community – the Regenerative Cycle

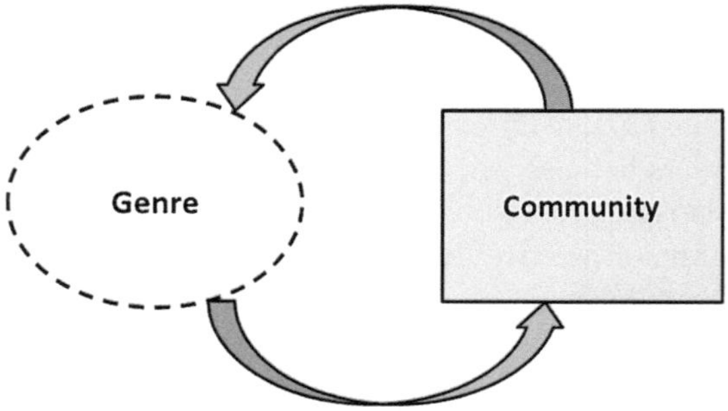

At the same time, we should not forget that members of a community *instantiate* a genre whenever they produce a text specific to the category (see Bateman 2011: 248). Every instantiation also innovates the genre. Innovations may, in turn, be taken up and reproduced by other members of the community. In this way, innovations may have long-term consequences regarding the community's genre knowledge. It's also possible for genre conflict to arise within a community, namely, when certain texts are seen as not "representative" enough of a genre category. Consequently, the relationship between genres and their community is certainly reciprocal, resulting in a regenerative cycle of innovation and reproduction as illustrated by Figure 1.

1.2 Genres as Socio-Cognitive Devices

In the last section, I defined genres as everyday categories grouping texts according to certain similarities. Categorisation is actually a cognitive process: blog author-readers draw on their knowledge about, for instance, personal weblogs in order to decide whether a certain blog belongs to that category. As I've also pointed out, other members of the community will share much of the knowledge these imagined bloggers employ for categorising the blog. Genres are therefore essentially a cognitive phenomenon; they are "intersubjective mental pattern[s] of knowledge" (Brock 2013: 63). Consequently, genre *description* is the reconstruction of a community's shared knowledge by analysing genre exemplars and, possibly, other sources (2.4).

Genre knowledge is an essential device in both text production and reception (see, e.g., Santini et al. 2011: 4; Karlgren 2011). It guides text production in that it sets the frame of what can be considered typical of a certain genre. On the recipient's side, it is a means of "complexity reduction" (Giltrow & Stein 2009a: 6) as it provides a "horizon of expectations" (Lomborg 2014: 3), and, thus, cues for sense-making. Readers of a personal weblog will, for instance, recognize the genre by referring to their knowledge of typical language and image use etc. (see chapter 6) and, thereby, form expectations on the topics and communicative functions of a certain blog.

Figure 2: Prototypical Clustering External Links vs. Words per Post (Weblogs 1997–2000)

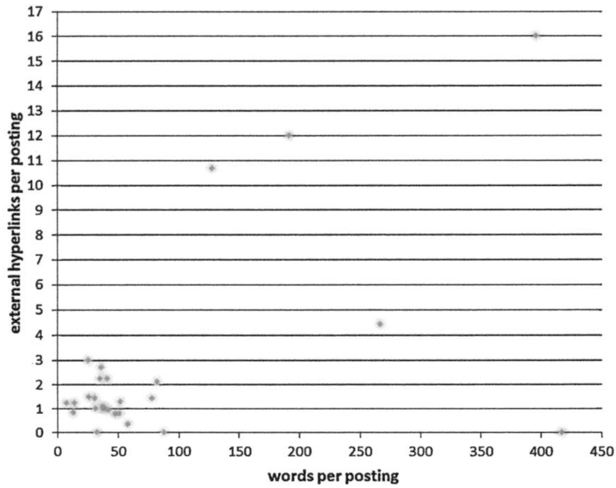

Most probably, the genre knowledge of a community is organised according to the principles of prototypicality (see, e.g., Swales 1990: 31; Lemke 1999; Sandig 2000: 101–108). Consequently, both "more and less representative members of a type and various degrees of family resemblance between them" (Brock 2013: 63) can be described. The most typical members of a genre category share features in several descriptive dimensions to a higher degree.

Figure 3: Prototypical Clustering External Links vs. Words per Post (Personal Weblogs, 2009–2012)

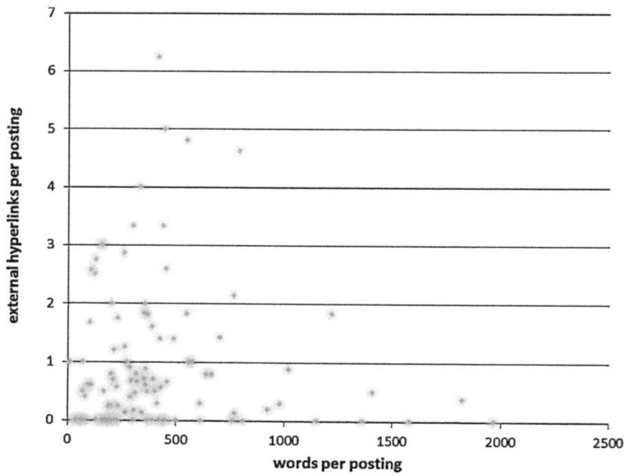

Lemke (1999) makes similar assumptions about the organisation of genre knowledge and develops a very intuitive model of genre prototypicality. He situates genres in a topological space which is defined by several dimensions. In this topological space, genres can be visualized as groups of text exemplars clustering around a prototypical core. Figures 2 and 3 take two features from the present study to exemplify Lemke's approach, namely the average number of words per post on a blog-page (x-axis) and the average number of links to external sources per entry on a blog page (y-axis). Two snapshots in the history of the personal weblog are compared; the oldest blogs of my corpus from the late 1990s and still labelled *weblogs* instead of *personal weblogs* (Figure 2), and the youngest exemplars, *personal weblogs* launched between 2009 and 2012 (Figure 3). The figures show a different clustering for these two groups: typically rather short entries with 1 to 3 external links for the 1990s weblogs versus rather lengthy posts with typically between 0 and 1 external links for the late 2000s personal weblogs. Both diagrams also show peripheral exemplars diverging notably from the central cluster.

This model assumes that features which re-occur with a high frequency over a number of texts in a sample are prototypical. There are two links from this frequency of occurrence to the genre as socio-cognitive device:

- Features occur with such a frequency because the authors consider them typical of a certain genre.
- Features which occur frequently are more likely to be encountered and can thereby take hold in the community's genre knowledge. The high frequency thus makes it more likely that this feature is cognitively salient and therefore possesses the high cue validity typical of prototypes and prototypical features (see also Löbner 2002: 181 on familiarity and prototypes; Źebrowska 2013: 138).[4]

I will also assume that category boundaries are fuzzy and show zones of overlap with neighbouring categories (see Mangasser-Wahl 2000: 27). Mixed genre terms such as *personal academic blog* are an indicator of these overlaps.[5]

4 This approach is not without risk. Stolt (1985, cited in Sandig 2000: 103), for instance, shows that even though the opening "Es war einmal" (Once upon a time) is considered prototypical of German fairy tales, it only occurs in one third of her sample. In this case, I assume that the opening acquired its high cue validity because it is a feature of those fairy tales most likely to be read (e.g., *Little Red Riding Hood* and others). In the current study, such prominent blog-texts everyone is most likely to read were not available (e.g., the very popular A-list blogs) due to the method of corpus compilation (see chapter 3).

5 The author of http://jasonrichards.odinlab.co.uk/ has chosen this label, for instance.

1.3 Genres as Multi-Layered Phenomena

Both Anglophone and German text linguistics usually model genre knowledge along several dimensions. A typical funeral speech could, for instance, be described by referring to a situation type (funeral), a function (commemoration) as well as certain formulae, for example, "We have gathered here today…" and a solemn style. Usually, typical features in all dimensions coincide. If someone, however, wished for a funeral speech entitled "Another one bites the dust", this speech would be regarded as exceptional. This status would, however, only be due to the fact that this person chose to avoid typical formulae and style; situation and function would still resemble a typical funeral speech. This example of broken expectations shows how useful it is to model genre knowledge on several dimensions.

Text linguists vary in the numbers of dimensions they propose: Devitt (2009: 30) suggests three – "form, substance and situation". Adamzik (2004) uses four: situation, function, topic and language.[6] Raible (1996) postulates seven and is followed in that by Bittner (2003). Mostly, the dimensions boil down to three central aspects, as Gansel (2011: 39) also suggests: function, situation and structure. In the remainder of this book, I will follow this proposal. I will, however, somewhat modify and redefine the individual dimensions in order to render them more applicable to the study of personal weblogs. I will also add a fourth dimension which is generally treated separately: communication form.

1.3.1 Communication Form

In German text and media linguistics a distinction is made between genres and communication forms (see, e.g., Bittner 2003; Dürscheid 2005; Holly 2011b; Meiler 2013; Pentzold et al. 2013).[7] The term communication form dates back as early as Ermert's (1979) study on letters. However, with the advent of digital media, the concept has recently enjoyed both a renaissance and further development. Therefore, the term is currently used in a variety of slightly different ways. Here, I conceptualize *communication form* in a simplistic manner as a technical constellation which gives rise to communicative potentials. Potentials include the semiotic systems available for message production, the possible number of participants and

---

6 Similarly: Heinemann & Viehweger (1991) and Heinemann & Heinemann (2000).

7 There is a variety of different terms, which however denote similar concepts: Herring et al. (2005: 164) refer to the technological basis of blogs as *socio-technical format*, Hutchby (2001) chooses the term *affordances* and Lomborg (2014: 18) opts for *software genre*. For a more detailed view on these terms and the development of the term *communication form*, see Schildhauer (2014: 27–28) and Meiler (2013: 52–67).

the extent to which distance in space and time can be bridged. The potentials can be used by several genres to a varying extent. That blog-software such as *WordPress* increasingly provides the opportunity for embedding pictures, for instance, does not necessarily mean that all authors of Personal Weblogs will do so.[8]

Adopting Thaler's (2007) view on media,[9] I assume two layers of the communication form relevant for blogs:

Table 1: Layers of the Communication Form Relevant for Blogs

1st Layer	• the infrastructure of the Internet, including protocols such as TCP/IP and standards like HTML
2nd Layer	• software building on the infrastructure, for instance blog-software such as *Blogger* or *WordPress* as well as • the specific implementation of this software: *WordPress.com* and *WordPress.org* are different implementations of essentially the same software package, with considerable consequences for usability and potentials.[10]

Several blog genres, but also others such as personal or corporate websites, can build on the specific communication form just outlined (see, e.g., Meiler 2013).

Via the potentials they create, communication forms certainly influence the shape of genres building on them. This relationship is, however, more complex. Genres, that is, complex patterns of usage, may exert an influence on their communication form, too: for instance, the typical reverse chronological order of posts was selected by first-generation blog-systems such as Blogger as *one* structural pattern used by blog-authors at that time and has been the default option ever since. At that specific point, a decision could also have been made in favour

8 See also Luginbühl (2014: 40). Vice versa, considering these potentials may resolve a number of questions arising from the analysis of text exemplars only. For instance, Eckkrammer's (2002: 43) surprise about her observation that in 2000 an increase of visual or auditive information in web-based genres is barely noticeable may probably be explained with reference to constraints of the communication form such as bandwidth, webspace, and data volume in these early years of the www. See 4.4.2 for further discussion of these factors.

9 The term *medium* itself is highly polysemous (see, e.g., Dürscheid 2005; Luginbühl 2015). In order not to get trapped in several readings of the term and because of the wide acceptance of the term *communication form* in German media linguistics at least, I will refrain from writing about media and use *communication form* instead.

10 Thaler (2007: 156–157) exemplifies this by referring to different implementations of chat technology, e.g., by granting specific operator-rights to individual participants in a specific chat environment.

of the page-paradigm used by some other early bloggers who presented each new entry on a new page (6.3.4). The introduction of the @-syntax in tweets, enabling Twitter users to directly address others, also follows this pattern: Twitter created the technical feature by taking up a convention which had already taken hold among Twitter users some time before (see boyd et al. 2010: 3).

Both examples also underline how the communication form, or changes to it, gives rise to certain communicative potentials (easily addressing tweets with an auto-alert feature, for instance). *To what extent* these potentials, provided by the communication form, are typically exploited by a genre is part of the genre description within the dimensions of structure, situation and function.

1.3.2 Structure

In the light of current developments on the WWW, increasing visual content, the embedding of sound files etc., it becomes obvious that, besides language, sign systems (or: *modes*) contribute, through their unique potential, to the overall meaning of a text (Meier 2002: 89; Źebrowska 2013: 228; Luginbühl 2014b: 34–35). Stöckl (2004b: 10) states: "[T]he purely monomodal text has always been an exception."[11]

I will therefore regard texts as multimodal entities, with language being *one*, probably central, but certainly *not the only* sign system to be taken into account. Most importantly, however, a holistic multimodal analysis does not merely *add up* meanings contributed by individual modes but rather takes account of a complex interplay of several facets of meaning (Bateman 2011: 54).[12]

It is also essential to note that both the presence and the specific interplay of several modes have to be considered as a central aspect of genre description (Stöckl 2006: 22). So far, the modes of language and image as well as their composition in space (*layout* in the sense of Kress & van Leeuwen 2001: 183) have been vividly investigated, which led to an abundance of applicable and empirically tested analytic categories in these fields. For this reason, and because of the specifics of my research corpus (see chapter 3), I also focussed on these modes.

In order to establish a framework for the analysis of the structural dimension, I established three sub-levels of the structural dimension:[13]

11 See also Kress (1998: 60).

12 This view is supported by Steinseifer (2011: 184), Nöth (2000: 483), Pflaeging (2013: 93, 96) and others.

13 In doing so, I followed Steinseifer (2011: 177–185), who proposes a macro- and a micro-perspective for the analysis of print texts.

Table 2: Levels of the Structural Dimension

Macro	This level focuses on the website[14] as a unit of several pages which are linked to each other within a certain domain, for instance *www.bump.net*. From this point of view, a personal weblog appears as a complex web-based document; either a subordinate or central part of a larger network within a domain, with the other pages fulfilling either independent or subsidiary functions (for example, *about-sites* explaining the purpose of the blog).
Meso	This level focuses on the blog-page: the blog-page comprises the content which can be reached by horizontal and/or vertical scrolling, without clicking on hyperlinks or entering a new URL. On the meso-level, the basic elements of a blog-page such as header, sidebar, footer and body are viewed as individual language-image texts contributing to the whole blog-page. Within these basic elements, further building blocks can be examined, for instance posts[15] in the body and a blogroll in the sidebar. The meso-level also focuses on the design of these elements: layout, colour and typography.[16]
Micro	On this level, the focus lies on specific linguistic features of blog-posts and on language-image-clusters in posts. Language-image-clusters are often characterised by a spatial contiguity of language and image.[17] Sometimes, however, the verbal passage referring to an image and the image itself occur at quite distant points within a post.[18] In these cases, semantic links (such as key words or deictic expressions referring to the image)[19] have to be taken into account in order to spot relevant language-image constellations.

14 See also Androutsopoulos (2010: 427).

15 Postings can be defined structurally by their headings, timestamps and metalinks, sometimes even by frames or horizontal lines separating individual posts. They can also be conceptualised as a topically and functionally coherent unit which is published as a whole (e.g., by hitting the *publish*-button of a blog-software). This view on posts as coherent unit is apparently also shared by blog-authors. The author of *Ask Jewels!* (II.A), for instance, publishes several posts in a few minutes, which are even linked by cohesive ties. Despite that, the author seems to view the products as individual posts: "Ok, I lied, I will post 1 more after this, because I just remembered I was going to, but anyhow…" (*Ask Jewels!* 38, II.A).

16 Stöckl (2004b: 12) subsumes these sign systems under the term "peripheral modes"; Steinseifer (2011: 171) calls them "heteronome Modalitäten". According to the "resource integration principle" (Baldry & Thibault 2006: 18), they interact in order to integrate the "core modes" (Stöckl 2004b: 12) of language and image in a genre-specific way.

17 This view on language-image-constellations is in line with a number of current approaches: Contiguity is part of Stöckl's (2004a: 34–39) account of multimodal reception processes, forms the basis of Schmitz's (2011: 28) characterisation of *Sehflächen* and furthermore plays a central role in Bateman's (2011: 67–73) visual-filter-approach.

18 This happens frequently, for instance, in the personal weblog *In a Silent Way* (II.C), which will be analysed in 6.4.4, Example 111.

19 See also Jäger's (2002) transcription theory on the complex interplays between connected semiotic systems. See also Holly (2006; 2009; 2010; 2011a) and Siefkes (2015).

1.3.3 Situation

This dimension comprises a diversity of aspects all concerned with the context in which a certain kind of usage of multimodal means typically occurs. Firstly, the *wider communicative context* has to be described. Is a text, for instance, written in an institutional context, part of a leisure activity or, like the funeral speech mentioned above, part of a ritual? It is also essential to analyse typical partner constellations. Whereas Wikipedia articles typically exhibit multiple authorship, diaries are frequently single-authored. Whereas a love letter is typically directed at one addressee only, open letters address a multiplicity of potential readers. Furthermore, characterising authors and readers contributes to a sound genre description. As far as the blog-readers are concerned, Levinsons conclusion that "the reception-role set [...] is especially resistant to analysis" (Levinson 1988: 177) is still more than valid. Puschmann (2010: 25) points out that, usually, very little is known about the actual readership of an individual blog[20] and argues (e.g., 2009; 2010; 2013) for focussing on the bloggers' mental concept of their audiences as it is *this* concept *only* which influences the writing process and thereby continuously shapes actual blog posts. This mental concept of the audience (or conceptual audience, for short) is focussed on here as well. In this respect, I also take into account how authors manage the background knowledge necessary for rendering their posts coherent (see Giltrow 1994).

Internet-based communication forms provide the authors with the opportunity to keep a rather high level of anonymity with ease (see, e.g., Anonymous 1998; Gallery 2000; Qian & Scott 2007). Therefore, web-based genres like the personal weblog are specifically characterised by aspects such as self-presentation and disclosure, authenticity and identity-play (see, e.g., Buckingham 2008; Hollenbaugh 2008, 2010; Hollenbaugh & Everett 2013; Kitzmann 2003; Newitz 1995; Reed 2005 and others).

Until now, I have shown implicitly that I view a text (such as a blog-post) not only as a static product but also as a process.[21] This view entails that texts are seen as a means by which authors and readers work *together* towards meaningful interaction, adhering to certain communicative guidelines. One influential attempt at reconstructing these guidelines is offered by Grice (1975), who states

20 This is particularly true for *lurkers*, that is, readers who do not leave comments. See Stegbauer (2000: 23–24) on the term *lurker* and Preece et al. (2004: 202–203) on the phenomenon in general as well as reasons for lurking in particular.

21 This view also becomes apparent in 1.3.4 where I argue for taking the writing process into account.

that participants in an interaction orient towards a cooperative principle (CP): "Make your contribution such as is required, at the stage at which it occurs, by the accepted purpose of the talk exchange in which you are engaged." (Grice 1975: 45) This principle translates in maxims of quality, quantity, relevance and modality (see below). I have discussed the CP and its applicability to several communicative modes in detail in Schildhauer (2014: 58–64) and, as a result, modified the cooperative principle in order to account for the following observations:

- The purpose of a communicative interaction is often negotiated among the participants alongside the interaction (just think of a conversation between two people who have just met in the street).
- Purposes can change (for example, if conversation partners decide to switch from small talk to planning an event).
- Initiating an interaction can be seen as an *offer of cooperation*. Participants may accept this offer temporarily and reject it later.
- Grice's maxims account for situations in which an effective exchange of information is the primary purpose. This is, however, not always the case (as in comedy, for instance, see Brock 2004).

In this study, I used the following modified version of the cooperative principle and slightly altered forms of the maxims (the recipient-oriented formulations, for instance, are not given in Grice's account):

Table 3: Generalised Gricean Maxims

Cooperative Principle	Make your contribution such as is currently required by the jointly established (or established-to-be) purposes of the communicative event in which you are engaged.	
	Producer	**Recipient**
Quantity	Make your contribution as informative as currently necessary for the jointly-established (or established-to-be) purposes of the communicative event in which you are engaged. Don't make your contribution more informative than currently necessary for the jointly-established (or established-to-be) purposes of the communicative event in which you are engaged.	Interpret your partner's contribution as containing the right amount of information which is currently necessary for the jointly-established (or established-to-be) purposes of the communicative event in which you are engaged.
Quality	Be truthful.	Interpret your partner's contribution as truthful. If you have reasonable doubts then look for a motif for not telling the truth which is in line with the general assumption of cooperation. Adjust your idea of the communicative purpose to that motif.
Relevance	Be relevant regarding the current jointly-established (or established-to-be) purposes of the communicative event in which you are engaged.	Interpret your partner's contribution as relevant regarding the current jointly-established (or established-to-be) purposes of the communicative event in which you are engaged.
Manner	Express yourself in a way which serves the current jointly-established (or established-to-be) purposes of the communicative event in which you are engaged, for example, be brief, be orderly, avoid ambiguity and avoid obscurity.	Assume that your partner's contribution is adequately shaped regarding the current jointly-established (or established-to-be) purposes of the communicative event in which you are engaged.

Let me briefly comment on the maxim of quality: it gains a powerful position in the model above because of its straightforward formulation "Be truthful". It is meant to reflect that a basic assumption underlying communicative interactions is one of truthfulness (see Searle 1999: 143 and Yus 2011: 41). Only if doubts are raised, for example, by listening to a joke or reading a novel dealing with dragons) do we usually change this default setting and search for some new quality (for example, being funny in the case of a joke, see Brock 2004: 116). I'd like to argue that this "presumption of honesty" (Yus 2011: 41) also holds for blog-posts: when the readers of the blog *Living Colours*, for instance, discovered that they had not been following a dying girl's fight against cancer but had actually been fooled, they reacted in a hurt and angry way (Rosenberg 2009: 236–238), probably because they had assumed the validity of the quality maxim "Be truthful".

To what extent and in what way these maxims are oriented to is an interesting question for genre description. Answering this question will also help to reconstruct the complex interaction between blog-authors and readers.

1.3.4 Function

Traditionally, the function of a text is viewed as *communicative* function on the basis of speech act theory[22] (see, e.g., Miller 1984; Brandt & Rosengren 1992; Brinker 2000a, 2000b, 2010) and is given a central role in the classification of genres (for example, Brinker 2010; see also Askehave 1999). Generally, research has tended to assign one, dominating illocution to a text. Brinker, for instance, differentiates between an informative, an appellative, an obligational, a declarative, and a contact function. This way of conceptualising the functional dimension works well for genres of institutional and professional fields (see, e.g., Bazerman 1994; Berkenkotter & Huckin 1995) and other, functionally clearly defined genres (see, e.g., Eckkrammer & Eder 2000; Rolf 2000). Particularly in professional settings, texts, for example, business letters, are produced with a pronounced focus on the *single* communicative act they are intended to perform (Motsch 2000: 415).

It has been shown, however, that genres such as the personal weblog cannot be fruitfully described in these traditional terms (see, e.g., Schildhauer 2013 and Table 43). In fact, even the communicative function of rather trivial genres such as shopping list may be not straight-forward at all (Askehave & Swales 2001: 200–201). Any text may exhibit a heterogeneity of functions not only for *different* recipients (Presch 1991: 85) but also for *one and the same* recipient at different points of time or even simultaneously (Klemm 2002: 155): a shopping list, to stay with Askehave & Swale's example, may *inform* on what is currently missing in the fridge, *order* to buy the missing items and even *prohibit* buying anything

22 See, for instance, Searle (1982; 1999).

else, thus being also *appellative* in Brinker's terms. Therefore, I assume that the function of a text is rather a mixture of several functional components in most cases, *informative* and *appellative*, often also *contact-oriented*.[23]

What is more, the traditional speech act paradigm tends to overlook that for some texts the writing process itself, including its potential benefits for the author, is also of considerable importance, and may even be the sole goal of producing a text at all. This insight has been voiced, among others, by researchers in the creative writing paradigm:

> Writing is best described as a process rather than a product, and it may be that very process that benefits the writer. The benefit may result from the self-discovery allowed by writing or the fact that writers must consider different options, find words, and think of various perspectives while writing. (Runco 2009: 188)

Besides these cognitive effects of structuring knowledge and generating ideas, writing psychology has also been able to show the possible benefits of releasing emotional tensions through writing (see, e.g., Baikie & Wilhelm 2005; Kohanyi 2009; Pennebaker 1997; Pennebaker & Francis 1996; Sexton & Pennebaker 2009). In writing therapy, for instance, texts mainly function in this process-oriented rather than in the reception-oriented way which is focussed on in the speech-act paradigm.

In Schildhauer (2014: ch. 9.5), I argue that benefits of the writing process should also be highlighted for personal weblog-posts, and that the overall function of a blog post may be a fascinating blend of both recipient- and process-oriented components, for example, when writing a post releases emotional tension (process-oriented) but also aims at asking for help in a difficult situation (recipient-oriented). This line of argument is taken up in chapter 7 of this book, particularly in 7.5.

1.3.5 Interim Summary

Figure 4 sums up most aspects discussed in this sub-chapter. All in all, genres are cognitive devices (the conceptual sphere at the top of Figure 4) which group texts according to similarities within several descriptive dimensions (1.1, 1.2), namely multimodal structure, situation, and function (the coloured layers within the conceptual sphere, 1.3). These cognitive categories probably exhibit prototypical structure (the black dots within the sphere cluster around a prototype). Genres are based on a *communication form* (orange socket in Figure 4, 1.3.1). In

23 See also Pflaeging (2015: 174–175) for a similar approach to the online genre *ListSite*.

addition, the levels of situation (1.3.3) and function (1.3.4) have been modelled with a process-oriented perspective in mind, paying attention to the complex interplay of text production and reception. In 1.3.2, I have introduced macro-, meso- and micro-levels providing different but intertwined perspectives for analysing the multimodal structure of genres. That texts are seen as multimodal rather than language-only entities is illustrated by including several layouts, images etc. on the textual layer in Figure 4.

Figure 4: A Genre Model of the Personal Weblog (visualised by J. Pflaeging)

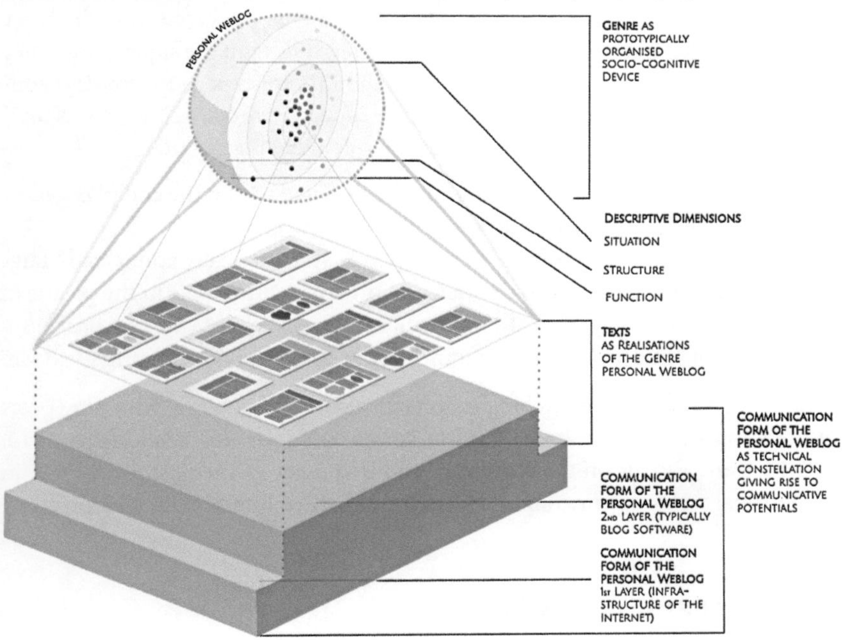

1.4 Genre Profiles and Genre Networks

Recently, text linguistics has increasingly been influenced by the idea that genres do not exist in isolation but are connected in several ways to other genres in so-called genre networks (see, e.g., Adamzik 2011; Hauser 2014).[24] In his seminal study on one particular *genre ecology*, Erickson (2000) focuses on several CMC-conversations within the intranet of a company, where it is apparent which genres

24 See also Bazerman (1994) on syntagmatic relations of genres in an institutional context.

can be described in terms of their interrelatedness. This approach can be extended to Social Media (Schildhauer forthc.) where it is not always obvious which genres should be treated as interrelated: if genre networks are also *cognitive structures* (Adamzik 2011), even apparently unrelated genres such as the personal weblog and the Facebook status update are connected in the minds of their users and thereby may influence each other in their development (see 8.4; see also Hauser 2014: 288).

Another adaption of the network idea is proposed by Luginbühl (2014a: 312–313; 2014b: 103–105), who argues that genres exist on different levels of complexity. For instance, the super-genre *TV news show* constitutes a constellation of several genres (for example, *interview, lead-in, package* etc.), which are more delimitated in terms of structural characteristics than the super-genre they are part of (Luginbühl 2014a: 316–317). Luginbühl's concept *genre profile* is concerned "with the contour of genres within a super-genre like a TV news show" (2014a: 313) and enables us to describe super-genres in terms of:

- *Repertoire* – what lower level genres can be detected within the complex genre?
- *Frequency* – what is the overall frequency of these genres?
- *Intertextual Relations* – how are these genres systematically connected? Luginbühl (2014b: 291–293), for instance, shows that genres within the profile of news broadcasts may occur in sequential clusters such as *lead-in – package – anchor item*. This aspect draws on the idea of genre networks outlined above.

I assume that the personal weblog *is*, in fact, such a super-genre, with blog posts instantiating genres on a lower level of complexity (see also Schildhauer 2014: ch. 9.1). Here, I focus on the repertoire and frequency of the post genres within the personal weblog genre, and address the aspect of intertextual relations only marginally.[25]

1.5 Patterns of Genre Change

In chapter 1.1.3, I've outlined a dynamic conceptualisation of genres: as complex multimodal patterns, genres are instantiated in specific texts. Every instantiation of a genre is unique and contains innovations for a number of reasons. For instance, slight differences in competence and genre knowledge among the community members may as easily be the reason for innovations as intentional deviations from the established convention (see, e.g., Croft 2000: 115; Keller 1990: 120–122). Brock (2009: 235) plausibly states that genres actually only exist in the

25 The intertextual relations between post genres are addressed in 7.6.1, investigating if (and what) post genres typically co-occur on blog-pages.

variations of which they constitute abstractions.[26] When these innovations are taken up and reproduced by other members of the community, this may eventually influence the community's genre knowledge. This regenerative cycle has been illustrated in Figure 1.

Current research shows a growing interest in *how* genres change[27] and whether there are certain recurring patterns of change. This strand of research has identified a variety of genre change patterns (see, e.g., Bolter & Grusin 2001; Brock 2009; Luginbühl 2014b; Stöckl 2010), of which I'll outline a few here.

1.5.1 Evolutionary Change

Stöckl (2010: 145) uses the term *evolutionary change* to describe a genre's gradual change regarding at least one feature. Taking up Lemke's (1999) metaphor of the topological space (1.2), we can model this change as a shift of the prototypical core of a genre category on one specific dimension. As some users may adhere to established patterns rather than instantly follow the change, the process usually involves a temporary widening of the genre category; for example, even in recent years, some bloggers have not joined the trend of embedding images in their posts (see 6.4.4).

Following Stöckl (2010: 162), I'll differentiate between *evolutionary change* as a gradual and rather slow process on the one hand, and metamorphose on the other hand. Metamorphoses are moments of revolutionary change at which recipients can easily perceive changes in a genre as there are sharp contrasts with expectations grounded in their established genre knowledge. At several points in this book, I'll refer to the spread of blog-software around the millennium as such a special moment in the history of the blog.

1.5.2 Genre Split

During a genre split some texts of a certain genre category gradually show differences with respect to at least one feature. This process works along the lines of the *evolutionary change* pattern just outlined. Other texts of the established genre category don't exhibit this change. Therefore, the source genre mainly remains in its former position in the topological space. After a phase of overlap, both genre categories are perceived as distinct. Consequently, separate names are assigned

---

26 "Textsorten existieren eigentlich nur in den Variationen, deren Abstraktion sie verkörpern." (Brock 2009: 235).

27 Many studies contained in Giltrow and Stein's (2009b) volume on genres in the internet and most recently Hauser et al. (2014) stress the importance of such a diachronic perspective on genres.

to them and individual texts are labelled accordingly. Rosenberg (2009: 24–28) describes such a genre split with regard to the development of blogs out of personal websites,[28] which I'll deal with in more depth later (8.2).

1.5.3 Pattern Embedding

Patterns are salient and clearly delimited aspects of a genre – a complex pattern itself – which can occur within all dimensions of the genre model. For instance, the rhyme scheme of a Shakespearean sonnet constitutes a distinct pattern. If this rhyme scheme is separated from the original genre *Shakespearean sonnet* and used, for example, to compile a shopping list, this is an instance of pattern embedding: the import of a pattern from one genre to another, which is usually perceived as such by recipients. Pattern embeddings can occur in one or just few texts of a category, or they can become firmly established and thereby part of the receiving genre.

Pattern embeddings can also occur in different ways,[29] of which I'd like to highlight three here:

- *Quotations* are clearly delimited pattern embeddings which are highly likely to be perceived as such by genre users. It is, for instance, a case of pattern quotation if a single entry of a blog is written in the form of a poem as in Example 4:

Example 4: Pattern Quotation – Blog Post as Poem

Winter
knotted
  like hair
    on a static windy day
numb
  like fingertips
    waiting for the bus
frozen
  like icicles
    dangling from a roof
dark
  like my brow
    when the memories return

(*A la Coque Wonderland* 77–80, II.A)

28 See also Lomborg (2014: 12) and Yus (2011: 95).

29 See, e.g., Sandig's (2006: 164–165) compilation of various types under the heading "Mustermischung" – *mixing patterns.*

- *Blendings*: a pattern from a source genre is consistently woven into a text of another genre category. Genre users may recognize blendings particularly if they occur only in single members of a genre, even though they are often less obvious than quotations. The personal weblog *Dandy Darkly*, for instance, blends the genres *personal weblog* and *ghost story* in such a skilful way that a recipient is only made aware that they're not reading a personal weblog "proper" by subtle cues in the text (see Example 162 for an excerpt from this blog).
- *Embedded Communication Forms*: particularly in the younger history of the blog, aspects of other communication forms are embedded into blogs. For the recipient, these embeddings result in modular websites with some parts of the screen taken by elements such as chat windows, recent tweets and others. More often than not, only part of the functionality of the source communication form is embedded: for instance, the Twitter widget in Example 5 only allows *reading* of recent tweets but doesn't offer retweet buttons etc. Embeddings of this kind allow for a convergence of the potentials of different communication forms (Fritz & Bader 2010: 337). As the embedded modules can be considered to be well-known building blocks of Internet communication, an almost intuitive handling is ensured. Integrated as they are into the architecture of the website, they are necessarily present until removed by the author.

*Example 5: Twitter Widget as Embedded Communication Form (*1 Ideal Life, *II.A, add. excerpt 28 January 2011)*

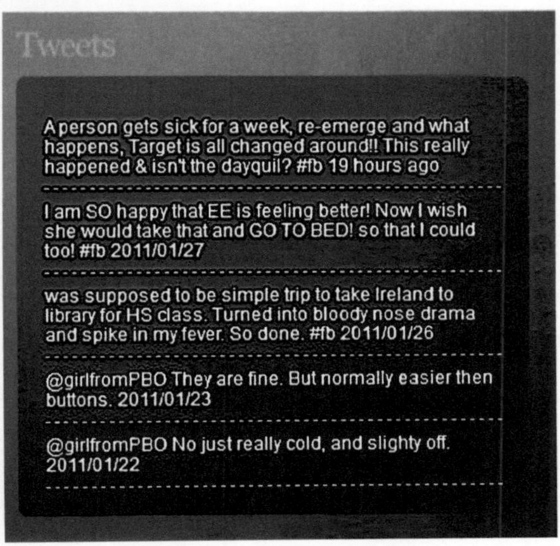

1.5.4 Migration

Several scholars have observed that, actually, there's not as much that's new about genres on the web as might be expected. Digital genres "are medially migrating genre instantiations that are typically based on antecedents in the traditional or spoken media" (Heyd 2009: 246).[30] Adopting Heyd's metaphor, I use the term *migration* to describe the process of transferring a *whole genre* as a complex multimodal pattern from one communication form to another. This transfer involves the application of established genre knowledge to the context of a new communication form. The resulting cognitive link between genre ancestor and migrated genre can be reconstructed when genre users explicitly refer to genre ancestry, as is, for instance, visible in the genre label *online diary*. Genre labels such as *online diary* also allow the assumption that genre users perceive some changed quality in the migrated genre and therefore feel the need for a new genre label. After all, an online diary strongly resembles its offline ancestor but is something different concerning, for instance, potentials such as hyperlinking or embedding video clips (8.2).

1.5.5 Why do genres change? Regenerative Cycle and Invisible Hand

While the previous sub-chapters have dealt with *how* genres may change, the question of *why* they do has been addressed only marginally. My understanding of genres is firmly grounded in a user-centred perspective, which is compatible with accounts of the reasons of genre change such as Croft's (2000) *Theory of Utterance Selection*, social network accounts of language change (e.g., Bergs 2005), and diffusion research (Rogers 2003). On these grounds I'd like to make the following assumptions on genre change:

- Genre change can often be modelled as a gradual shift of a genre category along one dimension in the topological space. Whenever we can observe such a shift, this is also linked (either by mirroring or by foreshadowing) to a change of the community's shared genre knowledge.
- Each shift within the topological space is caused by the sum of genre instantiations and therefore by the genre users.
- Every instantiation of a genre is innovative. Innovations may be produced deliberately (for example, in order to set a text apart from the norm) or may come about unconsciously.

30 See also Askehave & Nielsen (2005: 124–125), Baron (2008: ch. 6), Giltrow & Stein (2009a: 9); Miller & Shepherd (2004, 2009), Püschel (1997: 35).

Based on these considerations, one possible scenario for genre change is the following: genre change happens as the result of the regenerative cycle (Figure 1). Innovations are taken up and reproduced by genre users, particularly if genre users consider an innovation more effective, socially successful etc. than their previous usage. If an innovation is reproduced many times, it gradually becomes the typical way of realising a certain genre feature and thereby reaches the status of a new convention. For this scenario, the social network of the genre's community is decisive as an innovation is passed on along the links between the network members. While some community members are eager to adopt an innovation (so-called early adopters), others are more conservative and adhere to established practices; these are referred to as *laggards*.[31] This results in a (temporary) widening of the genre category (1.5.1).

Another account of genre change that is compatible with the perspective taken here is Keller's (1990) *Invisible Hand Theory*. In a nutshell, this theory assumes that language change is based on the sum of the actions of individual speakers. Every speaker follows individual goals and acts accordingly. For instance, a speaker might use the intensifier *bloody* in order to be slightly provocative and stick out of the mass in order to gain attention. Independently, others might do the same. What happens is that *bloody* is being used so frequently that it loses its taboo status and enters colloquial usage. The connotation of *bloody* as an intensifier changes as a result of the *cumulation* of the acts of individual speakers following their own personal goals. Of course, none of these speakers actually intended to trigger *language change* by their behaviour. Language change is therefore, according to Keller, the *unintended result of an accumulation of the communicative acts of individual speakers*. Each Invisible Hand process can be described in terms of motifs (for example, gaining attention), process (*bloody*'s provocative nature is slowly worn out) and result (*bloody* has lost its taboo connotation).[32]

Keller's scenario is compatible with the scenario of the regenerative cycle mentioned above in that it focuses on the acts of language (genre) users. However, the Invisible Hand Theory, in the narrow sense proposed by Keller, assumes that the speakers (or genre users) act *independently* from one another, that is, they're not influenced by other's previous communicative acts. The regenerative

31 The types cited here are the extreme poles of a more elaborate typology suggested by Rogers (2003: 282–285).

32 See the OED entry for *bloody*.

cycle, however, is exactly based on this momentum of influence of one communicative act (using a genre) on the next one(s).

Of course, both scenarios can also be combined in various ways and by no means exclude each other. In chapter 9 of this book, I'll discuss several developments in the history of the personal weblog in the light of these two scenarios.

1.6 Summary

In this chapter, I've outlined several facets of the genre concept which this book is based on. In doing so, I've also situated the current study in the landscape of genre research. In particular, I've expressed my affinity with approaches to genre focussing on

a) the genre users and a genre's community
b) genres as cognitive and prototypically structured devices
c) genres as complex multimodal patterns which can be described on several dimensions.

The focus on genres as an inherently socio-cognitive phenomenon has also been continued into the considerations on genre change in 1.5, where I've sketched some patterns and possible scenarios of genre change. In part B, I'll address each descriptive dimension of the genre model (Figure 1) in turn. The next chapter, however, takes another necessary preliminary step as it introduces the research corpus this book is based on and clarifies the decisions I made during its compilation.

2 The Diachronic Blog Corpus (DIABLOC)

Just as in every other corpus-based study, the results presented in this book are highly dependent on the corpus which was investigated and can only be interpreted with sufficient knowledge about this corpus in mind. I have used the Diachronic Blog Corpus (DIABLOC), and I'll use this chapter to clarify the decisions which led to DIABLOC's current design. These decisions draw primarily on theoretical assumptions I outlined in the previous chapter, but of course, there were also practical decisions connected to the purposes and circumstances of the overall study. The first sub-chapter introduces the gateway I used to enter the past of the personal weblog genre and also the stumbling blocks it contains: the Internet Archive.

2.1 The Internet Archive

For several reasons, a study dealing with the history of personal weblogs cannot just identify personal weblogs in the present, browse through their archives until the earliest possible point and use these entries for analysis:

- Entries may have undergone several changes in the meantime, or even have been deleted.
- Current changes to the layout of the blog also influence how archived entries are displayed. Just using the archives of the blogs would make it impossible, then, to make statements about what kind of layout was typical of a certain period in the history of the personal weblog.
- *Globe of Blogs* doesn't provide information on *when exactly* a blog was registered and assigned to a certain category. What if, say, authors registered their blogs in 2003, forgot about it, but kept blogging for 10 more years. Would they still, in 2013, say they kept a personal weblog? Would they know why they had classified it accordingly in 2003, and if, or at what point in time, their blog had ceased to be a personal weblog as they understood the term in 2003? Questions impossible to answer.

I was lucky enough to have a colleague, Dr. Jörg Wagner, who made me aware of the *Internet Archive* where snapshots of the Internet have been collected since 1996. Via an interface called *Wayback Machine*, users can visit websites by providing their URL and view these sites in several stages of their development. It is even possible to click on hyperlinks on the site and see where they lead – that's basically surfing the WWW of 2, 5 or even 20 years ago! The Internet Archive enabled me to look into the *Globe of Blogs* of 2002 and see what personal weblogs had only just been registered then – and, of course, to view them the way they looked back then.

Thus, the Internet Archive became my tool of choice for the study I present in this book. However, it also has its limitations, some of which I'll briefly outline because they've had influence on the compilation of the DIABLOC, or may have on future genre studies:[33]

- There is no search engine apart from the Wayback Machine. In other words, we can't just tell the Archive that we're looking for personal weblogs.
- Dynamic sites lose their functionality as they depend on their server to process information. Search engines (for example, *Google*) become useless, and password-protected sites cannot be accessed either. Similarly, some JavaScript-elements cannot be archived.
- The Archive employs a crawler, i.e. a program that follows the hyperlinks on websites to reach the next site and archives every site it passes. If no hyperlinks point to a website, it will only appear in the Archive if its owner submits it separately. A vast amount of blogs existing in isolation are therefore not included in the Archive.
- The crawling procedure also entails that sites are not archived at regular intervals; if the crawler doesn't happen to drop by for a couple of months, there won't be any new snapshots in the Archive.
- "Not every date for every site archived is 100% complete" (The Internet Archive 2011). In such cases, the Archive directs users to the closest available date with sufficient completeness; or even to the present-day's live web when the Archive cannot find any sufficiently archived version. From my experience, not even every date the Archive *considers* to be sufficiently archived can be used for analysis as layout structures might be broken, elements missing for some reason (unknown to me) etc.
- Sometimes, image files are not archived; either because files over 10MB are excluded automatically or because users protected the image folder of their domain by entries in the *robots.txt*.[34]

33 See The Archive's FAQs for more information (The Internet Archive 2011).

34 The robots.txt is a file in the main folder of a website that contains instructions for crawler software on which parts of the site the owner does not want to be crawled (and, e.g., indexed in search engines). See the "Standard for Robots Exclusion" on http://tinyurl.com/36hht3.

Despite these limitations, the Internet Archive is the best tool available for a diachronic genre study on the web.

2.2 Blog, Weblog, Personal Weblog – Genres?

Before thinking about corpus design issues at all, a profound question has to be answered: is the personal weblog a genre at all? This question is ever more important as the rivalling terms *weblog* and *blog* are also in use. In the light of what was said about genres, communities and genre labels above (1.1), that is, in the light of an ethnocategory-based approach to genres – all three terms can generally be considered genre labels: They are terms the community uses to group texts according to certain similarities. What remains is to unravel how the terms relate to one another. Are they, in fact, synonyms denoting the same groups of texts or does each have its own extension? Considering their etymologies within the blogging community, I'd like to differentiate the terms as follows:

2.2.1 Weblog

The term *weblog* evidently emerged first. Jorn Barger coined it in 1997 when he was looking for a suitable label for his website *Robot Wisdom*. *Weblog*, a compound of the clippings *web* (for *World Wide Web*) and *log* (for *logbook*, Schlobinski & Siever 2005a: 10) was well suited to Barger's purposes, as only an expert minority of system administrators used the term at that time (Rosenberg 2009: 78–79), but with a different meaning, of course. Jessie James Garrett (author of the website *Infoshift*) and Cameron Barrett (*Camworld*) adopted the term for their own websites, which looked similar to what Jorn Barger was doing.

They also widened the extension of the term: in 1998, Jessie James Garrett began to compile a list of "other sites like his" (Blood 2000). That same year, he sent a list containing 23 weblogs to Cameron Barrett, who published it on his weblog *Camworld* and invited others to get in touch if they authored similar sites. The sidebar of his weblog contained a *weblogs* section, to which he added a link whenever he found such a site. The Internet Archive contains a version of Barrett's list from April 1999, containing 26 weblogs.[35]

Jessie James Garrett also published, according to Blood (2000), a list of weblogs, which was probably an extended version of the list he had already sent to Cameron Barrett. Blood (2000) states: "Jesse's 'page of only weblogs' lists the 23

35 Afterwards (next entry in the Archive: October 1999) it was replaced by a section entitled "Sites I Visit Often".

known to be in existence at the beginning of 1999." The Internet Archive only contains a 2002-version of this "page of only weblogs", which, obviously, must have grown considerably in those three years, and presents tremendous lists under several headings. One of these categories is *ye olde skool*, which contains exactly 23 entries. As 14 of these also appear on the *Camworld* list, and some are even mentioned in Barrett's (1999a) essay "The Anatomy of a Weblog", we can assume these 23 to be the ones Barrett had published at the end of 1998 / beginning of 1999 under the heading "page of only weblogs".

What Garrett and Barrett did (following Barger's initiative) was exactly what I outlined in 1.1: they identified a common social practice, a complex multimodal pattern, and labelled it. The genre *weblog* was born. In this book I'll count the 30[36] websites we get from compiling both Cameron Barrett's and Jesse James Garrett's lists (with a considerable number of sites appearing on both lists) as the earliest instances of this weblog genre.[37]

In 1999, more and more weblogs were created (Blood 2000; Winer 2001). As early as in the first months of 1999, Brigitte Eaton, who wanted to compile a catalogue of all weblogs, withdrew to the single criterion "that the site consist of dated entries" (Blood 2000). Debates about what can be considered a weblog spread, as illustrated, for instance, by both Cameron Barrett's essays "The Anatomy of a Weblog" (1999a) and "More about Weblogs" (1999b) as well as Rebecca Blood's (2000, 2004), Dave Winer's (2001; 2003b) retrospective insider accounts and others. In terms of genre description, the category *weblog* contained more and more peripheral members exhibiting a low degree of family resemblance. Consequently, the fuzziness of the category boundaries increased.

It would be a highly interesting endeavour in itself to trace this evolution of the *weblog* genre. As this book is about the personal weblog, however, I'll confine myself to those 30 weblogs mentioned above and use these to investigate the roots of all later blog genres including the personal weblog.

2.2.2 Blog

As stated above, the extension of the term *weblog* started to grow considerably from 1999 onwards, promoted, among others, by Brigitte Eaton's catalogue project

36 Actually, both lists amount to a total of 35 weblogs. For reasons why the corpus only contains 30 out of these weblogs, see 2.3.1.

37 Many weblogs on these two lists are also mentioned by Blood (2000), Winer (2001) and Rosenberg (2009), which makes it more likely that we really deal with central members of the early weblog genre.

EatonWeb. It's around this time that Peter Merholz created the pun "wee-blog" (Rosenberg 2009: 101) and decided to use the clipping *blog* as label for his weblog. The blog system *Blogger*, launched in August 1999 and quickly becoming very popular, adopted the label and contributed to its rapid spread. Blood (2002: 6) still uses the term *blog* to refer to a particular diary-like genre, which she sets apart from first-generation weblogs with their main purpose of collecting and presenting interesting hyperlinks. Sometime later – McNeill's (2009: 145) estimate is roughly 2003 – *blog* appeared as a general cover term, a hyperonym for several blog genres. Compounds such as *travel blog*, *corporate blog* (Puschmann 2010), *science blog* and others also attest to the use of *blog* as an umbrella term for more specific blog genres. I assume that the development of this general reading is connected to the growing fuzziness of the *weblog* term in 1999. In this book, I'll adopt this reading of *blog*, also in compounds such as *blogosphere*, *blogger*, *blog-page*, and use the term whenever I'd like to refer to blogs in general and not to a specific blog genre.

2.2.3 Personal Weblog

Now and then, this term is already attested in the discourse of the first generation bloggers. To my knowledge, however, it is only from 2002 onwards that there is sound evidence for the term being used as genre label: The blog directory *Globe of Blogs*,[38] which claims to be the oldest blog directory, contains a system of categories which authors can use to classify their blog. Apparently, authors are not confined to using existing categories only, but are also allowed to suggest new ones. Even in the 2002 version available on the Internet Archive, there are many different, mostly topic-related categories such as *travel blog*. Besides these, the directory also offers the meta-category *personal weblog*, which is apparently not primarily topic-related. The fact that *Globe of Blogs* allows the creation of new categories tells us that the personal weblog category may have been suggested to the directory by blog-authors, that is, active members of the blogging community, as a label to classify blogs according to certain similarities. When authors classify their blog as personal weblog in this directory, they probably do so because:

a) They are convinced that their blog fits this category. This is because the author's assumptions about what features constitute a personal weblog show enough overlap with their own blog for the author to decide on this category.
b) Registering a blog in a directory is something bloggers do to increase their readership. It is therefore quite likely that they assign their blog to a category

38 www.globeofblogs.com.

where others might look for particularly *this* kind of blog because of the expectations they have concerning this category.

In other words: when registering their blog for the category *personal weblog*, authors draw on their (more or less explicit and elaborate) *genre knowledge*. We can therefore assume that the blogs in this category are instances of the genre *personal weblog* and can be used to identify the similarities and reconstruct the genre knowledge which made authors classify them that way. In summary: In this book, personal weblogs are those blogs that were classified accordingly on *Globe of Blogs*.[39]

2.3 Corpus Design

2.3.1 Corpus Periods

The previous sub-chapter already anticipated a profound decision concerning the corpus architecture. It's because I'm convinced that describing the root genre of the personal weblog is a necessary part of working on the history of this genre that my research corpus contains two parts.

Part I assembles 30 specimens of the weblog genre as defined in 2.2.1. Here, we find the websites of blogging pioneers such as Dave Winer (*Scripting News*), Jorn Barger (*Robot Wisdom*), Brigitte Eaton (*Eaton Web*), Cameron Barrett (*Camworld*) and Jessie James Garrett (*Infoshift*). In 2.2.1, I already mentioned that the number of potentially available weblogs was higher (35) than the 30 now contained in the corpus. This is partly due to the fact that some of the 35 are protected by a *robots.txt* prohibiting the Archive's crawler from archiving the respective website (2.1). Others were only archived after 2000, i.e. after the weblog genre had already started to grow increasingly fuzzy, and even after the launch of blog systems (particularly *Blogger*) further fuelled this development. In other words, I could not be sure to what extent weblogs archived after 2000 still mirror the root genre which I'd like to describe here in order to show where the personal weblog came from. Therefore, I decided not to include any weblog on the 35-list archived only after 2000. For the remaining 30, I always collected the

39 At several points in this book, I'll use the label (personal) weblog. When I do so, I am referring to both the 30 first-generation weblogs mentioned in 2.2.1 *and* personal weblogs as defined in 2.2.3. The term *(personal) weblog* is a bit more specific than *blog* as it (a) only refers to blogs contained in the DIABLOC and (b) explicitly excludes other blog genres such as the corporate or the science blog.

earliest version available on the Internet Archive which was also fully archived (and doesn't exhibit a broken layout structure, for instance).[40]

Part II contains 300 specimens of the genre *personal weblog* as defined in 2.2.3. This part, then, was compiled with the help of the directory *Globe of Blogs*. The procedure should have been quite simple: open the *Personal Weblog* category in this directory for every year between 2002 (launch of the directory) and close-to-present (2012 in the case of the current study), work through the resulting list and collect every blog sufficiently well archived. Figure 5 provides a screenshot of such a list, archived in 2004:

Figure 5: List of Personal Weblogs in the Globe of Blogs *Directory, Archived in 2004*

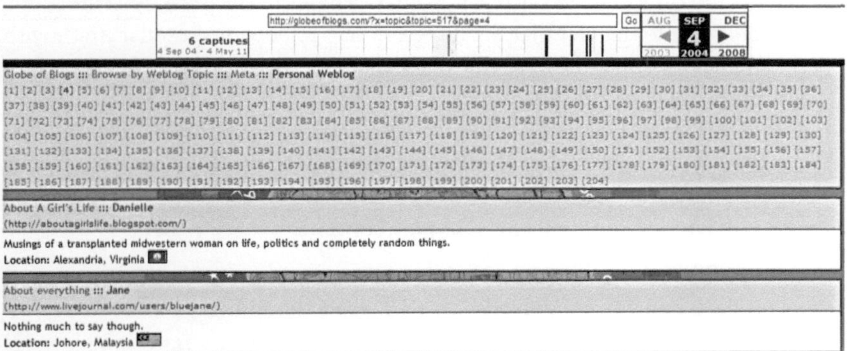

Usually, however, the *simple* plan doesn't work out and my study was no exception for the following reasons:

- Figure 5 shows that the Archive usually contains only a few snapshots of each list (2004, 2009, 2010, and 2011 in the example). It was therefore not possible to just choose a year (e.g., 2004) and then go through the lists one by one. Rather, the availability of list pages in the Archive had to be taken into account.
- Frequently, a blog's hyperlink on a list does not lead to a blog page of the same year as the list page, either because the blog wasn't archived at all in that year or because the archived version is not of sufficient quality.

40 *Scripting News* is an exception: There is a 1996 version of the website on the Archive, which, in fact, is only an advertisement for the launch of the project. Therefore, I collected the first version of 1997 – no advertisement anymore but a healthy weblog by then.

In other words, the collection of corpus texts had to take into account not only the availability of list pages in the Archive but also that blogs identified on a list page could often only be found within a range of about one year before or after the archived date of the list page. Quite an issue for a study in the history of a genre, which naturally depends on some sort of accuracy in dating sources and spotting sources of a particular date.

The original plan was therefore dropped and I decided on subdividing part II of the corpus into three sub periods, trying to take account of the issues just mentioned as well as the aim of setting corpus periods of rather equal length:

- Period II.A naturally begins in 2002 with the launch of *Globe of Blogs*. However, I could only detect very few personal weblogs in the years 2002 and 2003 (probably due to the fact that the directory had to become popular first), with a first cluster forming around the years 2004 and 2005. Period II.A therefore comprises the years 2002 to 2005.
- Periods II.B and II.C were actually designed as 3-year periods: 2006 to 2008 and 2009 to 2011. When I collected my data, however, there were also some blogs available for the early months of 2012, which I included to capture the most current developments for that point of time.

To sum up, Table 4 provides an overview of the corpus periods. Please note that I labelled part I and II as "periods" as well, even though there is no "smooth" transition from one into the other. However, period I clearly represents a stage in the history of the personal weblog – we could call it the "pre-natal" period.

Table 4: DIABLOC Periods

DIABLOC	**Period I** *Weblogs*		1997–2000
	Period II *Personal Weblogs*	**II.A**	2002–2005
		II.B	2006–2008
		II.C	2009–2012

2.3.2 Criteria for Selecting Period II Corpus Texts

The small number of period I weblogs available led me to include every blog from this period which I could get hold of. For period II, the situation looked a bit different. Every blog I could reach via a *Globe of Blogs* list page was, at first, a corpus *candidate only* and had to pass several tests before eventually entering the corpus.

First of all, only blogs which were available in the Internet Archive for a specific target period were put to the following tests. As stated above, a blog only archived in 2012 (and not some when between 2006 and 2008) could never have been used to represent period II.B as it might have undergone profound changes in the subsequent years, for example, layout or the deletion/modification of entries).

The second and most essential test is concerned with the validity of an individual personal weblog for a specific corpus period (II.A, II.B or II.C). *Globe of Blogs* does not provide information on when a blog was registered. It is therefore possible that a blog found on a 2007 list had been registered as early as 2002, developed further in the following years and wouldn't have been classified as personal weblog at all in 2007. Therefore, merely allocating every blog found on a 2007 list to period II.B would not have created a collection representative of what bloggers in 2007 thought a personal weblog looked like. For that reason, I've applied two activity tests:

- As a precondition to be selected for the target period at all, a personal weblog had to be active – i.e. show current entries – in the respective period.
- I selected only personal weblogs whose archives did not date back further than the period boundary. A personal weblog with archived entries from 2004 would not have been selected for II.B, for instance. If there were no archives in the sense of a list of links somewhere in the sidebar, I just browsed the blog for its first entry. If neither was possible (for example, pages with earlier entries were not available in the Archive), the blog did not pass the test.[41] I allowed a tolerance range of a couple of months. For instance, a blog found in 2006 with some entries dating back to November 2005 was still allocated to period II.B.

In order to narrow down potential variation caused by language and/or culture areas (Luginbühl 2014), I selected only blogs whose authors had located their blogs on *Globe of Blogs* in the area of one of the main varieties of English (USA, Canada, UK, Australia, New Zealand). This is quite broad a range and the test itself does not stand on very solid ground. However, this was the only option available to focus mainly on the genre-inherent instead of language- or culture-induced variation.

For the purpose of multimodal analysis, I collected only blogs which were archived with sufficient quality. In some cases, I tolerated missing images

41 One exception here is the personal weblog *it's ok to cry here* (II.B) whose archives even date back to 1976 to document the author's birth. As the *actual* entries set in right in period II.B, I decided to include the blog in the corpus.

(hyperlinked to other servers, for instance), but only if the rest of the blog was sufficiently archived.

Finally, I applied an ethical criterion: Whenever authors explicitly prohibited copying, processing or some other further use of their data, the blog was not collected. Additionally, I followed the guidelines of the Association for Internet Research (Ess & AoIR ethics working committee 2002; see also Paccagnella 1997; Marx & Weidacher 2014: 16–24).[42, 43]

2.3.3 Corpus Size, and: What did I Collect Anyway?

A question which has yielded several different answers among corpus linguists is concerned with how many texts should be collected (see, e.g., Marx & Weidacher 2014: 33). For this study, I used a formula proposed by Raithel (2008: 62) for studies in the social sciences:

$$n \geq 10 \bullet K^V$$

In this study, *n* is the number of blogs, *V* the number of features (*Variables*) to be analysed simultaneously and *K* the number of different possible manifestations of a feature which can be anticipated on average (for example, number of different global topics for the variable *topic*). This formula is designed to ensure, theoretically, that even in small-scale studies, each cell of a cross-tabulation represents at least ten cases. The following example gives $n \geq 60$:

Table 5: Example for Calculating Case Numbers in Small-Scale Studies

		Variable y	
		Manifestation y_1	**Manifestation y_2**
Variable x	**Manifestation x_1**	$n \geq 10$	$n \geq 10$
	Manifestation x_2	$n \geq 10$	$n \geq 10$
	Manifestation x_3	$n \geq 10$	$n \geq 10$

42 Of course, I use only blog titles or nicknames in this book and don't refer to real names (if available at all), email addresses and the like.

43 Six personal weblogs did not pass the validity test but were collected in an *additional* section of the corpus because they are very illustrative of some phenomena. I cite them without corpus period under the label "additional excerpt". See 11.1 for a more detailed account.

The present study looks primarily at one feature and its manifestations in relation to the variable *corpus period*. A cross-tabulation therefore contained the period (variable x) and the respective feature (variable y). If the number of blogs for *one* period only is focussed on, then $V = 1$ (as only variable y is relevant, then). I anticipated some features (especially *function*) to yield around 10 manifestations ($K = 10$). Therefore: $n \geq 10 \cdot 10^1$, i.e., $n \geq 100$ for each of the periods II.A to II.C.

I considered Adolphs's (2006: 20) suggestion and collected a complete blog-page for every blog, each containing several entries.[44] Collecting more than a blog's homepage, i.e. pages with further entries, was, again, often not possible as the links to these pages frequently led either nowhere or to a different archiving date. Table 6 gives an overview of the design of the DIABLOC:

Table 6: DABLOC Overview

				Blog-Pages	Posts	Word-Count
DIABLOC	**Period I** ***Weblogs***		1997–2000	30	775	approx. 34,075
	Period II ***Personal Weblogs***	II.A	2002–2005	100	1,091	approx. 224,025
		II.B	2006–2008	100	786	approx. 211,420
		II.C	2009–2012	100	901	approx. 302,017
			Total:	330	3,553	approx. 771,537

According to corpus linguists such as Adolphs (2006: 20), Gries (2009: 24–25) and Sinclair (2004), the DIABLOC is neither representative (reflecting all different parts of the population) nor balanced (reflecting the size of the parts of the population). Instead of a random sampling, I used an *all-you-can-get* method.[45] All results in the following chapters need to be qualified regarding the specifics of the DIABLOC. This is no exception for corpora in general (Adolphs 2006: 8) and in particular not for diachronic corpora. I can therefore only join the authors of the Helsinki corpus of Old, Middle and Early Modern English texts, who state:

44 See 1.3.2 for a definition of the term *blog-page*.

45 The random sampling in which every text of a population has the same probability of entering the corpus is the only way of achieving representativeness for Raithel (2008: 61).

> We acknowledge the restrictions of our corpus humbly but not too apologetically. We see our work as one of the first steps in the field of diachronic [for the current study: diachronic web-based, P. S.] corpus compilation, which may encourage the creation of a series of new historical corpora [for the current study: of web-based genres, P.S.]. (Rissanen 1993: vi)

2.4 Extended Corpus: DIABLOC + X

According to chapter 1.3, a genre description doesn't only extract patterns of language (and image) use out of corpus material but also needs to take into account recurring features of the situation this use of multimodal resources is embedded in. Based on Giltrow (2013: 724), I'd like to argue that a diachronic approach to genre has to reconstruct past contexts of language use and therefore necessarily has to make use of historical sources. Consequently, I enriched the data available through the DIABLOC by bloggers' insider accounts – the meta-discourse of the blogging community – which answer questions such as "How do bloggers talk about their own purposes and audiences?" (Miller & Shepherd 2004: 10) For this purpose, I used introspective accounts such as Efimova's (2009) *Passion at Work* as well as Efimova & Moor (2005), but also the accounts of bloggers such as Rebecca Blood (2000; 2002; 2004), Cameron Barrett (1999a; 1999b) and Dave Winer (2001; 2003a; 2003b; 2004). Benton (2006a; 2006b) provides an extensive collection of answers given by bloggers to the question *Why I Blog*. Ethnographic studies (e.g., Gumbrecht 2004; Karlsson 2006; Nardi et al. 2004a; Nardi et al. 2004b; Reed 2005 and others) offer interpretations and citations of interviews conducted with bloggers.[46] Meta-comments contained in the DIABLOC itself and concerning, for instance, remarks on the intended function or conceptualised audience were also of great value, of course.

The communication form was reconstructed with the help of blogging guides such as *We Blog: Publishing Online with Weblogs* (Bausch et al. 2002). These guides provide instructions for creating blogs, for using certain functionalities etc. and therefore can be seen as historical documents providing insights into the communication form at a particular point of time. As these (printed) manuals might have reacted to current developments with some delay and as there were only very few manuals available for period II.A, I also collected online tutorials and websites provided by blog systems (for example, *WordPress*'s *Codex* site) via the Internet Archive. See 11.3 for a complete list of these sources.

---

46 I was very careful in using these accounts as they were often not primarily focussed on the personal weblog but on blogging in general.

2.5 Summary

In this chapter, I provided an outline of the Diachronic Blog Corpus (DIABLOC), on which the present book is based. I did so because I am convinced that the results and interpretations contained in the following chapters can only be judged on the grounds of knowledge about the research corpus which gave rise to them.

In summary, I compiled the corpus using the Internet Archive (2.1). I consistently applied an ethnocategory-based approach – a text is a member of a genre as soon as it is *declared* as such in some way by members of the community – and sketched my understanding of the terms *weblog* (2.2.1), *blog* (2.2.2) and *personal weblog* (2.2.3) accordingly. In the remainder of this book, *weblog* refers to the 30 blogs I could extract from Cameron Barrett's and Jessie James Garret's lists, whereas *personal weblog* denotes blogs which were listed under this category in the directory *Globe of Blogs*. Generalisations concerning the genre beyond the texts I collected can certainly be made, but we need to be careful in doing so. This is particularly true as the DIABLOC is designed for primarily qualitative analysis (and is therefore rather small, 2.3.3) and was shaped by a number of decisions concerning corpus periods (2.3.1), and which blogs to select (2.3.2). The DIABLOC is complemented by a collection of historical sources (2.4). The next chapter will both give an outline of main methodological decisions and close the introductory part of this book.

3 Methodological Framework

Efimova (2009: 18) opens her methodology chapter by voicing the insight that "[t]alking about one's research paradigm is similar to talking about one's religion." Indeed, there have been profound debates between proponents of qualitative and quantitative research as the two basic methodological paradigms. While quantitative research aims at testing hypotheses at large amounts of data, qualitative studies focus on interpreting small samples and case studies in order to generate theories in an inductive way (Brüsemeister 2000: 21). However, more recent publications stress that, depending on the specifics of the respective object of research, integrating methods from both paradigms proves most beneficial (e.g., Mayring 2010: 124; Dang-Anh & Rüdiger 2015; Klemm & Michel 2015).

Similarly, the current study rests on three methodological pillars, which I'll outline in the next section. Sections 3.2 and 3.3 will then elaborate on two of them as they will be relevant for all the chapters to follow. Please note that every chapter in the main part is introduced by a section *What I Did | What I Read*, which provides detailed information on the methods applied to reach the respective results.

3.1 Mixed Methods: Three Pillars

This study rests on three methodological pillars.

- First, it draws on a variety of approaches which have been established in linguistics and, more particularly, in text and media linguistics.
- A second pillar is provided by the *Grounded Theory* framework, a bundle of qualitative methods and premises developed in the social sciences. The Grounded Theory concept is applied here to correct some blind spots in traditional linguistic methods (see below). Furthermore, Grounded Theory provides a highly transparent framework, which helps structure and aids reflection on the whole research process. It's actually aimed at analysing the statements of social actors on their own practices in order to extract concepts for a theory grounded in everyday life (Feistel 2013: 160). Thereby, important and highly relevant insights can be gained, for instance concerning the purposes of blogging, which can hardly be analysed by relying on textual indicators alone (Askehave & Swales 2001: 208–210). Bloggers' statements are also very revealing as far as the genre split weblog → personal weblog is concerned (8.2). However, if we focussed on what bloggers said about blogging alone, we

could get trapped in several ways. For instance, blogger Rebecca Blood (2000; 2002) has proposed a typology of blogs which had become highly influential in blog-related research until, recently, Puschmann (2013: 90) criticised it as "somewhat prescriptive." Additionally, a pure Grounded Theory approach would not have been able to reveal how textual practices emerge, change, and blend. Therefore, the first two pillars mentioned here, Grounded Theory and established linguistic methods, have to complement each other and enrich each other's limited perspectives.
- The third pillar this study relies on includes quantitative methods that enable the trace of changes in features over time, and therefore allow for sound statements concerning genre change. The input to these quantitative, or, rather, *quantifying* methods and the descriptive statistics carried out in that respect was mainly provided by categories generated by qualitative analysis, that is, the other two pillars.

In the following, I'll elaborate on Grounded Theory and its modification for the current study as well as the third pillar, that is, quantitative methods.

3.2 Grounded Theory: Basic Principles and Circular Framework

As outlined above, Grounded Theory is actually a bundle of qualitative methods aimed at generating theories about the 'everyday' from empirical data. This approach is compatible with the idea of genres as categories of the everyday and socio-cognitive devices outlined in 1.1 and 1.2. In the following, I'll summarise some major Grounded Theory premises, without, of course, claiming to provide a comprehensive introduction (see, e.g., Glaser & Holton 2004).

Most importantly, Grounded Theory conceptualises research as a circular process. Research begins with minimal knowledge about the subject with collection and analysis of first chunks of data. The results provide initial insights, increasing knowledge about the subject and leading to new questions and desiderata, which provide the basis for further data collection and analysis, deeper insights, new questions, and so on. Thereby, an oscillating movement between theory and data emerges during which concepts and conceptual networks are generated and refined step-by-step. According to the principle of *saturation*, this process ends when new data cannot contribute new insights to the emerging theory. The decision *when* this moment is reached is entirely in the hands of the researcher (Feistel 2013: 161).

The simultaneity of data collection and analysis just described is referred to as *theoretical sampling* and is most distinct from other methodologies. In the context of the study presented here, I haven't *entirely* adhered to that principle. The DIABLOC was collected following corpus linguistic principles in order to, among other reasons, make it usable for later studies and comparable to other corpus-based work (see Schildhauer 2014: 121–122 for a more detailed argument).[47] The additional sources (11.3), however, were collected according to the theoretical sampling principle. For instance, questions concerning the development of the communication form led to including blogging guides; issues left open (especially in period II.A when still only few guides existed), led to collecting tutorials and FAQ-sites etc.

The core of Grounded Theory work is *coding*, which refers to selecting relevant text passages, extracting their basic message and labelling them with a code stating the respective concept expressed in the passage. The codes are later structured, summarised, related to each other, etc. in order to arrive at core categories. Glaser & Holton (2004: 13, 15) distinguish between open and selective coding. While open coding is used in early phases (minimal knowledge about the subject), selective coding is applied later when relevant concepts have been identified and the material can be approached by applying the established framework.

Coding is essentially based on constant comparison: the concepts generated during analysis as well as their corresponding text passages are constantly compared with each other in order to further differentiate the concepts and allow for refined descriptions. In this context, it's important not to exclude cases that contradict the emerging theoretical construct but to deal with these cases in a transparent way (*negative case analysis*, Schwartz-Shea 2006: 107). In line with this principle, this book also presents cases that qualify, contradict and challenge general patterns.

Guided by the basic principles of Grounded Theory, I've developed a general methodology for the study presented here, summarised in Figure 6. There are, of course, slightly modified implementations for each of the different descriptive dimensions of the genre model outlined above (1.3). In Figure 6, I used the analysis of post genres (chapter 7) as an example.

---

47 In order to take account of that principle regarding the research corpus, I have, nevertheless, collected some additional blogs for each period in order to test the concepts I gained in previous analytical steps on their saturation.

Figure 6: Grounded Theory Framework for the Present Study

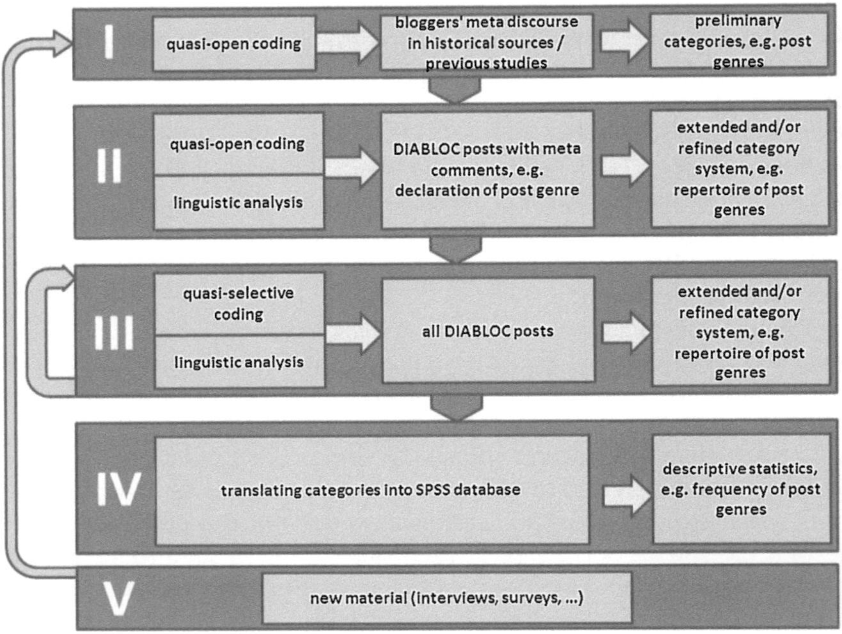

Figure 6 depicts a circular process, structured by several consecutive (and sometimes circular) steps, which aims at saturation. In step I, preliminary categories are generated from the meta discourse of the blogging community to serve as general orientation in the analysis of step II. Results of previous research and categories generated in earlier studies can play a similar role. In step II, the focus shifts towards meta comments in DIABLOC posts (for example, on the purpose of a particular post, on ideas concerning the audience, etc.). In the case of post genres, the respective posts were analysed linguistically (for example, use of hyperlinks, pronouns, coherence, etc.). The resulting extended and refined category system (i.e. repertoire of post genres) serves as input for step III – the analysis of *all* DIABLOC posts. Step III is circular; cases are constantly compared with each other until no further refinements can be gained. The respective codes are, wherever possible, labelled with terminology used in the blogging community to remain as close to the data as possible. This becomes apparent, for instance, when post genres in chapter 7 are termed *sharing experience*, *filtering*, and so on. These labels have been directly transferred from the discourse of the blogging community.

The coding in step I and II is *quasi*-open as, in fact, even the beginning of the research process was not a *tabula-rasa-situation*. For instance, the focus was already determined by the respective descriptive dimension of the genre model to be analysed. Furthermore, previous results were not ignored but incorporated actively into the current study. Step III makes use of *quasi*-selective coding. Here, the material is approached with a preliminary framework in mind. However, I tried to keep the analysis as open as possible in order not to miss new and conflicting cases or concepts not covered by the meta discourse / meta comments analysed in steps I and II. Therefore, the coding was not entirely selective.

Whenever new material can be brought into play, the process (at least theoretically) starts anew by the analysis of new material and generation of new codes. In practice, previously gained knowledge can, of course, not be excluded, so the new coding procedures would be more selective than the initial approaches.

Step IV quantifies qualitative results and transfers them to descriptive statistics. I will turn to that phase in the next section.

3.3 Quantifications and Statistics

In step IV of the circular process (Figure 6), I transfer features and their variants to the statistics software SPSS. Usually, I used a binary system with *1* as *feature present on the blog-page* and *0* as *feature not present*. In some cases, I used *2* as a value to indicate that a particular feature could not be analysed on the respective blog, for example, due to archiving issues. These cases were then excluded from the calculations. In each table in the following chapters, *n* documents the number of cases actually used for the respective statistics. Generally, I applied cross-tabulations with the corpus period as independent variable.

As posts are *the* decisive unit of production and reception of blog content (see 1.3.2, fn. 15), metrical variables (for example, *number of images in posts*) were usually normalised regarding the number of posts. For instance, I was interested in *how many images per post* a particular personal weblog contained (see 6.4.4). In some cases, I additionally applied the *occurrences per 1000 words* measure to make the results comparable with other corpus linguistic studies.[48]

I would like to highlight that the normalised values were calculated for each blog-page separately and only then embedded in the context of the respective period by descriptive statistics. The values presented in the tables do not, therefore, relate to some nebulous mass of posts but to the blog-pages of the DIABLOC.

48 See Schildhauer (2014: 125–126) for a detailed argument concerning the normalisation measures chosen in this study.

Generally, I intended to describe individual (personal) weblogs *first* and *then* investigate how their specific features relate to other blogs in their respective period.

In order to be able to talk about *changes* of a genre regarding a certain feature, I used statistic tests. In the case of nominal variables (*present* vs. *not present*),[49] I employed *Cramèrs V* (given as φ_c), which measures the association between two nominal variables – in this case, a particular feature and the corpus period. If the test suggested such an association, this allowed for the assumption that there are, indeed, differences among the corpus texts of the individual periods. This association was also tested for significance (SPSS automatically performs the Chi Square test) in order to assess the probability with which the association has to be attributed to chance. The significance level was set at $p = 0.05$. Therefore, associations were interpreted as significant if the probability that they *did not* arise by chance amounted to at least 95%.

For metrical variables, I applied the t-test (including the Levene Test, see Meindl 2011: 181–184). This test compares the mean values of two populations (here: two corpus periods). It returns a probability value, allowing for interpretations as to what extent the two populations differ significantly.

Apart from quantifying the results of qualitative analytical steps, I also made use of corpus linguistic methods, which are also quantitative in nature (frequency analysis, keywords, type-token ratio etc.). I will elaborate on these measures in 6.1.

3.4 Summary

This study rests on three methodological pillars: firstly, it combines qualitative linguistic approaches (and also corpus linguistic methods). Secondly, it adopts key concepts from Grounded Theory. Thirdly, it quantifies the results of qualitative analysis by means of descriptive statistics. This mixed methods approach is aimed at combining the strength of various approaches and gaining deeper insights than promised by one method alone (3.1). I've highlighted the principles

49 See Benninghaus (2007: 113–116) for more information on Cramèrs V. The variable *corpus period* is actually *ordinal* (as the values show a specific – temporal – order). However, in order to apply Cramèrs V, the variable was downscaled and treated as nominal variable. In other words: the corpus periods were statistically treated as equal groups of texts. The value returned by Cramèrs V can, therefore, not be interpreted 1:1 (e.g., the later the period, the more of a certain feature) but only via a detour to the underlying cross-tabulations. See Meindl (2011: 69–72) for more information on types of variables and this practice of downscaling.

of theoretical sampling, constant comparison, and saturation as well as coding procedures as key aspects of Grounded Theory. In addition, I've shown how they have inspired the circular methodology of this study (3.2). What is more, I've outlined how the results of qualitative steps are quantified and in what way statistical tests can allow for plausible claims on genre change (3.3).

Part B: Facets of the History of the Personal Weblog

4 The Technical Side of the Personal Weblog: Communication Form

4.1 What I Did | What I Read

In this chapter, I'll turn to the technical constellation which forms the basis of the personal weblog genre and show which communicative potentials arise from this. Several cross references will point to later sections in this book which deal with the use of these potentials; the discrepancy between potential and use will also be sporadically addressed in this chapter.

As there is no deterministic 1:1 relation between the technically-induced potentials and their typical use in a specific genre, it's nearly impossible to reconstruct the potentials from looking at texts making use of them to an initially unknown extent. Consider, for instance, one of the most prominent structural characteristics of blogs in general – reverse chronological order. Table 32 (6.3.4) clearly shows that this way of presenting posts is the only one to be found in DIABLOC posts from II.A onwards. From that result, we would have to conclude that the potentials don't offer any other option. However, the situation is more complex in II.B and II.C, where there are, indeed, other options provided by several blog services.

The current chapter is, therefore, mainly based on a qualitative analysis of a collection of blog manuals,[50] online tutorials and FAQ-sites, some of which were added in the course of the analysis to fill emerging knowledge gaps (see 2.4 and 3.2). While reading, I noticed that what I got was a description of several kinds of blog software at several points in time, with many issues re-occurring again and again; for example, options for embedding images, for allowing and editing comments, and so on. I used the grid which emerged successively to create a data sheet for each period, aiming at filling as many gaps in the grid as possible. Eventually, I grouped the categories of my grid into larger clusters which were partly inspired by Herring's (2007) *faceted classification scheme*. In fact, Herring's *medium factors* provide a neat grid for describing communication forms. However, some aspects I discovered in the material (for example, *modularity*, 4.9) are

50 Some aspects such as the use of blog software (4.2), or widgets (4.9.2), were analysed by accessing the source code of the respective blogs (see also 6.1 for more general information on that issue).

not covered by it. I also included Thaler's (2007) account of *synchronicity* in order to be able to reflect on my results on a richer theoretical level.

Now and then in this chapter, I make reference to some literature on blogs. You will find remarks concerning the communication form of blogs in Herring et al. (2005), Meiler (2013), Puschmann (2010), Rosenberg (2009) and Schlobinski & Siever (2005b).

4.2 The Spread of Blog-Software

Essentially, a blog is not different from other documents on the WWW: what the browser presents as amalgam of language and image structured according to a certain layout is actually nothing but a program script written in HTML (*Hypertext Markup Language*).[51] The blog post on the left is depicted as originally displayed in the screenshot on the right:

Example 6: random and odd *(II.A) as Rendered by a Browser (left) and in Source Code View (right)*

In principle, it's therefore possible to keep a blog without using any special software apart from a text editor.[52] Diagram 1 shows that the vast majority of period I authors didn't use any blog software.[53] In fact, there were only few blog services

51 It's also possible to use languages such as PHP (*Hypertext PreProcessor*, used for interacting with databases). PHP scripts are run on the server on which the website is stored and, eventually, create an HTML document. Such scripts can therefore not be traced by looking at the HTML source code of a website only.

52 Due to the fact that the use of blog software has become highly common over the years, this fact is often neglected. Puschmann states, for instance: "The types of website that refer to themselves as blogs are *generally maintained and updated with a specialized publishing tool* (blog publishing software) which is either installed by the user or available for immediate use as part of a web-based blogging service (e.g., Blogger, Wordpress, LiveJournal)." (2010: 14, my italics, P.S.)

53 70% of the period I weblogs do not show any evidence of a blog software.

available at that time anyway, with *Frontier* (designed by Dave Winer – the author of the weblog *Scripting News*)[54] being the most prominent one. Later, however, the use of blog services gained momentum: I could find evidence for blog software in 77% (II.A) and 96% (II.B and C) of the personal weblogs.

Diagram 1: Overview of DIABLOC Blog Systems

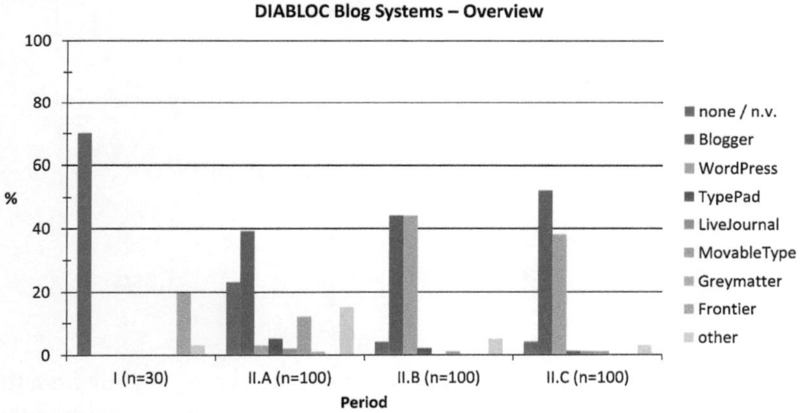

Diagram 1 also shows that *the* blog service for authors of personal weblogs is clearly *Blogger* followed in II.B and II.C by *WordPress*. Blogger was launched in August 1999, shortly after its rival *Pitas* (July 1999).

Essentially, both services offered a way to relieve potential blog authors of the tedious business of hand-coding their website, which involved updating the archives by hand every time a new entry was published. On its platform *pitas.com*, *Pitas* also offered a free domain and server space (Rosenberg 2009: 117). *Blogger* drew on this idea a bit later (Schildhauer 2014: Fn 243). What followed was a "mini-boom in weblog services" (Rosenberg 2009: 112). This led to the creation of a whole landscape of blog systems mirrored in Diagram 1 (see also Figure 7), all of which provided a technically more or less simple solution for blogging without needing to know how to code HTML, but differing widely regarding the potentials they offered concerning interaction with other blogs, privacy, etc.

54 See 8.1 for more on the role of *Scripting News* in the emergence of the weblog genre.

Figure 7: Blog Systems and Dimensions of Accessibility

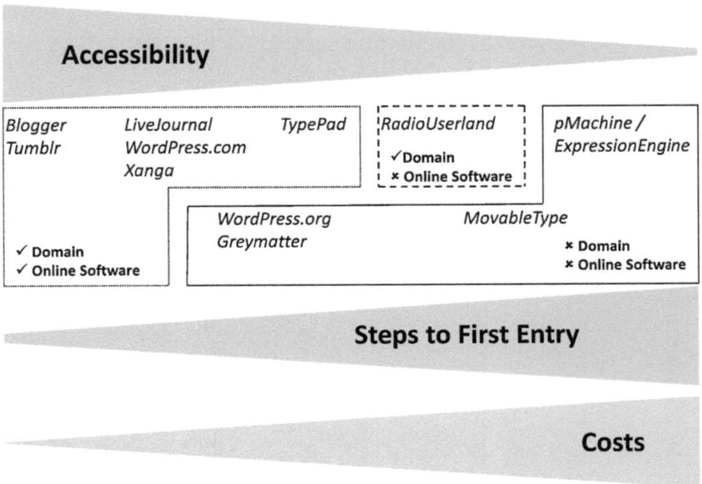

For the purposes of this chapter, it's necessary to abstract away slightly from this heterogeneity of blog services and provide a description of shared and/or rather general features. One way to do so is to refer to the different blog services in terms of how *accessible* they present themselves to lay bloggers (see Figure 7).

Highly accessible services offer online software so that newbies don't have to download anything to their computers. They also provide their users with a domain and server space. The number of steps to take in order to be able to publish the first entry is pretty low for accessible systems. With under 5 steps, *Tumblr* (launched in 2007) is the most accessible in this respect. Additionally, the most accessible services such as *Blogger* are entirely free. Others charge their users for additional options and plug-ins (for example, *WordPress*), raise subscription fees (*RadioUserland*, *TypePad*) or offer their software only at a rather high price (*ExpressionEngine*). In what follows, I'll frequently refer to the accessibility scale as a way to provide a sensible degree of abstraction *and* a detailed picture of the history of the blog communication form at the same time.

4.3 Blog-Postings: Production and Presentation

One of the most salient features of blogs – the reverse chronological order of blog posts – is often attributed entirely to the blog system as if blog software offered no other way of structuring posts (Herring et al. 2005: 145; Puschmann 2010:

33; 55–56). This sub-chapter will show that this explanation doesn't hold equally throughout the whole history of blogging.

Example 7: Blogger's *Textbox in Period II.A (Stauffer 2002: 79)*

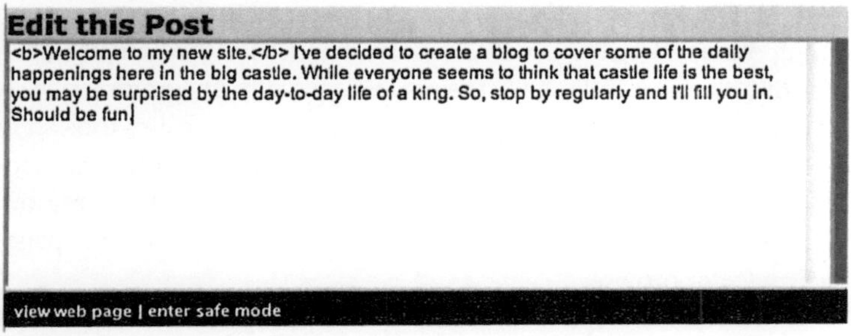

As stated above, blogs were increasingly maintained by using blog systems from period II.A onwards. For this purpose, blog systems provided a textbox such as Blogger's period II.A textbox (Example 7) and a *publish* button. Blogger's early textbox, by the way, is still quite rudimentary. Formatting is only possible via HTML-tags. The comfortable WYSIWYG surface (*what you see is what you get*) with formatting buttons, available in all systems today, was first offered by less accessible blog systems such as *RadioUserland* and became the standard only in II.B. No matter what sort of textbox is used, whenever an entry is produced, it's eventually stored in a database. In a purist sense, each blog is a program script with database queries which is compiled by the blog system. The database queries serve the purpose of retrieving the individual entries and placing them somewhere in the basic layout structure of the blog. This is an essential point: any database query can apply a set of criteria to widen or to narrow the search, but it can also modify the way the output is presented. Presenting the results in reverse chronological order is also based on such a database command: the entries are sorted according to their record number, namely in descending order. That way, the entries which entered the database last are presented first (Puschmann 2010: 55–56). Theoretically speaking, it would, therefore, be fairly easy to manipulate the output differently, for instance sorting the records according to their number in ascending order. In II.A, the most accessible systems, however, don't allow any changes to the reverse chronological order. *MovableType*, on the other hand, allows fiddling with the blog's architecture. The default setting of the attribute *sort_order* can easily be overwritten by the user.

If reverse chronological order is based on a particular database query and output manipulation, then why choose expressly this particular way of presenting posts?

First of all, presenting data in reverse chronology was not a far-fetched idea at all at the end of the 1990s but actually a very common practice. Even in those early days, Already Tim Berners-Lee, the father of the World Wide Web, maintained a site which he regularly updated with new entries on the growth of the young WWW (Rosenberg 2009: 9). This site was structured in reverse chronology. Among others, Berners-Lee chose this structure for the benefit of his readers. Generally, it's easier to look for the newest stuff at the beginning of a site and not at its end. Additionally, at that time – around 1993 – websites took so incredibly long to load, building from top to bottom, that this structure was necessary in order to save time from a technical point of view. For the same reasons, this principle was also employed later on, as well, for instance on the homepage of the *Netscape Navigator* browser.

Period I weblog authors could therefore make use of an established pattern. They, too, had to meet the challenge of presenting dynamic content in a way which immediately showed the recipient what was new without plastering their site with *NEW!* banners or deleting old content. As 6.3.4 will show, many first generation bloggers chose reverse chronology, among them the leading figure Dave Winer, whose weblog *Scripting News* will be characterised as a catalyst of early blogging in 8.1. As period I weblogs were mainly hand-coded, the implementation of a reverse chronology has to be interpreted as reproducing a sensible convention:

Example 8: Considering Reverse Chronology

> It's just an intelligent way to structure a webpage that will be updated frequently, since your browser automatically starts at the top of each page it visits. No one wants to scroll down to the bottom of the page (or even the current day's section) to see if any new content has been posted. With the new content at the top, a visitor can see at a glance whether your page has been updated and easily begin reading your latest entries without any additional effort. A few webloggers prefer to create a new page each day they add content, but weblogs will most commonly feature several days' content in the front page.
>
> (Blood 2002: 44)

We can conclude, then, that the reverse chronology was *not* determined by technological limitation at the beginning of the history of blogging, but only after the developers of the first blog systems decided to implement it in period II.A. In periods II.B and II.C, reverse chronology remained the default setting but many blog systems started to offer additional options in II.B. By the end of II.B, all blog systems apart from *Blogger* offered *sticky posts* which remained at the top even if new content were added. Also, from II.B onwards, *WordPress* and *MovableType* offered a straight chronological order for the first page of a blog: newest entries on the bottom. In II.C, *WordPress* plugins allowed for choosing *every* possible order for posts, for instance, ordering them alphabetically.[55]

Even though chronology is at the core of blogging, additional ways of structuring content developed as early as in period II.A, when *categories* and *tags* were introduced. Categories can be characterised as follows:

Example 9: On Categories

> Categories are a hierarchical method of organizing the site's posts. For instance, if you have a site that offers reviews on automobiles, your categories would likely include 'Cars,' 'Trucks,' 'Motorcycles,' and 'Recreational Vehicles.' You can have subcategories as well; hence, under 'Cars,' you might have 'Sedans,' 'Luxury,' 'Sports,' and 'Hybrids.' An author can assign a post to any number of categories.
>
> (Cole 2010: 11)

Cole's (2010) examples show that, from a semantic point of view, categories are hyperonyms of terms used in the respective entry which can be located on different levels of abstraction. Cole describes *tags* as something different:

Example 10: On Tags I

> Tags are a way of attaching keywords to blog posts. Unlike categories, tags aren't organized into any sort of hierarchy. Essentially, they allow you to be more granular in your classification of content.
>
> (Cole 2010: 11)

An entry which deals with a film featuring George Clooney could therefore be categorised under *film reviews* and *male actors*. Tags would be far more fine-grained and could comprise *George Clooney* and *Burn after Reading*. Stauffer (2008) adds on tags:

Example 11: On Tags II

> Tags give you a way to create free-form associations between your blog entries, and they can also provide hooks into social networking websites such as Technorati.com. And tags are the heart and soul of some multimedia sharing sites like Youtube and Flickr, where the tags help you to locate and share related content with the online community of users.
>
> (Stauffer 2008: 288)

55 This was, by the way, already offered by *MovableType* already in period II.A – the command *sort_by* allowed users to choose a criterion for ordering the posts.

In other words, both tags and categories can lead to the emergence of semantic networks of blog posts. They can connect entries on one blog, but also among different blogs. Thereby, reception processes different from reading chronologically become possible.

Categories appeared first. In II.A, only the less accessible systems offered them (*pMachine, MovableType,* but also *RadioUserland*). *pMachine* allowed one category per post only and *MovableType* understood them as merely a tool for the blog author and required fiddling with the HTML code if categories were also to be presented to the reader. In II.B, however, categories had already spread to all blog systems, which often allowed more than one category per entry and the presentation of categories in a category cloud (presenting frequent categories in a larger font than the ones less frequently used). *Blogger*'s categories are called *labels*; there is no equivalent to tags in this system.

Tags originated with *Technorati*, a blog search engine founded in 2002. As well as a global categorization of blogs, *Technorati* developed the tagging of individual posts with key words. All bloggers needed to do was add a piece of HTML code to the entry containing the key words: <a href="http://technorati.com/tag/NAME" rel="tag">NAME</a>. The *Technorati* robot did the rest. Clicking on a *Technorati* tag on a blog led to entries of other blogs tagged in the same way. Until II.B, therefore, tags were, rather, an *external* key word system, turning the whole blogosphere into a semantic network of posts. When *Technorati* collapsed due to the massive increase of blog posts, tags still survived in other blog systems. In 2007, *WordPress* 2.3 was the first blog system to implement its own tags and a tag cloud– initially also as an external means of connecting posts from different blogs. Later, this situation apparently changed and tags became a way of internal structuring in addition to categories.

Both tags and categories can serve as a semantic guide for a recipient, accompanying the primary chronological principle. Experienced designers can also use them to manipulate database queries in particular ways to only show posts of specific categories on a particular page or to allocate posts to layout spaces according to their category. Thereby, the former chronological order can be broken up entirely for the sake of alternative structures.

However, 6.3.4 will show that chronology, and in particular reverse chronology, is THE basic principle along which personal weblogs work. An important aspect of this which I haven't mentioned yet is the *timestamp*. As early as period I, weblogs usually added the publication date and/or time at the end of an entry. This convention was taken up by blog systems and continued from II.A to II.C. An interesting issue in this respect is backdating. In II.A, timestamps couldn't usually be manipulated by the blogger and invariably gave the publication time of an entry. Only *pMachine* allowed its users to publish an entry pretending it had already been published, say, five months previously. By II.C, this option had spread into the more accessible systems such as *WordPress*. This doesn't seem to be true for *Blogger*, though. Backdating allows bloggers not only to document their lives as they unfold, but also their past. The author of *it's ok to cry here* (II.B), for instance, adds an entry for 1976 to testify to his own birth.

To sum up, this passage has dealt with the question of how much reverse chronological order, a prototypical structural feature of blogs, is determined by the communication form. In contrast to voices blaming it all on communication form, I've suggested a more differentiated perspective: in period I, the main reason to choose reverse chronological order was recipient design. This was a matter of free choice and alternative ways were also chosen, as 6.3.4 will show. In II.A, however, blog systems usually didn't offer alternatives to reverse chronology. Here, the communication form acted in a rather deterministic way. The influence decreased again in II.B and II.C, with new options being provided also by accessible blog systems. If, as 6.3.4 suggests, reverse chronology dominated nevertheless, factors apart from the communication form have to be taken into account, for instance the users' competence (not knowing about options besides the default settings) or laziness (not caring about them) or willingness to follow a reasonable convention.

4.4 Multimodality and Layout

4.4.1 Layout

As far as period I weblogs are concerned, the influence of the communication form on the layout can be estimated just as stated above regarding chronology. As the weblogs are coded mainly by hand, the limits to layout design are more likely to be set by factors such as the individual blogger's competence, creativity and considerations of recipient design.

Period II.A blog systems provided without any exception a template system. Templates were (and still are) given designs which defined the location and measurements of all elements of a blog page (header, sidebar, main part, footer) and their features, for example colour, font and others, even though not all elements actually had to be used (Gerdes 2005: 100). In a template providing two sidebars, one could be used, for instance, while the author decided not to fill the second one.

When a blog was published, the entries were retrieved from the database and filled into that basic framework. The framework was, eventually, nothing more than a given HTML-code, which even back in II.A could be edited by the blogger. Yang (2006) states in II.B:

Example 12: On Templates

> A blog template is a pre-designed page layout. Most blog hosts provide a selection from which you can choose, and it's usually not difficult to modify them by accessing their source code. With the right coding knowledge, or by seeking out blog templates from a third party, you can gain control over what your blog looks like by changing backgrounds, images, fonts, colors, and more. *Staid, generic blog designs are a thing of the past.*
>
> (Yang 2006: 33, my italics, P.S.)

Obviously, the template system was extended after II.A, with some third parties seeking economic profit. At the end of II.B, some of the less accessible systems (for example, *Expression Engine*, but also *WordPress*) still favoured this approach. Others, such as *Blogger*, started to implement a drag-and-drop alternative. In II.C, *Blogger* offered the *Template Designer* and *Visual Editing*, which meant that users could edit layout elements directly within the output version of their blog. These features meant it became fairly easy to change given templates, even for those who weren't experienced in HTML.

In II.B, *WordPress* developed the *theme* approach – a very powerful extension of the earlier template system. *Themes* are a collection of php and css files which describe the elements of a site and different types of sites (for example, *about*, *blog*, *homepage*). Thus, experienced bloggers were provided with a high amount of flexibility. From II.B onwards, the *WordPress* community has been developing countless themes alongside the standard *WordPress* themes, partly for free, but sometimes at fairly high prices. As far as the layout is concerned, *WordPress* themes functioned just like templates in that they mainly defined the arrangement of the individual elements; some themes also offer various options. *WordPress* offered a search template with options to filter for layout types, for instance, sidebar left vs. sidebar right. Because of the large amount of available themes, bloggers in II.B and even more in II.C could choose out of a pile of themes for nearly every constellation of header, sidebar, body and footer imaginable. In II.C, another interesting possibility was introduced as bloggers were allowed to edit a file called *functions.php*. Thereby, they could influence their *dashboard*, that is, the appearance of their *WordPress* user interface, for instance, by adding new menus or options concerning the choice of layouts, colour schemes and the like. That way, the members of the blogging community, at least those using *WordPress*, got the power of shaping the blog system itself.

4.4.2 Multimodality

From period I onwards, there are three profound technical constraints which played a decisive role regarding the multimodality of blogs until period II.C and still do so today:

- *Bandwidth*: This is a measure of the total amount of data drawn from a server account, usually measured per month. If an image of 1 MB is viewed five times in a month, this amounts to 5 MB. Why is this important? Every blog needs a home base. For the most accessible systems, this is provided by the blog systems themselves. But it is also possible to rent such a server space from some other party. Usually, these providers only offer a limited amount of bandwidth per price category. If this amount is exceeded, the blog is either made unavailable for the rest of the month or the transmission speed is reduced tremendously. In all periods, therefore, bloggers have to take into account how many image files and the like they offer as each file constitutes a potential threat to overdrawing the bandwidth account.
- *Storage space:* Additionally, bloggers have always had to consider how much space they rent on a server – again, something related to how much money they're willing to pay for maintaining their blog. Blog systems, too, have always restricted the storage space available for media files. In II.C, for instance, *Blogger* offered image hosting in cooperation with *Picasa* with a maximum storage space of 1 GB per blog. In the same period, *WordPress* users needed the *VideoPress* plugin in order to be allowed to upload video files. This is still true at the time of writing (2015). Of course, *VideoPress* is not part of the default package but of a premium offer currently priced at €99 per year.
- *Transmission Speed*: The larger the files that have to be loaded when viewing a blog, the longer the site needs to fully show. This factor was obviously something to take into account in II.A, when one large file could cause a tediously long wait:

Example 13: Considering Transmission Speed

> To those of you on dial-up: I'm sorry. I'm sure the loading time is horrible. I think this shot is worth the wait, though, especially since calling myself an amateur photographer is, at best, a stretch.
>
> (*(sometimes) cynical nature* 78, II.A)

Besides these infrastructural constraints, all blog systems took part in a general trend of increasing the possibilities of embedding media files from II.A to II.C. While in II.A at least uploading image files was the standard for all systems apart from blogger,[56] only few accessible systems offered thumbnail options. Thumbnails are small-sized versions of the original image which can be enlarged by clicking on them. Blogs employing thumbnails can still be viewed much faster, with the user deciding which images to enlarge. In II.B, thumbnails spread to more accessible systems as well.

As late as II.C, *Blogger* only offered quite restricted options for positioning images within a blog entry (right, left, and centre). *WordPress*, on the other hand, provided more flexibility in this period as a drag-and-drop approach was employed and, additionally, the tool *EditImage* enabled an easy way of editing images (for example, cropping).

WordPress also became more flexible in handling other file types besides images (for example, *pdf*), when a file manager was introduced in II.C. This tool allowed easy hyperlinking of all sorts of files within the blog entry. Additional plugins such as *WordPress*'s *VideoPress* made embedded players available so that audio and video files could be played directly from the blog. Apart from these sometimes rather costly plugins, it became increasingly common to make use of *Youtube*'s embedding option: today *Youtube* still provides a special hyperlink for each video. Inserting this link results in embedding *Flash Player* so that the video can be viewed without the need to leave the blog and switch to the *Youtube* platform entirely. *Tumblr* (founded in 2007) tremendously eased handling of a variety of different media types. *Tumblr* users have always been able to choose among various entry types depending on what modality to focus on (image, audio, video, plain language), with different sets of options provided in the next step.

4.4.3 Summary

This sub-chapter traced the steady increase in potentials concerning layout and embedding a variety of media files. Concerning layout, II.A is (just as in the previous chapter) the most restrictive period, as the given templates dominating this period became more flexible and increased in variety only in II.B and II.C. In period I, there were no restrictions apart from the scope provided by the HTML-standard. However, in this period the HTML competence of an author was often decisive in being able to launch a weblog at all. Regarding media files, the potentials steadily increased alongside the improvement of the infrastructure. In all periods, the general constraints of storage space, bandwidth and transmission speed have to be taken into account.

---

56 With *Blogger*, images had to be embedded directly into the HTML code by using the <img> tag, which referred to another server where the image was stored.

4.5 Synchronicity and Interactivity

According to Herring's (2007) definition of *synchronicity*, the communication form underlying blogs is *asynchronous* throughout all periods. The blog communication form differs in that respect, for example, from the *chat* communication form, which provides the potential of quasi-synchronous communication (Garcia 1999) of users mutually logged in to a chat service. The blog communication form has never required, and in many cases even enabled,[57] the co-presence of author and reader in the sense that both are logged in at the same time. Puschmann (2009) states:

> Similarly, blogs are characterized by affording their users unlimited floor time in a quasi speech situation that is potentially interactive but not encumbered by the constraints of synchronous communication. (Puschmann 2009: 2)

The interactive potential mentioned by Puschmann was already available in period I, mainly because of the most crucial feature of the World Wide Web: hyperlinks. Due to this functionality, period I weblogs could cite and comment on each other and even point to cited posts to some extent (Blood 2004: 54).

4.5.1 Comment Function

At the beginning of II.A, the interactive potential increased immensely via the introduction of the comment feature. It allowed leaving replies to posts directly on the respective blog. The feature emerged between 2000 and 2002 out of the need for simplifying the interaction. At first, commenting was made possible by special systems which were developed by hackers, run on a different server and only connected to the respective blog via a hyperlink. These systems were, however, not very stable or comfortable, especially due to the poor infrastructure of the servers involved (Bausch et al. 2002: 183; Blood 2004: 55). In 2001, the developers of *MovableType* (one of the less-accessible systems) reacted and integrated the comment function in their software package. From then on, *MovableType* blogs offered a box for leaving comments under each entry, with comments to be displayed directly underneath in linear, non-branching structure (Rosenberg 2009: 148). With the beginning of II.A, this function had already established itself in all blog systems apart from *Blogger*, which caught up with this development in 2004 (Meiler 2013: 75). From II.B, this functionality has been one of the

57 It's rather exceptional that readers have to log in to view a blog. See 4.7 on privacy options.

indispensable standards of blogging, with blogs truly being "potentially interactive" (Puschmann 2009: 2).

The comment function created the potential of quick, though not immediate, feedback (as I've stated above, there has never been anything resembling chat-like co-presence of author and reader, a precondition for immediate feedback). In II.B, the immediacy of feedback by comment was potentially reduced when nearly all systems started to implement features for moderating comments.[58] In most cases, these features allowed authors to check comments before releasing them. Since II.C, many blog systems have additionally offered word and link filters designed to prevent spam and other unwanted comments.

4.5.2 Multiple Authorship

Apart from the lack of co-presence and the design of the comment function itself, other features of the blog communication form have also contributed to a rather delayed feedback. In period I, this was due to the effort it took to hand-code each new post, with slight changes to the whole site possibly necessary until everything showed correctly. From II.A onwards, blog systems started to offer ever-increasing options of formatting and editing, which also invited some investment of time into writing posts. For instance, a spell checker was part of the standard in all systems as far back as II.B.[59] In II.A, *Blogger* queued new posts to be edited before publishing. Bloggers could, however, also circumvent the queue by hitting the additional *post & publish* button.[60]

Delayed feedback has also been promoted in many blog systems since II.A because of the potentials of multiple authorship. These options were also offered by *Blogger* as early as II.A. At the other end of the accessibility scale, *pMachine* and *ExpressionEngine* offered not only rather complex systems of access and editing permissions but also an editor function which allowed the blog administrator

58 Again, *Blogger* lagged behind a bit. In II.B, this system only provided the opportunity of deleting comments retroactively, with full comment moderation only to be implemented in II.C. Despite that, it can be stated that Serfaty's claim that "the weblog software is in charge of displaying reader's answers" (Serfaty 2004: 66) did not hold (anymore) in II.B.

59 This also holds for *Blogger*, even though spell checking in II.B was rather uncomfortable because users had to switch between editing and spell checking mode when revising their entries. This probably increased (at least in some cases) the amount of time for producing an entry considerably.

60 From II.B, most blog systems have offered options of editing posts *after* publishing. This procedure, however, has not been looked at very favourably by the blog community.

to review all posts before publishing. From II.B, *WordPress.org* has also offered comparable tools for team blogs. In II.C, the support for multiple authorship can be considered a standard feature for all blog systems.

4.5.3 Permalink

A major pre-condition for the development of extended blog conversations over different blogs is the possibility to hyperlink blog entries. In period I, this was highly complicated as bloggers could, in fact, only hyperlink another weblog's blog-page.[61] In 2000, *Blogger* introduced the permalink feature which immediately facilitated hyperlinking blog *posts* instead of *pages*, and which was found in all blog systems only a few years later. The permalink feature allocates a new page to each new post so that each one receives its own hyperlink. Clicking on a hyperlink does not open the actual blog-page but a page showing the specific entry only. The impact of this technology on blogging was judged as tremendous even fairly early:

Example 14: On Permalinks

> It [i.e. the permalink, P. S.] may seem like a trivial piece of functionality now [i.e. 2003! P. S.], but it was effectively the device that turned weblogs from an ease-of-publishing phenomenon into a conversational mess of overlapping communities. For the first time it became relatively easy to gesture directly at a highly specific post on someone else's site and talk about it. Discussion emerged. Chat emerged. And - as a result - friendships emerged or became more entrenched. The permalink was the first - and most successful - attempt to build bridges between weblogs. It existed way before Trackback and I think it's been more fundamental to our development as a culture than comments... The creation of the permalink built-in [sic, P. S.] memory - links that worked and remained consistent over time, conversations that could be archived and retraced later.
>
> (Coates 2003)

The permanent availability of blog entries and even whole strands of conversations also takes pressure off bloggers: it's not necessary to be particularly quick (like in chats, Grube 2011: 54) to make a relevant contribution to the topic at hand. Contributions won't get lost and, provided bloggers use hyperlinks, their connection to a strand of conversation can be recognised.

---

61 6.3.4 will show that some period I weblogs created one page for each new entry. In these cases, hyperlinking was, of course, fairly easy and similar to today.

4.5.4 Trackback

The benefits of the permalink addressed above were further increased when the trackback was invented in 2002. Trackbacks enable bloggers to monitor where and when posts are published which cite one of their own entries: As soon as an entry is cited somewhere, a link to the citing entry appears below the cited post. Many blog systems don't send trackbacks automatically by inserting a link to the cited entry in the new post, but require bloggers to provide the respective link in an additional field, for instance *TypePad* in II.B. As *MovableType* developed this technology, it worked only among blogs of this system at first. It was not before the end of II.A that trackbacks also appeared in other systems (Efimova & Moor 2005: 1), but by II.B, all blog systems supported the technology. Usually, authors can decide for each entry individually whether trackbacks should be shown or not.

4.5.5 Summary

Blogging was already potentially interactive in period I. The spread of the comment feature as well as the permalink and trackback technologies are further milestones on the way to the high interactive potential which can be attested for the blog communication form in II.B. This sub-chapter has also shown that the blog communication form is rather "relaxed" as compared to chatting. It promotes delayed feedback because of features like comment moderation, editing and formatting, as well as options for multiple authorship. Permalinks and trackbacks also relieve bloggers of some pressure as contributions to blog conversations won't get lost and, additionally, can always be traced back to their reference posts. The features discussed here all developed in the early years of blogging shortly after the millennium and were established as common standard in II.B, also taken up also by newcomers such as *Tumblr* (2007).

4.6 Number of Participants

Already in period I, the communication form provided the potential of a *many-to-many* communication. It was perfectly possible to maintain a blog from different locations, provided all authors possessed a user name and password for the blog domain. Concerning readership, there were also no limits in period I and subsequent periods.[62] Many blog systems all along the accessibility scale had

---

62 Please see the following section 4.7 on opportunities on setting limits on the circle of readers.

already implemented functionalities for multiple authorship by II.A and elaborated on that in later periods.

The spread of the comment feature in II.A (4.5.1, 6.3.4) also supported the readers' participation in the blog. Their contributions could, from then on, be voiced directly within the blog communication form and didn't have to take a detour via other forms such as e-mail anymore, as was still the case in period I. As comments could now be read by everyone, the many-to-many communication on blogs was no longer fixed to the constellation *author – reader* but could be extended to *reader-reader* communication, with conversations developing their own dynamics loosened from the author[63] and, because of *trackback* technology, even detached from the original post (Efimova & Moor 2005: 7).

4.7 Privacy

Even though Puschmann (2010: 31) claims that "[t]he facet of private messaging does not apply to blogs," I wouldn't exclude this aspect from the description of the blog communication form *per se*. Already in period I, weblogs could be protected by setting a password. It was also perfectly possible to make some changes to the website's *robots.txt* and thereby exclude crawling software, which would have indexed the website for search engines.

For period II.A, the sources mention that *Blogger* allowed the choice of whether a blog should be public or private. *Public* meant that a new blog appeared on lists maintained by the *Blogger* platform – some sort of showcase of *Blogger*-generated blogs for other *Blogger*-bloggers.[64]

According to the sources, *LiveJournal* offered a range of options of private messaging at the beginning of II.B – probably even earlier. For instance, individual entries could be protected by a password or made visible only to specific audiences. Additionally, the system allowed flagging an entry as absolutely private so that it would show to the blog's owner but to no one else. A similar range of options was offered by *TypePad* in II.B:

63 But see 4.5.1 on monitoring comments, a functionality which put the authors again in a powerful position. This asymmetry between bloggers and commentators reminds Baron (2008: ch. 6) of the constellation typical of *talk radio*.

64 We can assume that visibility for search engines is connected to this option, too. However, the sources are silent on that matter.

- *Publicized:* everyone can view the blog. It also appears in the list of recently-updated *TypePad* blogs. *Technorati* and other blog search engines are notified about new entries.
- *Non-publicized*: everyone can view the blog but it doesn't appear in the lists and neither are search engines notified.
- *Password-protected*: only readers in possession of the password can view the blog.

WordPress, too, offered several options similar to *LiveJournal* and *TypePad* (also in II.B). If *WordPress.org* users were experienced enough to install some plugins and modify a file called *htaccess*, they could even exclude certain users or groups according to their IP addresses. They could also require their readers to register for the blog if they wanted to read entries.

In II.C, at least a minimal set of privacy options was part of the standard of all blog systems. *Blogger*, too, offered more than the initial *public-private* option mentioned above. Considering the privacy facet is, therefore, more than relevant for a description of the blog communication form.

However, looking at the blog data typically used in studies, it doesn't come as a surprise that Puschmann, for instance, doesn't consider privacy an issue for blogging. Researchers usually find blogs in blog directories such as *Globe of Blogs*, via search engines as *Technorati* or with the help of crawlers. Blogs which can be found that way are those with the fewest privacy restrictions. The same holds for the current study as I compiled the DIABLOC with the help of a blog directory. The DIABLOC, therefore, doesn't allow any conclusions on how frequently personal bloggers made use of the privacy options outlined here.

4.8 Anonymity

I understand anonymity here as "the degree to which a communicator perceives the message source is unknown and unspecified" (Anonymous 1998: 387). While *privacy*, then, is concerned with the message itself, *anonymity* applies to the source, or rather, to the recipient's perception of the source. An important dimension in this respect is *source knowledge*, i.e. "the degree of familiarity between the source and the receiver" (Anonymous 1998: 390), part of which is knowing the source's name.

It's not a matter of the communication form which degree of anonymity bloggers actually aim for. I'll turn to this question in 5.6. However, it's important to note that the communication form allowed concealing the blogger's identity, thus keeping the source knowledge at a rather low level. Regardless of blog system and period, authors could always decide to conceal their true name and write under a pseudonym so as not to show author information in the blog's metadata.

4.9 Modularity

This last facet describes the scope which a communication form provides for its own modification and complementation, when further modules can be added to the software core. Regarding blogs, there are two main types of these modules:

- *Plug-ins* are small programs which add some functionality to the original blog software. A typical plugin is, for instance, *Akismet*, which is currently part of *WordPress*'s basic configuration and merely needs to be activated by users. *Akismet* is a spam filter for comments. Just like this spam filter, plug-ins usually don't reveal themselves to the blog readers and rather work backstage.
- *Widgets*, on the other hand, have a graphic output interface and appear as small modules typically in sidebars and footers.

4.9.1 Plug-ins

Plug-ins were already present in II.A in nearly all blog systems. They enabled, for instance, desktop publishing – users could write and edit their entries offline and connect with the blog system only for publishing. Generally, the more accessible blog systems have never exhibited a high compatibility with plug-ins because they provide online software which has to remain stable for all users relying on it. Adding new snippets of code from the outside always constitutes a security risk. For that reason, there were no *WordPress.com* plug-ins even in II.C.

For *WordPress.org*, however, which is the DIY-version of *WordPress.com* with software to be installed on the user's server, there were already numerous plug-ins in II.B. They were mostly created by members of the blogging community and shaped according to the community's needs, as the following example illustrates:

Example 15: Plug-ins and Blogging Community

Another experiment in academic blogging has been the Academic Citations wordpress plugin, which began as an idea in a WRT post but was brought to fruition by reader and talented developer Julie Meloni. The concept for the plugin was that serious blogs should (like e-journals) provide their own professionally formatted citations. Through adding them, we felt we were helping transform the system of citations endemic to blog posts into formal claims of academic legitimacy. Ironically, we discovered in the process that most surfers landing on our project were not interested in helping others cite their blog posts - instead, they were looking for a way to format bibliographic citations to elsewhere.
(*Writer Response Theory* in Benton 2006a)

WordPress's open source approach (providing users with the *WordPress* source code) has always made it rather easy for experienced members of the community to identify gaps in its functionality and write modules to fill them. It has also always been the community itself taking responsibility for the quality of the plug-ins by evaluating them with a scoring system. Such a pronounced focus on the community is rather exceptional. Blog systems such as *MovableType*, *TypePad* and *ExpressionEngine* only offered plug-ins written by their own developers. Even these less accessible systems, however, retained the community's role as gatekeeper.

4.9.2 Widgets

Actually, widgets are older than the World Wide Web and were already part of *Apple's* early graphic operating systems. However, the idea was transferred to blogs only reluctantly. In II.A, *pMachine* offered a tiny module called *pBlock*, which could be added to a blog. *pBlocks* were usually small boxes, situated in the sidebar, which could, for instance, show photos or something similar. *pBlocks* could be configured in such a way that they could take different states, for instance several photos in succession, or in randomised order, which are retrieved from a folder on the server. *pBlocks* could also be used in more creative ways, for example, to change the blog's background colour randomly.

In II.B, widgets could be found also in *WordPress* and *MovableType*. Both systems delivered some widgets such as a search box and a calendar as part of the core software package. Depending on the constraints of the current theme, the blogger only needed to activate these widgets. There were already widgets developed by members of the community and released in user forums as well. *Blogger*, too, allowed use of some widgets, which were part of the online software system. A *Blogger* widget, still typical today, connects blogs with the image platform *Flickr* and shows image galleries.

In II.C, *Blogger*'s standard widgets were comparable to those of *WordPress* and others. Typically, widgets were added, arranged and removed by drag-and-drop. This made adding snippets of code superfluous, but nevertheless still possible and important for developers of *WordPress* themes.

Probably due to their easy handling, using widgets became so popular that the sources contain warnings against their exaggerated use:

Example 16: On Exaggerating Widget Use

> I can't stress enough that although widgets are awesome, and I have lots on my own blog, it's easy to get carried away and have too many widgets on your blog. When people start mentioning how long it takes for your blog to load or that your blog 'looks funny', it's probably time to take a hard look at those widgets, especially the custom ones, and see what you truly need to have and what is just blog bling.
>
> (Hussey 2011: 161)

The next sub-chapter investigates the extent to which DIABLOC blogs follow this trend.[65]

4.9.3 Widgets in the DIABLOC

Example 17: Widgets in Asian Polyglot (II.C)

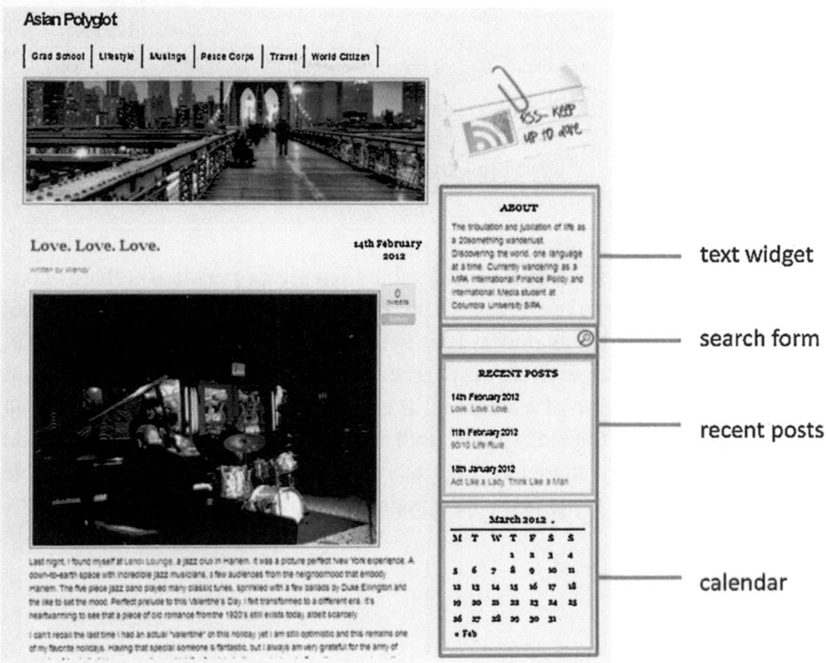

---

65 This is actually an aspect of *using* rather than providing potentials and could therefore also appear in chapter 6 instead of in this current chapter, which deals with the potentials provided by the communication form. However, I decided for this spot here as widgets are so closely associated with the technical constellation of the communication form.

A typical widgeted blog in II.C showed a modular structure similar to Example 17. However, not in every case were these building blocks realised by widgets – sometimes they were already implemented by the blog system, hand-coded by theme designers (particularly navigation bars) or by experienced bloggers. The following data is therefore based on an investigation of the source code of the DIABLOC blogs. As widgets are usually activated by commands containing the word *widget* (for example, the *register.widget* command in *Blogger* blogs), I searched for these lines in the source code. Quite probably, some of the more fancy hand-coded widgets escaped my view due to that approach, but it provides a good picture of what can be considered typical of personal weblogs.

Table 7: Modularity I - Presence of Widget-*Commands in Source Code*

Period	**Widgets**				**Total (valid cases)**	
	no		**yes**			
I	100.0%	(30)	0.0%	(0)	100%	(30)
II.A	99.0%	(99)	1.0%	(1)	100%	(100)
II.B	47.0%	(47)	53.0%	(53)	100%	(100)
II.C	7.0%	(7)	93.0%	(93)	100%	(100)
$\varphi_c = 0.776 \mid p < 0.0001$						

As could be expected, there is a considerable increase of personal weblogs containing such *widget*-commands from 1% in II.A to 93% in II.C. The one personal weblog in II.A may strike as odd as blog systems actually didn't offer widgets in that period. The one widget in II.A is part of the personal weblog *The Asylum* and embeds the search engine of a webring. It is therefore a third-party embedding and nothing offered by the blog system itself. With $\varphi_c = 0.776$ and $p < 0.001$ we can assume an evolutionary change of the personal weblog in this respect. As Table 8 shows, the *number* of widgets per blog page also shows a significant[66] increase:

66 The t-test yielded significant differences between the mean values of II.A and II.B as well as of II.B and II.C.

Table 8: Modularity II – Number of Widgets per Blog-Page

Period	Widgets per Blog-Page				N (of total)
	Min.	Max.	Mean	σ	
I	0.00	0.00	0.00	0.00	30 (30)
II.A	0.00	1.00	0.01	0.01	100 (100)
II.B	0.00	24.00	4.95	6.359	100 (100)
II.C	0.00	47.00	13.82	10.891	99 (100)[67]

On the other hand, there are blogs in each period (even in II.C) for which the use of widgets could not be attested at all. Quite probably, we observe a case of widening the genre category here (see 1.5.1), which is reflected in the rise of standard deviation.

Table 9 provides an overview of which widgets are actually used. Please note that this survey was based only on those personal weblogs only which contained at least one widget.

Table 9: Modularity III – Use of Selected Widgets in Personal Weblogs Containing Widgets

Period	Twitter	Search Feature	Text Widget	Current Entries / Comments	Category Cloud	N (of total)
II.A	0.0% (0)	0.0% (0)	0.0% (0)	0.0% (0)	0.0% (0)	1 (100)
II.B	0.0% (0)	17.0% (9)	45.3% (24)	34.0% (18)	54.7% (29)	53 (100)
II.C	10.8% (10)	30.1% (28)	64.5% (60)	28.0% (26)	45.2% (42)	93 (100)
	$\varphi_c = 0.206$ $p = 0.044$	$\varphi_c = 0.152$ $p = 0.180$	$\varphi_c = 0.209$ $p = 0.040$	$\varphi_c = 0.083$ $p = 0.603$	$\varphi_c = 0.122$ $p = 0.337$	

All widgets apart from the *Twitter* widget[68] can already be traced in II.B, with text widgets being most popular. They can be used, for instance, to provide a short author biography or a blog description in the sidebar.

In summary, the DIABLOC mirrors the growing popularity of widgets, which is assumedly due to the integration of widgets in the more (and most) accessible blog systems and their ease of use.

67 I decided not to include *Gentle Apocalypse* (II.C) as it uses a very exceptional number of 84 widgets to display images in the sidebar (one image per widget).

68 As Twitter was only launched in 2007, this result is not surprising.

4.9.4 Widgets as Embedded Communication Forms

According to what was said in 1.5.3, widgets can be seen as a case of embedding communication forms. We can assume that both bloggers and their readers mainly perceive a widgeted blog as containing elements of different communication forms such as *Flickr* image sharing, the *Twitter* news feed, a search engine and others. We can roughly distinguish three categories of embedded communication forms on blogs:

- Implementations which recognisably reproduce communication forms: these are probably the most salient widgets which evoke thoughts like "This blog even has a chat!" or "There's a blog within the blog!" I'd like to subsume *Sideblog*, *ChatBox*, *RSS Feeds* and the *Twitter* widget under this category. However, sideblogs don't occur at all in the DIABLOC; only one personal weblog (*Cocktail Nerd*, II.B) contains a chat box.
- Universal navigation elements: these elements have often been used for years and even decades in human-machine-interaction. This category comprises *navigation bars*, link lists (for example, *blogroll*, *category cloud* etc.), *share buttons* as well as *search feature* and *calendar*.
- Text widgets, which are offered as empty spaces to be filled with literally everything from a short biography to an *Amazon* wish list.

Widgets particularly of the first two categories are building blocks of the World Wide Web (and even beyond) and therefore widely known. They can therefore most probably be used intuitively. Implementing elements of the known ensures stability while advancing and enriching the blog communication form.

4.10 Summary and Conclusions

4.10.1 Multiple Layers of the Blog Communication Form

Summing up this chapter, we could observe how the communication form underlying blogs gradually gained more complexity. For most period I weblogs, the communication form comprised only one layer, namely the infrastructure of the Internet combined with the software, protocols and standards constituting the World Wide Web. The constraints at work in this period were therefore mainly of a purely infrastructural nature: bandwidth, transmission speed and storage space. Furthermore, what bloggers could and couldn't do on their weblogs was limited by the potentials of the HTML standard and soft factors such as creativity and competence.

This was the basis on which, in the transition to period II.A and later on, blog systems were implemented. These systems facilitated launching and maintaining a blog, but also provided additional constraints imposed by the respective software. On this layer, plug-ins could be added to an increasing extent, which lessened the constraints of the blog-software. Period II.A blog systems reproduced and *codified* existing blogging practices, for example, reverse chronological order. In some cases, blog systems didn't only reproduce but also improved established practices, as the comment feature illustrates. Additionally, the permalink and trackback functionalities were implemented, increasing the interactive potentials provided by the blog communication form. From II.B onwards, the complexity increased again, when some blog systems (for example, *WordPress*) implemented themes, each with a special frame of design options. Themes could partly exert influence on their own basis, modifying the user interface of the underlying blog software. Within the limits set by a certain theme, users could also implement certain widgets, which are, figuratively, placed on a socket formed by infrastructure and World Wide Web, blog software and theme.

Figure 8: Complexity of the Blog Communication Form

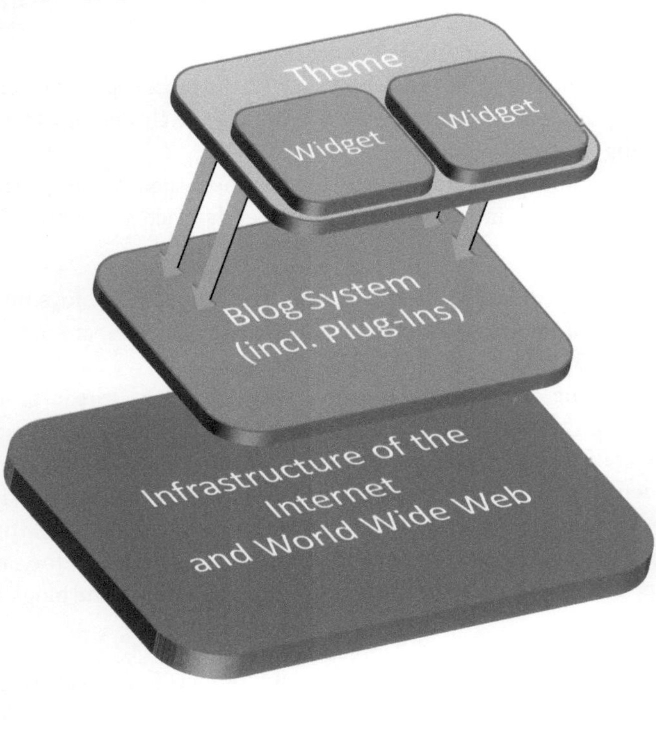

For those bloggers who made use of themes and widgets, the communication form therefore took the complex, multi-layered shape illustrated in Figure 8. This model shows the highest degree of complexity possible for the communication form of a particular blog. Please note that authors were always free to act on lower levels of complexity. Rebecca Blood, one of the early bloggers, states that in 2004, she was still hand-coding her blog, while facing increasing difficulty of keeping up with software-powered blogs though.[69] However, as most personal weblogs from II.A onwards apparently used some blog-software (Diagram 1, p. 49) and widgets were also increasingly popular (Table 8, p. 67), the complex structure in Figure 8 was probably typical of II.C personal weblogs.

4.10.2 The Influence of the Blog Communication Form on other Dimensions of the Genre

Most certainly, the blog communication form exerted some influence on how blogging took place in every period. Regarding the structural dimension, we can make the following general statements:

- The frame of potentials provided by the communication form was most flexible in both period I and II.C, so that we should assume a rather loose relation between communication form and structure.
- II.A, on the other hand, has shown itself to be the most restrictive period. This became especially obvious when considering reverse chronology (4.3) but also concerning multimodality.
- In II.B, the frame of possibilities provided by the respective blog system gradually widened until, in II.C, some systems nearly reached a status of *anything goes* (Grube 2013).

All in all, *deterministic* views explaining the characteristics of blogs by referring directly to the communication form (e.g., Herring et al. 2005) are most valid for II.A, but certainly have to be qualified for I and II.C.

Concerning the dimension of *situation*, first of all, the spread of accessible blog systems led to a considerable increase in potential bloggers as no specialist knowledge was no longer needed (Kumar et al. 2004). The development of the comment, permalink and trackback functionalities considerably increased the interactive potential of the blog communication form in II.A, with authors increasingly gaining control over conversations on their blog. At the same time, privacy options also increased and allowed authors to define the blog's audience

69 In 2014, Rebecca Blood used *MovableType* (http://www.rebeccablood.net/).

more and more if they wished to do so. In all periods, there was the potential of multiple authorship.

Period I weblog authors have blamed a shift of communicative purposes on the spread of blog systems. The original function to filter and comment on interesting hyperlinks had been, according to them, replaced by reporting the mundane:

Example 18: Controversy in First Blogging Community on New Ways of Blogging

> So, with the overwhelming adoption of Blogger, and without an interface that emphasized links as the central element of the form, the blog-style Weblog was born. Much controversy ensued in the original Weblog community: These are diaries, not Weblogs; Weblogs are about links.
>
> (Blood 2004: 54)

I don't doubt that the spread of mainstream blog systems encouraged a shift in the functional spectrum. However, I'd characterise the situation as more complex and less deterministic: as I've shown in Schildhauer (2014: 154), some early blog systems, among them *Blogger*, actually *provided* tools for collecting and commenting on hyperlinks, without interrupting the current "voyage". In 8.2, I'll also discuss that the functional shift which distressed many early bloggers started way before the launch of *Blogger*. The spread of accessible blog systems can rather be described as a catalyst further fuelling a development which had already started.

4.10.3 Accessibility, Innovation, Blogging Community

At the beginning of this chapter, I ordered the blog systems analysed in this study along a dimension of accessibility. Now, I'd like to take up that thread again in Figure 9. This chart lists important features of the blog communication form and states when the sources mention it as part of a specific blog system.[70]

70 As sources were mainly silent on *Tumblr*, I haven't included it here.

Figure 9: Origin and Spread of Selected Innovations in Blog Systems

	Accessibility (high → low)						
	Blogger	***WordPress***	***TypePad***	***Greymatter***	***Radio Userland***	***MovableType***	***pMachine/ Expr.Engine***
backdating posts	-	II.C	II.A	-	-	II.A	II.A
static pages	II.C	II.B	II.B	II.A	II.A	II.A	II.A
sticky posts	-	II.B	II.B	II.A	-	II.A	II.B
tags / categories	II.B	II.B	II.A	-	II.A	II.A	II.A
comment feature	II.B	II.B	II.A	II.A	II.A	before II.A	II.A
moderating comments	II.B	II.B	II.B	II.A	-	II.A	II.A
trackback	II.B	II.B	II.A	-	II.A / II.B[71]	II.A	II.B

The colouring divides the chart into roughly two halves: Dark grey, indicating earliest occurrences of functionalities, dominates in the right part and, therefore, among less and least accessible systems. All these dark grey cells are potential innovations (i.e. *first* occurrences) as the sources were not clear about where exactly a feature originated. This could also be stated for comments and trackbacks – both *MovableType*. There is evidence that *MovableType* was a system in which innovations were first implemented and tried with a rather experienced user group: The website of *TypePad* (produced by *SixApart* just like *MovableType*) stated in 2003 that *TypePad* was meant to be a system of high accessibility but with the range of functions provided by *MovableType*. *WordPress* was launched only in 2005 and

71 As the earliest archived versions of the *radiouserland.com* site are from the beginning of II.B, it cannot be stated with certainty whether trackbacks were offered by this system only in II.B or already earlier.

therefore only had to implement the existing functionalities. *Blogger* is also only a *receiver* of innovations tried out elsewhere.

Apparently, innovations were generated and tried out by less accessible systems and spread to the mainstreamers only later. This may be due to user demographics. The less accessible systems were probably used by experienced and maybe even professional users. On the one hand, they were experiences and/or motivated enough to meet the challenges concerning both finance and IT-competence. On the other hand, these users probably depended on innovations in order to remain competitive.

The most accessible systems provide stability and accessibility for users with less ambitions and the wish *to only blog*. As these systems are the most frequently used in the DIABLOC (Diagram 1, p. 49), we can assume that authors of personal weblogs are more likely to belong to that group.[72] In the terminology of social network theory (Milroy 1987) and diffusion research (Rogers 2003), the *innovators* of the blogging community use less accessible systems, while the (late) majority frequents systems at the opposite end of the accessibility scale.

However, members of the blogging community are not only important for testing and spreading technical innovations. The developers of the blog systems described here are, for the most part, bloggers and central members of the community themselves, for example, Evan Williams and Meg Hourihan (*Blogger*), Dave Winer (author of *Scripting News*, period I, and developer of *RadioUserland*) as well as Matthew Mullenweg (*WordPress*). These bloggers took and still take up patterns of common blogging practice and also provided and continue to provide solutions to everyday blogging problems:

Example 19: Bloggers as Innovators – Mullenweg on Planning WordPress

> What to do? Well, Textpattern looks like everything I could ever want, but it doesn't look like it's going to be licensed under something politically I could agree with. Fortunately, b2/cafelog is GPL, which means that I could use the existing codebase to create a fork, integrating all the cool stuff that Michel would be working on right now if only he was around. The work would never be lost, as if I fell of the face of the planet a year from now, whatever code I made would be free to the world, and if someone else wanted to pick it up they could. I've decided that this the course of action I'd like to go in, now all I need is a name. What should it do? Well, it would be nice to have the flexibility of MovableType, the parsing of TextPattern, the hackability of b2, and the ease of setup of Blogger. Someday, right? Update, 2003–12–26: This became WordPress.
> (Mullenweg 2003)

72 See also 5.5 on author demographics.

This innovative role of the blogging community was strengthened even more in II.B and II.C, when plug-ins and widgets were developed by bloggers for the needs of bloggers – and eventually judged by no one but bloggers (4.9). As *WordPress* theme designers could (and still can) even influence the graphic user interface (4.4.1), it is important not only to investigate *How Blogging Software Reshapes the Community* (Blood 2004), but also to keep in mind the importance of the blogging community with regard to the development of blog systems – and, thus, the communication form.

5 The Communicative Situation of Personal Weblogs

5.1 What I did | What I Read

This chapter will attempt to describe the characteristics of the communicative situation in which personal weblogs are embedded. Several aspects of this descriptive dimension have already been covered for blogs in general by a range of studies. The following tables provide a summary of this blog research. These charts are also the basis for the structure of the remainder of this chapter.

In order to address these aspects I made use of a range of methods: The DIABLOC blogs were coded for number of authors, author demographics (if information were available), identity indicators such as choice of names or pseudonyms, and grades of intimacy of self-disclosure in order to allow for a quantitative analysis.[73]

Qualitative content analysis was applied to meta-comments in DIABLOC texts as well as to the extended corpus to acquire insights into communication spheres, self-disclosure (particularly considerations of selectivity), conceptualised audience and orientation towards communicative maxims. The analysis of linguistic indicators such as deictic elements and the use of pronouns enriched the analysis of the conceptualised audience and was also essential for sub-chapter 5.3 on the *immediacy* of blogging. The investigation of implicatures, presuppositions, frames and scripts paved the way for assumptions concerning the management of background knowledge and complemented the results of qualitative content analysis concerned with communicative maxims. These considerations were based on the analytic construct of an *objective observer* as developed by Claridge (2011: 38):

> all recipients/listeners, including the researcher [...] all of whom are less emotionally involved than the speaker. 'Objective' is thus to be understood as not being affected by the disposition and motives of the speaker and the immediate communicative situation.

Assuming such a position of a reader *not* immediately involved allowed me to make plausible assumptions about the reception of a particular text, which includes, for instance, reconstructing *if* and *how* implicatures arise during that process. The management of background knowledge can also be analysed from that perspective as knowledge gaps that would become apparent for non-insider readers are also notable for a researcher.

---

73 I limited the quantitative analysis to these aspects as they could be coded with the highest degree of transparency and reliability.

Table 10: Synopsis – Research on the Communicative Situation of Blogs I

	Studies	**Key Words / Observations**	**Section**
Communica-tive Sphere	Lenhart & Fox (2006), Lomborg (2014), Reed (2005)	• blogs (and personal weblogs, respectively) as leisure activity that sometimes also uses available time slots at the workplace	5.2
Immediacy	Myers (2010) Reed (2005), Serfaty (2004), Puschmann (2013)	• blogs and personal weblogs as tightly bound to the situation which is reflected (esp. Reed 2005: 227) • *staged* immediacy (Serfaty 2004: 67) • importance of the timestamp and of deictic expressions for linking blog posts and represented situation (Myers 2010: 67–70; Puschmann 2013: 83–84)	5.3
Partner Constellation	Herring et al. (2005), Puschmann (2010, 2013)	• predominantly single authorship (rather than multiple authors) • authors and readers are aware of the fact that an author does not obtain information on the reception of a particular post	5.4
Presentation of Self	Baumer et al. (2008), Blood (2004), Bruns & Jacobs (2006), Chesher (2005), Efimova (2009), Gerdes (2005), Gumbrecht (2004), Herring et al. (2005; 2006), Hollenbaugh (2008; 2010), Hollenbaugh & Everett (2013), Huffaker & Calvert (2005), Kendall (2007), Lenhart & Fox (2006), Miller & Shepherd (2004), Nardi et al. (2004a), Puschmann (2013), Qian & Scott (2007), Reed (2005), Rosenberg (2009), van Dijck (2004), Viégas (2005)	• increasing range of users due to the spread of blog-software (Blood 2004: 55) vs. increasing numbers of IT-workers as blog-authors • authors are mainly in their mid-20s and male, students (or *teens* acc. to Herring et al. 2005: 152) • high importance of authenticity of self-presentation as a tight link between *electronic self* (Miller 1995: 7) and the self which is created discursively in blog posts (see also Yus 2001: 36 as well as Newitz 1995: 18 on web-genres based on the creation of an identity loosened from the offline-self) • selectivity of self-presentation – only certain aspects of an identity are presented (Reed 2005: 230) • intimacy of self-presentation in relation o conceptualisations of blogs as public or private • assumed relations between intimacy and conceptualised audience (Hollenbaugh 2010: 1664) as well as anonymity of the author (Hollenbaugh 2008: 1664; Hollenbaugh & Everett 2013: 293; Viégas 2005); perceived social norms (Efimova 2009: 225) and potential consequences of published information play a role as well	5.5, 5.6

Table 11: Synopsis – Research on the Communicative Situation of Blogs II

	Studies	Key Words / Observations	Section
Audience	Baumer et al. (2008), Brake (2007), Efimova & Moor (2005), Efimova (2009), Gumbrecht (2004), Hoffmann (2010), Hodkinson (2006), Karlsson (2006), Lenhart & Fox (2006), Marlow (2004), Myers (2010), Nilsson [Hendrick] (2002), Puschmann (2009; 2010; 2013), Rosenberg (2009), Scheidt (2006), Serfaty (2004), Stefanone & Jang (2008)	• blogs between monologue and dialogue, *conversation without partner* (Puschmann 2010: 65), divergent assumptions on whether bloggers write for themselves or others (or both, Nilsson [Hendrick] 2002: 3) • publication of blogs reflects a conscious decision for posts to be read (Efimova 2009: 81) • typical audience: friends and family (Puschmann 2010: 66) • complexity of conceptualised audience, possibility to address several sub-groups (Efimova 2009: 155; see Myers 2010: 79–80 on the use of pronouns in that respect) • importance of audience as source of recognition and appreciation • the audience expects new and original content in high frequency • managing background knowledge (e.g., by using hyperlinks) as a means of managing readership (Myers 2010: 91; Nilsson [Hendrick] 2002: 26); hyperlinks as *glue of weblog texts*(Hoffmann 2010: 68) • specific audience roles: witness of self-disclosure (Puschmann 2009: 4), motivation for writing process (Brake 2007: 6, 17; Reed 2005: 232), identity formation (Serfaty 2004: 40, 125), typology of roles such as witness, therapist etc. offered by Scheidt (2006) • formation of a relatively stable community (Hodkinson 2006: 192), principle of similarity (Karlsson 2006: 29)	5.7
Maxims of Communica-tion	Baumer et al. (2008), Nilsson [Hendrick] (2002), Karlsson (2006), Kitzmann (2003), Myers (2010) Puschmann (2009; 2010; 2013), Rosenberg (2009)	• Gricean maxims are not valid for at least a part of personal weblogs (Puschmann 2010: 71–72); it can only be assumed that bloggers follow the cooperative principle when an orientation towards a specific readership is evident (Puschmann 2009: 4) • Nilsson [Hendrick] (2002: 36), however, argues for the validity of Gricean maxims and interprets the use of hyperlinks, among others, as indicator for orienting towards the quantity maxim (see also Myers 2010: 86–89 for examples of implicatures based on Gricean maxims in blogs) • particular importance of quality maxim (Baumer et al. 2008: 1116; Kitzmann 2003: 59–60), especially concerning trust by audience (Karlsson 2006: 9) • what is relevant is determined by the author (Rosenberg 2009: 64)	5.8

5.2 Communicative Sphere: Leisure Activity and Workplace Distraction

I'd like to assume that the blogs of all corpus periods typically constitute a leisure activity. Blood (2002: 4), for instance, characterises period I bloggers as web enthusiasts who spent their time in front of their computers even after work, testing the potentials of the new communication form. Their weblogs were, most likely, a hobby distinct from their professional lives. The author of *Genehack* writes at the end of an apparently long day at work:

Example 20: Blogging as Hobby I

> I really should be going to bed instead of blogging, but...
>
> (*Genehack* 27, I)

In period II, too, many authors draw a clear line between their everyday professional lives and personal blogging. For instance, the author of *Deglaced* apologises for the lack of entries by referring to challenges in the workplace. Thereby, he confirms the distinction between blogging (as a hobby) and working, even though many of his posts deal with his work life:

Example 21: Blogging as Hobby II

> Sorry I have been away for so long, but this past week - the "six" I had to pull - was more like an "eight" as I had two double shifts in there as well.
>
> (*Deglazed* 182, II.B)

The problem of time management addressed in this post was apparently resolved by some authors by using free time at work to write posts:

Example 22: Blogging as Hobby III – (Personal) Weblogs as Workplace Distraction

> I'm back at work this morning, but I'm already tired from just driving in so I may have not made the best decision in coming in at all. [...]... We are having our big Thanksgiving lunch at work today.
>
> (*Bump* 8–11, I)
>
> Now, I gotta tell you guys about the fight I had with the secretary a day later....
> gotta go now, my supervisor is on his way in!
>
> (*Andrena's Ankh* 16–17, II.A)

A number of other DIABLOC blogs similarly served as a welcome distraction from everyday life. Apparently, not only the routine in the office was made less monotonous by blogging, but also housework or study phases. Entries of this kind are embedded in the rhythm of everyday life, which, in some instances, doesn't leave much room for elaborate writing:

Example 23: Blogging as Hobby IV – Integration into Everyday Routines

I have about 2 minutes to write this post so a quick overview of what I've been doing... again in the form of a list!

(*amy's little life* 64, II.A)

crap gotta make a phone call. finish this in a bit.

(*AtomicPup's Blog* 9, II.A)

However, II.B and II.C authors increasingly discovered the hobby *personal weblog* as a way of earning money, for example, by advertising or reviewing products (see 7.6.2). In these cases, the firm line between leisure and workplace activity, drawn by the bloggers cited here, apparently became more permeable.

5.3 Immediacy

The excerpts from *Andrena's Ankh*, *amy's little life* and *AtomicPup's Blog* quoted above also show that blog posts often relate to the author's current situation in an immediate sense: All three posts provide information about the *now* of the author and seem to follow what Reed (2005: 227) calls an "ethos of immediacy" at "the heart of journal blogging". The quotation above, taken from *Bump*, allows the assumption that this ethos of immediacy was also rooted in some period I weblogs already. As other period I bloggers stress the craftsmanship of weblog posts (e.g., Blood 2002: 17), however, *and* push-button-blogging became possible only with the spread of accessible blog systems (see 4.2), I'd like to assume that the ideal of immediacy became an important or even central feature only in the *personal* weblogs of period II.[74] According to Karlsson (2006: 24), this feature constitutes a difference between personal weblogs and online diaries, which are, apparently, not typically composed in the heat of the moment.

Language wise, the adherence to immediacy becomes particularly evident in the use of proximal deictic expressions, for instance the adverbs *here* and *now* as well as the present progressive in the following examples:

74 This assumption is supported by Viégas (2005): "Because the cost of publishing is low, and changes can be broadcast instantly over the web, authors tend to add entries to their blogs frequently and spontaneously, creating highly dynamic sites."

Example 24: Stressing Immediacy through the Use of Proximal Deictic Elements

And now? Now all soapy and mellow from the bath what I really fancy is a glass of merlot. But I'm not going to do that. I'm going to go to bed.

(*All back to mine* 26, II.A)

So here I am, on Christmas night. My family is asleep, and I'm laying on my stomach listening to Sarah McLachlan

(*Alone in Tacoma* 50, II.B)

The deictic centre for the interpretation of these expressions is provided by the entry's timestamp (Puschmann 2013: 91).

Table 12: WordSmith Match of Frequency Counts - DIABLOC vs. BNC (a: $p = 0.01$, otherwise $p < 0.0001$; LLH = Log Likelihood, see Dunning 1993)

	Freq. BNC	Period I		Period II.A		Period II.B		Period II.C	
		Freq.	LLH	Freq.	LLH	Freq.	LLH	Freq.	LLH
I	0.74	1.26	69.87	2.63	2560.01	2.74	2899.02	2.66	2839.78
WE	0.30	–	–	–	–	0.41	28.50	0.42	38.61
HERE	0.07	–	–	0.12	28.26	0.18	110.07	0.18	123.69
NOW	0.14	0.21	7.8[a]	0.22	37.29	0.20	19.21	0.19	13.86
TODAY	0.02	0.05	6.27[a]	0.09	101.14	0.07	53.13	0.06	31.76
YESTER-DAY	0.02	–		0.03	9.90	–	–	–	–

Table 12 lists proximal deictic elements of person (*I*, *we*), place (*here*) and time (*now*, *today*) and compares their frequencies in the BNC (British National Corpus, 100 Mio tokens) and the respective DIABLOC periods. The table was calculated using a *WordSmith* word list match, which returns only items that are used significantly more often or less often than in the reference corpus (here: the BNC). It becomes apparent that the frequency of proximal deictic expressions is indeed significantly higher in personal weblogs than in the reference corpus. This holds, to a limited extent, also for period I weblogs. *Yesterday* is not a proximal deictic element as it points away from the deictic centre. It was, however, included under the assumption that blog authors would use it frequently to talk about the immediate past. Interestingly enough, it is only listed in period II.A. This supports the assumption of an "ethos of immediacy": Bloggers apparently prefer tell us what has happened *today*.

Of course, there are also posts which deal with events that are further away, in a temporal sense, from the now of the author at the time of composing the post. *Asian Polyglot* (II.C) contains an end-of-year review each year, for instance, and the author of *50 years of angst* (also II.C) reflects on a past that stretches over several decades. However, even entries of that kind are, actually, related to the author's now at the time of writing:

Example 25: End-of-the-year Review

> This is always my favorite post to write each year. A lot happens in a year, and I am always amazed at what all took place when I write this post. 2011 was a good year. My life faced new changes and challenges, and I walked away a stronger, and more experienced person than before.
>
> (*Asian Polyglot* 64–69, II.C)

In some posts, immediacy is *staged* as the following example illustrates:

Example 26: Staged Immediacy I

> I was amazed to find that your normal household Brasso and a piece of micro fiber cloth, some elbow grease and 20–30 minutes of "polishing" can bring your Nano back into the spotlight of gorgeousness.
> I didn't have Brasso, but I did have a bottle of Silvo (same polish, only for silverware), the piece of microfiber cloth that came with my PSP, and 30 minutes to kill.
> [copious amounts of rubbing, polishing and 30 mins later...]
> **ALL** of my scratches are gone - GONE! It looks like the first time I took it out of the box.
>
> (*brit blogger* 60, II.B)

The first lines of the posts point to the fact that it was composed *after* the polishing. However, the parenthesis in square brackets evokes the impression that the entry was produced alongside the process of polishing and, therefore, a pause of 30 minutes has to be imagined. The reader gets the feeling of being a first-hand witness to the polishing process and to take part in waiting for the result. Another example of staged immediacy is the following:

Example 27: Staged Immediacy II

> Let me introduce you. This is Cathy. She ripped open her presents with the enthusiasm of a game show contestant. She absolutely loved her new jogging suit. [...]
> This is Nathan. He's new to Reedy Place. He welcomed us by singing a song he wrote. He has a beautiful voice. He loves to cook in his new kitchen. He asked for a coat, food and a CD player.
>
> (*The Honeymoon Phase* 5–8, II.B)

Formulae like *let me introduce you...*, *this is...* stage an introduction situation, which the reader is made part of.

Such a staging of immediacy can also be found in other DIABLOC blogs. I would like to assume that this mirrors the fact that immediacy was a feature of personal weblogs in II.A to II.C – maybe even a central, prototypical one.

5.4 Single vs. Multiple Authorship

Even though the blog communication form in all periods allowed for *many-to-many* communication, with multiple authors contributing to one blog, this option was only used by very few bloggers in the DIABLOC.

Table 13: Multiple vs. Single Authorship

Period	Multiple Authorship				Total (valid cases)	
	no		Yes			
I	85.7%	(24)	14.3%	(4)	100%	(28)
II.A	97.8%	(89)	2.2%	(2)	100%	(91)
II.B	94.8%	(92)	5.2%	(5)	100%	(97)
II.C	92.8%	(90)	7.2%	(7)	100%	(97)
$\varphi_c = 0.142 \mid p < 0.097$						

As Table 13 shows,[75] only a small percentage in each period was composed by multiple authors. In period I, *Memepool* was a weblog project with contributions by 31 authors, who compiled news from the World Wide Web. Similarly, *Need to Know* and *Linky & Dinky* apparently contained contributions from multiple authors. In that, and in their weekly publication rhythm, these two weblogs mirror patterns of the e-zine genre. Even though single authorship was typical of period I, there still seemed to be more scope of variation than in period II. Still, there was a small but steady increase in multiple authorship blogs from II.A to II.C, which may be related to the extension of multiple authorship options in accessible blog systems. The entries on *Hello Interloper* (II.C) were written by a couple and *Flying Confessions* (II.C) is even labelled *International Group Blog* as it contains contributions from a whole team of eleven female authors. Additionally, period II witnessed the spread of *guest blogging*: Bloggers were invited to publish posts, usually related to their particular fields of expertise, on other blogs

75 Coding was based on author signatures in the timestamp as well as metadata on profiles and *about* sites. In case of pseudonyms, I assumed one pseudonym to relate to one author each. If none of these indicators could be found, the blog was coded *0* and not included in the descriptive statistics.

(for instance in *Jenn's Travel Closeup*). Usually, no additional author account was created but posts were published by the blog's owner and marked as guest posts.

To sum up, personal weblogs have always typically communicated in a one-to-many fashion. In contrast to the genre label *personal* weblog, the genre's scope of variation allowed for multiple authorship, both in a temporary (guest blogging) and a permanent version.

5.5 Who's Blogging? Author Demographics

Let's now turn to the question of *who's blogging* in an attempt to characterize the authors of the DIABLOC blogs. Of course, the following can only relate to the data offered by the bloggers themselves and has to *rely* on that metadata. What follows is, therefore, a profile of what the blog authors *chose* to convey. Assuming an ethical code of truthfulness (see 5.6.1; 5.8.1), we can, however, suppose that this data mirrors actual blog authorship to some extent.

Concerning gender, the distribution is particularly striking for period I as nearly all blogs that contained data on the author's gender were kept by males. In period II, the fraction of female bloggers grows considerably. In II.B, more than half of the authors were female.

Table 14: Author Gender

Period	Authors: Gender				Total (valid cases)	
	male		Female			
I	91.3%	(21)	8.7%	(2)	100%	(23)
II.A	53.8%	(35)	46.2%	(30)	100%	(65)
II.B	41.0%	(32)	59.0%	(46)	100%	(78)
II.C	41.3%	(38)	58.7%	(54)	100%	(92)
$\varphi_c = 0.287 \mid p < 0.0001$						

In the light of the high numbers of blogs for which no such data could be gathered, I'd like to interpret these results only cautiously. Herring et al. (2005: 152) assume a correlation between the author's gender and the functional profile of a blog. While so-called *filter blogs* were kept typically by men, women would rather opt for *personal journals* in Herring et al.'s terminology. In 7.6.1, I'll show that this distinction between *filter blogs* and *personal journals* is not easily made, but that there are indeed significant differences between period I weblogs and period II personal weblogs concerning their core functions. The male dominance in period I would thus relate neatly to Herring at al.'s results. In period II, a statistic association between post genres and gender can only be given for II.A, where filter posts (see 7.2.1) can be detected in 30% of blogs kept by females as opposed to 62.9% of male-kept blogs ($\varphi_c = 0.328 \mid p = 0.008$). In other words: For later periods, the picture seems to be more complex than Herring et al. suggest.

Table 15: Author Occupation

Period	Authors: Occupation								Total (valid cases)	
	Student (Highschool or Similar)		Student (University)		Professional		None			
I	0.0%	(0)	11.8%	(2)	88.2%	(15)	0.0%	(0)	100%	(17)
II.A	3.8%	(2)	17.0%	(9)	77.4%	(41)	1.9%	(1)	100%	(53)
II.B	0.0%	(0)	9.1%	(6)	84.8%	(56)	6.1%	(4)	100%	(66)
II.C	3.4%	(2)	8.6%	(5)	74.1%	(43)	13.8%	(8)	100%	(58)
$\varphi_c = 0.150 \mid p=0.155$										

Data concerning *occupation* could only be obtained from roughly half of the blogs in each period. Table 15 shows that students in secondary and tertiary education are clearly the minority. If this is interpreted as an indicator for age, it becomes less likely that personal weblogs were kept mainly by teens.[76] Additionally, typical topics covered on weblogs and personal weblogs also point to adults of twenty-something and older (see 6.3.4). These results are supported by Lenhart & Fox (2006: 4), who state: "[M]ore than half [of the bloggers, P. S.] are between 18 and 29 years old."

Concerning the areas of profession, safe assumptions can only be made for period I, where many authors presented themselves as web designers (e.g., Rafe Colburn, *rc3.org*) or programmers (Jacobs Anderson, *Genehack*). Rosenberg (2009: 90), as an insider of the early blogging community, supports this assumption (see also Blood 2002: 4):

> Aside from Dave Winer [*Scripting News*, P. S.] and Jorn Barger [*Robot Wisdom*, P. S.], nearly all of the people who started weblogs in 1997, 1998, and early 1999 were young laborers in the booming Web industry. (Rosenberg 2009: 90)

IT aficionados can also be found among period II authors (e.g., *AskmyPaul*, II.A, and Dan from *askingforthirds*, a "computer science major"). However, besides IT, there are many professional fields ranging from housewives (*E-Housewife*, II.B),

76 Herring et al. (2005: 152) found that "females and teens create them [i.e. personal journals, that is, personal weblogs, P.S.] somewhat more often than do males and adults".

journalists (*Bill Bennett*, II.C) and artists (*ArtLove*, II.C) to teachers (*Atomic Raygun*, II.A), Avon consultants (*As a Star*, II.C) and even sitcom authors (*Comedy Writer*, II.B). This supports the assumption which I voiced in 4.10.3 – that the majority of personal weblog authors was not part of a web-savvy group of technological innovators.

5.6 Self-Disclosure

With their pointed question *Would you let 900 Million People Read Your Diary?*, Nardi et al. (2004a) address a key paradox of blogs: disclosing private information to a potential mass audience. Another question raised in this respect is concerned with the authenticity of the contents presented on blogs.

Indeed, some DIABLOC authors show that they are aware of this peculiar situation. What's more, they voice concerns that relate to one common denominator: that an unknown mass audience is presented with personal information, thoughts and emotions:

Example 28: Considering the Paradox – Personal Information vs. (Mass) Audience

so, my dad told my sister how wonderful my blog was and made her read it too. they both told me, separately, that they've learned more about me than they ever knew before. odd, and kind of scary. the 3 or 400 people who read my blog daily know me better than my family. i hope it doesn't make me feel like i need to censor myself.

(*EatonWeb* 23, I)

Actually, strangely, the thing that held me back more was that people I knew read…or more likely *could* read, once in a while, this thing. And it might be strange for them to read about things here before I've talked to them about it. Then again it might not…but it would be strange for me.

(*Ash says* 1, II.A)

Brigitte Eaton (first example) reflects on the strange experience that her audience might know her better than her family, while Ash voices concerns about threatening real life social relationships by blogging. Others, for instance Cheré (*Cheré takes on the world*, II.B) point out that potential employers might use blogs to get a first impression about their applicants. The author advises keeping the source knowledge (Anonymous 1998: 389–390) as low as possible by choosing a pseudonym and being careful about information on profile pages.

All these concerns presuppose a close relationship between the authors' offline- and blog-selves. Only if what is disclosed on blogs closely mirrors a blogger's offline personality can (personal) information or statements about others become dangerous. In what follows, I will look at this construction of blog-selves in more detail and deal with three aspects of self-disclosure: *authenticity*, *selectivity* and *intimacy*.

5.6.1 Authenticity

Some blog researchers argue in a direction similar to the one taken above. They assume that bloggers stage a close link between their offline and their blog identity (see, e.g., Karlsson 2006) and thereby give the impression of authentic self-disclosure (Baumer et al. 2008: 1116). An important role in this respect has been assigned to the bloggers' choice of online names, which usually appear as a signature in the timestamp (see, e.g., Viégas 2005). Herring et al. (2006: 5) interpret the variable "choice of name" as "identity indicator". They apparently assume that a full name is a stronger indication of offline identity than, say, a pseudonym.

Diagram 2: Choice of Names (n: blog-pages)

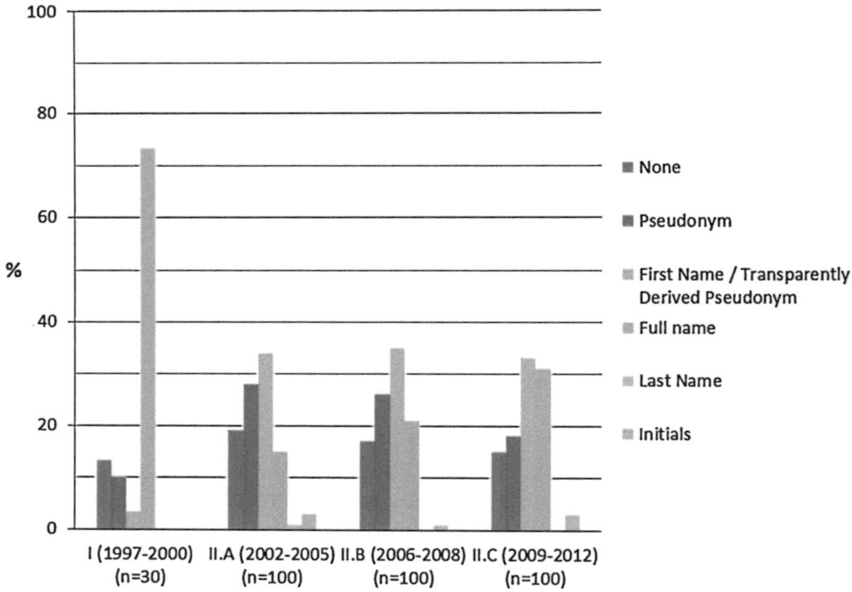

In period I (Diagram 2), it seems to be conventional for bloggers to provide their full names. The name can often be found as part of the copyright statement at the bottom of a site or in short biographies on *about*-sites. This observation does not hold for period II. Even though there is a tendency towards the full-name-convention, this fraction is generally much smaller for the personal weblogs of period II. Most period II-bloggers tended to give *some* higher identity indicator, that is first, last or full name. Pseudonyms such as *Linky* (I) and *linearchild* (II.C) decreased after a temporary rise in II.A. Interestingly, the *no-name*-fraction is well above 10% in each period. This fraction obviously mirrors the concerns pointed out in the introduction of this sub-chapter.

A name on a blog-page can usually not be proven to be identical with the author's real name. However, if we assume with Yus (2011: 41) a "presumption of honesty" in online environments, the choice to display a full name *creates the impression* on the recipients' side of increased knowledge about the author's identity. Karlsson (2006, p. 9) reports that in her "survey [of weblog readers, P.S.], a mere 5% of the respondents had ever distrusted the truthfulness of the identity presented in the weblog."

Images of the author are another identity indicator – and possibly an even stronger one than the choice of names. Similarly to Herring et al. (2006: 9), who found that around 80% of their sample didn't provide an image of the blogger, the DIABLOC authors were rather hesitant to provide such an image, as Table 16 shows.

Table 16: Author Images

Period	**Authors: Images**								**Total (valid cases)**[77]	
	None		**Photo**		**Visual Representation**		**Other**[78]			
I	73.3%	(22)	26.7%	(8)	0.0%	(0)	0.0%	(0)	100%	(30)
II.A	71.6%	(68)	26.3%	(25)	2.1%	(2)	0.0%	(0)	100%	(95)
II.B	69.1%	(67)	27.8%	(27)	1.0%	(1)	2.1%	(2)	100%	(97)
II.C	41.0%	(41)	47.0%	(47)	5.0%	(5)	7.0%	(7)	100%	(100)
$\varphi_c = 0.183 \mid p < 0.0001$										

An exception is period II.C, which exhibits a steep increase in the category *photo*. Apart from photographs, a minority of authors uses visual representations such as the avatar from *Being Alexus* (II.C), which is even headlined with *My Self portrait*. The author of that blog explicitly reflects on her avatar in one post:

77 Some blogs had to be excluded because the images on their *about*-sites had not been archived.

78 This category subsumes pictures of, e.g., cats (*Around My Kitchen Table*, II.C), which apparently do not show the blog's author.

Example 29: Commenting on Visual Author Representations

> A few weeks ago I got my hair kind of chopped off because it was so hot. I decided my avatar should also reflect the chopping so here is how my hair looks now. I only wish I were as young and "waif-like" as my avatar... *sigh*
>
> (*Being Alexus* 49, II.C)

Obviously, the visual representation of the avatar is both linked to the "real" blogger *and* uses the design options to deviate from the "original". Thus, visual representations might serve as an identity indicator – a rather weak one, though.

Photographs and visual representations taken together amount to 52% in period II.C. This tremendous increase can certainly be explained by referring to technological developments (see 4.4.2) to some extent. In connection to what was said on the choice of names, I'd also like to assume that authors, especially in period II.C, tried to use all means available to decrease the perceived anonymity by increasing their readers' source knowledge. Indeed, 46.2% of the bloggers with photograph or visual representation (52 in total in period II.C) provided their full name, another 36.5% gave their first name or a transparent pseudonym. 17.3% didn't provide any hint to their offline name and apparently were torn between striving for anonymity and generating trust by offering identity indicators.

In sum, authors of all periods made use of names and/or images to present themselves as identifiable. This can be interpreted as presenting a close relationship between an author's offline- and blog-self in the sense of "This is really me – you can trust what you see." The importance of authenticity is also highlighted by insiders of the blogging community (e.g., Bausch et al. 2002: 29; Blood 2002: 72; Rosenberg 2009: 236) and can – particularly in comparison with other genres of computer-mediated communication such as chat conversations – be highlighted as a specific of blogging in general and personal weblogs in particular.

5.6.2 Selectivity

Stressing authenticity as a tight link between offline- and blog-self is also mirrored in the way bloggers present themselves in their posts. When they characterise themselves, they address fields such as family, friends and profession, which are apparently also relevant in the offline world. Consider the following example:

Example 30: Activating Several Identity Components

> I have a good life. A fun, loving family, a decent job with fair pay, a few good friends, a really great husband who puts up with my grouchiness in the mornings.
>
> (*Excessively Diverted* 2, II.B)

The author presents herself as successful in a number of fields. She does not stop there, however, but moves on to her body self-concept:

Example 31: Activating the Body-Related Self-Concept I

The fly in my ointment is my health. Ah, heck, let's call a spade a spade. My weight. The fly in my oinment is my weight. I was chubby from the ages of 6–17, during which time I thought I was the fattest person ever. Then I went to college and got fat for real. Then I got married and crossed the line into obese. And then we come to a few days ago, when I saw a number on the scale that almost made me faint.

(*Excessively Diverted* 2–4, II.B)

She's obviously not satisfied in this respect at all, and the enumeration of positive aspects appears to be a compensation for this part of her self-concept.[79] In terms of self-disclosure, the author uses a number of aspects of her offline-identity to create her blog-identity. According to Yus (2011: 30), it's especially remarkable that the author doesn't use the opportunity, which computer-mediated communication offers, of excluding the physical body from her self-presentation. Interestingly, she is, by far, not the only one who addresses shortcomings of body and health:

79 The term *self-concept* is used in psychology to describe people's perception and knowledge about themselves. The self-concept is a complex knowledge structure comprising several components (Zimbardo & Gerrig 2008: 531, see also 531–536). Past, present and even future self-concepts are an integral part of a person's identity. I use the term here as a useful tool to show how several components of an identity are activated and presented. See Yus (2011: 39) on the construction of online-identities by activating several aspects of offline-identities: "Users do not necessarily have to reproduce their offline identities when they are online, but stress or favour certain aspects of their identities depending on the environment where they are interacting."

Example 32: Activating the Body-Related Self-Concept II

I am down more than 10 pounds in the diet. Although I did cheat a little over the weekend.
(*Bump* 84, I)

Well in other news I feel like a fat cow, my boobs aren't getting any bigger, but my thighs sure are. Don't you love how nature works?
(...*Life of L...* 3, II.A)

I have this pair of jeans that just don't quite fit. Actually I have nearly an entire wardrobe that doesn't fit. I want it to. Sometimes I even try to make it fit. It doesn't. But it's not a bad thing. It is though time to stop trying to make it fit and simply get rid of the clothes.
(*Experiencing the Journey* 46, II.B)

I have body issues. When you grow up hating what is on the inside, it's only a matter of time before you project it to the outside. I am working through this and now I can say that I think my rack is pretty awesome. They're real and they're spectacular!
(*Living authentically* 75, II.C)

It's striking that a *positive* presentation of the author's body can seldom be found in the DIABLOC, with the exception of *Bboy*, II.C, in which a dancer reports on his fitness and progress in training. This is also apparent from the posts cited above. Integrating negative aspects concerning their body into their blog-identity, which, according to Yus (2011), could have been avoided so easily, also points in the direction of authentic self-disclosure à la: "This is me. Take it or leave it."

At the same time, such a comprehensive activation of identity components as can be found on *Excessively Diverted* is rather exceptional in the DIABLOC. More often, authors addressed selected aspects of their identity and thus constructed their blog-identity in an authentic but *selective* way, affiliated with their offline-self. They used the veil of the monitor[80] in order to decide which identity components they'd like to incorporate. The author of *Blushes and Shimmy Shakes* (II.C), for instance, used her blog to report on her path to acquiring burlesque dancing skills. Her first post provides us with a biography, but limited to everything burlesque-related. Information gaps such as college, profession, age, family etc. are not filled as they are not relevant to her blog (see Schildhauer 2014: 214, Example 42).

This mixture of authenticity and selectivity can be found on many DIABLOC blogs. The author of *BankruptDad* (II.C), for instance, presented himself as divorced father whose life is focused on his kids. What he does for a living or what his new relationship is like are aspects that were backgrounded: no information is given beyond the mere existence of a job and a new relationship. In period I weblogs such as *Whump*, which Blood (2002: 9) labels *filters*, the weblog-identity

80 The credit for this nice metaphor goes to Serfaty (2004).

was constructed by selecting and commenting on hyperlinks. The authors thus presented themselves as experts in a certain field (see also Blood 2002: 29–36 and Yang 2006: 10).

In sum, blog-identities typically emerged in close relation to the authors' offline-selves. Regarding how far the veil was lifted, that is, how many identity components were activated, the genre personal weblog apparently offered a broad scope of variation from comprehensive to highly-selective.

5.6.3 Intimacy

Some bloggers cited in the introduction of this sub-chapter voiced concerns about providing *too much* information. Therefore, while the last chapter focused on the breadth of self-disclosure, I'd like to investigate how *intensively* bloggers self-disclose on personal weblogs here. Hollenbaugh (2010) states:

> Blogging to archive and organize one's thoughts characterized disclosive bloggers, both in amount and depth. Study participants who blogged for this reason used their blog as an online diary [...]. Much as one would write freely in a diary, bloggers disclose larger amounts of intimate information in their blogs. (Hollenbaugh 2010: 1664)

Hollenbaugh's statement, and the voices of Eaton as well as Ash cited above, allow for the expectation of a highly intimate way of self-disclosure on personal weblogs. In order to investigate this issue, I've ranked the self-directed posts of DIABLOC bloggers on a scale used in psychology. The scale is based on conversation topics.[81]

Table 17: Intimacy Scale Adopted from Sollie & Fischer (1985)

Value	0	1	2	3
Topics	no self-related statements	politics, hobbies, habits, likes etc.	religion, morals, professional life, finances, health, outer appearance etc.	personality, own weaknesses, emotions such as guilt and anger, sexuality

I introduced the zero-category as there are blog-pages in the DIABLOC which do not contain *any* self-related utterance in their posts. Particularly the majority of period I weblogs can be assigned to this category as their posts were often written without any reference to the author's self. The following excerpt illustrates this:

81 Please see Sollie & Fischer (1985: 919–921) on the design of that scale.

Example 33: Posting of the Zero-Category on the Intimacy Scale

Jesus Christ is PETA's new "spokesman"
The **People for Ethical Treatment of Animals** group is touting Christ as a politically correct eater, but columnist **Bill Citara** is skeptical. Reared a Catholic, the SF Examiner scribe writes: "I must admit I find the whole idea vaguely insulting, making God's only begotten son out to be **some sort of wandering nut cake** with too much time on his hands."

(*The Obscure Store and Reading Room* 2, I)

Self-related posts in period I were often focused on the author's opinion regarding developments on the World Wide Web, programming and politics and can thus be assigned to category 1:

Example 34: Posting of Category 1 on the Intimacy Scale (Period I)

November 20, 1998
A font that's like me: Periodically Coherent.
Sun's much-hyped Jini is now available for download. I have yet to see an official announcement and Slashdot is down, so maybe you heard it here first.
I'm looking through the new Jini specs and I don't see where it configures IP addresses. I'm not sure how Jini devices are supposed to communicate if they don't have IP adresses.

(*Hack the Planet* 16–18, I)

In period I, it was the author of *Bump* alone who published information about health and diets. Therefore, *Bump* can be assigned to category 2 as the only one in that early period. Table 18 gives an overview of all periods:

Table 18: Intimacy of Self-Disclosure

Period	Authors: Intimacy								Total (valid cases)[82]	
	0		1		2		3			
I	36.7%	(11)	60.0%	(18)	3.3%	(1)	0.0%	(0)	100%	(30)
II.A	6.1%	(6)	50.5%	(50)	24.2%	(24)	19.2%	(19)	100%	(99)
II.B	11.0%	(11)	50.0%	(50)	30.0%	(30)	9.0%	(9)	100%	(100)
II.C	12.0%	(12)	50.0%	(50)	27.0%	(27)	11.0%	(11)	100%	(100)
$\varphi_c = 0.183 \mid p = 0.0001$										

82 In period II.A, I excluded the personal weblog *ache* as it only contains one post saying "Hello". For *Astronaut Ambition* (also II.A), whose blog-page contains a list of hyperlinks leading to the respective posts, I checked a sample of entries.

In period II, half of the blogs were assigned to category 1 and roughly a third to category 2. Only a minority was coded as category 3. Personal Weblogs of that category contain memories of sexual adventures (*Dig Your Own Whole*) or deep emotions of regret and guilt (*The Core*):

Example 35: Postings of Category 3 on the Intimacy Scale

I'd say that Saturday night was the best sex I've ever had. Probably won't forget it for ages, in fact - being a bloke it's been the only thing on my mind for a number of days and I can't wait for a follow-up session another day. She enjoyed it too, which is the main thing! I reckon she was surprised, thinking I wasn't capable of such stamina. Now she's calling me the energizer bunny. Haha..

(*Dig your own hole* 29, II.B)

My regrets in life are so few, but the one that hangs heavy on me now is the way I spent my years in high school. Words were said, time lost, and people were hurt; all things I can never go back to change.

(*The Core* 19, II.B)

The fraction of the zero-category dropped significantly from period I to II.A. However, and most interestingly, this fraction then increased steadily while category 3 declined again. Maybe a trend can be assumed: after a first phase of highly intimate self-disclosure (II.A), personal bloggers rather settled for a medium level on the scale. With Serfaty (2004: 88), Viégas (2005) and Hollenbaugh (2010: 1664), I'd like to speculate that this development was at least partly caused by an increasing awareness of everyone being potentially able to read the posts, including friends and family. Conformity with social norms became, therefore, rather advisable. It can further be assumed that this medium level of intimacy established itself as typical of personal weblogs as a genre. Indeed, authors seemed to be quite wary of disclosing intimate information, which sometimes even meant some reluctance in bringing themselves to actually do so:

Example 36: Announcing the Disclosure (and Non-Disclosure) of Intimate Information I

You know, people. I've come to think that I don't share much of myself with you guys... well, not the real juicy stuff! Anyway, today I've made a difficult decision. It's time for me to do the "coming out of the closet" thingy... you know, let the truth be known. I've chosen to write it in a form of a poem. For some reason, it seemed proper*s*...

(*reborn by design* 38, II.A)

Apart from that, its all quiet on the Western front. Apart from amazing and unexpected sex on Saturday <u>Ill leave it to your imagination</u>!

(*andrewf my life* 103–104, II.A, my emphasis, P. S.)

And Sunday? <u>Sunday was my beautiful secret.</u>

(*Hello Stranger* 168, II.B, my emphasis, P. S.)

The author of *reborn by design* introduces a poem, of highly emotional content, with the title *How I fell in love with her*, which reflects openly on that degree of intimacy. The other two authors demonstrate their wariness by merely hinting at apparently sensitive information.

I'd also like to highlight the minority group which apparently enjoyed high degrees of intimate self-disclosure. These singular cases, to be found from II.A to II.C, show that the genre offered some scope of variation also regarding the intimacy dimension. One personal weblog of this group is *At her master's feet* (II.A), which opens as follows:

Example 37: Announcing the Disclosure of Intimate Information II

On my knees at his feet....
Who would have thought that my journey would begin so easily.... I knew what I didn't want.. but was unsure what I did want. S replied to an advert I placed and from his first reply we had a connection that others may spend their whole life seeking.
He is kind, and gentle and his knowledge of what I need and how he understands me brings me to my knees in gratitude.
Our journey has begun, we share it with you the reader... I hope you enjoy it as much as we will. Kxx

(*At her master's feet* 100–103, II.A)

The "journey" was in fact a sadomasochistic relationship which was shared with the reader in alternating posts by *him* and *her*. The authors shared sexual experiences as well as the emotional hardships of the male partner when the relationship broke up after six months. The blog also contained links to close-to-pornographic pictures. The high intensity of self-disclosure probably corresponds to the use of initials as a relatively weak identity indicator.

5.6.4 Summary

In all corpus periods, authors used their blogs for a form of self-disclosure whose central feature appears to be *authenticity*. There seems to be a convention to stress a close relation between offline- and blog-self. This was, among others, achieved by choosing identity indicators suitable to increase the source knowledge and thereby decrease the perceived degree of anonymity on the recipient's side. In terms of name selection, this tendency was particularly strong in period I weblogs. Personal weblogs (period II) tended to choose some kind of higher identity indicator in this respect (first / last / full name), paired with a photograph or visual representation.

Selectivity describes the breadth of self-disclosure in terms of how many identity components are presented as part of the blog-identity. Period I weblogs were usually highly selective; authors focused on pitching themselves as experts in certain fields. In period II personal weblogs, the scope of the genre ranged from highly-selective to rather comprehensive, when a great number of identity-components were addressed.

Intimacy deals with the intensity of self-disclosure. While period I was dominated by the zero-category (no self-related utterances), the personal weblogs of period II typically contained information related to the bloggers' selves. Interestingly enough, personal weblogs usually ranged on a medium level of the intimacy scale.

There is probably a complex interplay between these three aspects, as for instance illustrated by Example 37 (*At her master's feet*): The high degree of intimacy in that example corresponds to rather weak identity indicators. The authenticity of self-disclosure is probably nevertheless underlined by offering photographs of *her*, at least. In general, striving for anonymity and, therefore, making use of a key affordance of computer-mediated communication, is quite likely to be a factor influencing the way authenticity is staged, and probably also the selectivity of self-disclosure. Hollenbaugh (2008; 2010) additionally points out that the conceptualised audience, which I'll turn to in the next sub-chapter, plays a decisive role in this respect.

5.7 *Hello Stranger*: How Bloggers Imagine their Audience

As stated in 1.3.3, it's not the *actual* audience of a blog that is of interest here. What actually influences the production of blog posts is rather the individual blogger's mental concept of their audience. This discrepancy is illustrated by the following example:

Example 38: Audience as Mental Concept

Today, WC is 16 months old. [...] Happy birthday, baby girl.

(*Amy L. Marr* 66–77, II.A)

At the time of writing, *WC* is certainly not able to read this line. Still, the child is part of the author's conceptualised audience. In the next sub-chapters, I'll try and reconstruct various aspects of this mental concept.

5.7.1 *if I could invite the internet over for dinner*: Who? And How Many?

The question of *who* bloggers imagine to be their readers becomes apparent both regarding the use of address forms such as pronouns, names etc. and in the way authors manage the background knowledge needed to render a certain post coherent. The more knowledge gaps, the less likely is a conceptualised audience encompassing utter strangers.

There are, indeed, authors addressing exactly that nebulous mass audience potentially encompassing all Internet users as the following examples of address forms show:

Example 39: Conceptualising the Largest Audience Possible

Hi Internet! I have to ask a very big favor from you. I have been listed at a site for mommy bloggers called Top Momma, and I have a chance to be on their front page. If some of you click on my button, it will help with traffic to my blog.

(*E-Housewife* 109–113, II.B)

if I could invite the internet over for dinner, I would.

(*Hello Stranger* 157, II.B)

In these examples, the authors explicitly address the Internet as a metonymy for all its users. Such a broad conceptualisation can also be found in other forms of address, for instance in indefinite pronouns such as *all* and *anyone* as well as *you* in its 2nd person plural reading:

Example 40: Unspecific Audience Concept

Hello to all you out there in all your homes by your computers…

(*all about eve* 8, II.A, my emphasis, P. S.)

So has anyone else heard any stories similar to the one I heard? Have you just been made redundant and are you finding it tough to get a new job?? Let us know…we'd love to hear from you.

(*Freya Bletsoe's Personal Blog* 40, II.B, my emphasis, P. S.)

In terms of knowledge management, where information needed for rendering a post coherent is supplied explicitly, we can assume a broad audience concept including strangers, newbies and lurkers. Bloggers follow mainly two strategies here. First, embedding hyperlinks can serve to supply, literally, the missing link for understanding a post:

Example 41: Providing Background Knowledge by Using Hyperlinks

I'm working on this weeks Super Delegates for FOTM.

(*Evan4sh* 11, II.B)

It wasn't that long ago when we stayed in a nice hotel in the middle of nowhere, that was a nice time.

(*David Parkinson* 78, II.B)

The author of *David Parkinson* makes use of permalink technology (4.5.3) in order to point to a previous post containing information not mentioned again in the current entry, thus exploiting the historicity of his own blog. Second, the missing knowledge can be spelt out verbally:

Example 42: Spelling Out Background Knowledge

> I'm worried about another miscarriage (I've had two)
>
> (*the asylum* 3, II.A)

Without the additional remark in brackets, readers would have to handle the presupposition *not the first miscarriage* triggered by *another* on their own. The statement in brackets both confirms the presupposition and supplies additional context knowledge by extending the presupposition from *one* to *two*. In some cases, authors blend both strategies, providing hyperlinks and in-post information:

Example 43: Providing Background Knowledge – Verbal and Hyperlink Strategy

> Last night I did some caricatures at Temple Shaaray Tefila's Purim Carnival. Purim, for those of you who choose not to follow the link I so kindly provided, is kind of like a Jewish Halloween.
>
> (*Evan4sh* 15, II.B)

Apart from these instances of broad audience conceptualisations, there are also posts in which a more focused concept becomes apparent. The following excerpt explicitly addresses (close) friends:

Example 44: Audience Concept of (Close) Friends

> I'm sorry, sweetheart. My body and I shall make it up to you. And my dear Cat, the books arrived! Thank you so much. They couldn't have come at a better time.
>
> (*August Dreams* 6, II.A, my emphasis, P. S.)

While *August Dreams* addresses two different addressees in succession, the following excerpt presents a multi-layered form of address:

Example 45: Multi-Layered Audience Concept

> Tomorrow, Will joins me in the ranks of the 30 somethings. Happy Birthday Honey! Xox
>
> (*all my tediousness upon thee* 15, II.A.)

The first sentence introduces *Will's* approaching birthday as a fact in the 3rd person. At most, a particular audience concept could be assumed from the fact that some context knowledge is needed to determine the reference of *Will*, but a broad and unspecific concept seems to be more likely. This changes in the second sentence when the author directly addresses *Will* as *Honey*. *Will* is therefore part of the conceptualised audience. I wouldn't assume that the broader audience concept from the first sentence is erased, but rather suggest a multi-layered audience concept which encompasses broader and more specific components at the same time. Puschmann (2010: 77) uses the metaphor of "concentric circles of narrower / wider audience" in this respect.

Concerning knowledge management, narrow audience concepts, for example, regular readers, friends and family, are shown by coherence gaps which result in the objective observer lacking background knowledge. In these cases, the authors rely on their audience possessing the needed knowledge or drawing the correct inferences, as is illustrated by the following examples:

Example 46: Coherence Gaps Due to Missing Background Knowledge I

I booted up Kendra last night and ten seconds into it, she freezes. I reboot, and she freezes again.

(*The AlmightyGuru* 11, II.A)

Only 1 month to Ireland's 3rd Birthday!

(*1 Ideal Life* 3, II.A)

The audience has to decode *Kendra* as the name of a computer and to identify *Ireland* as a child rather than a country in order to render the utterances coherent. The neglect of contextualization can be even more pronounced as in the following excerpt:

Example 47: Coherence Gaps Due to Missing Background Knowledge II

I am reminded today of how disappointing people are. Disappointing, unreliable, self-centered, phony. There was a time in my life, however brief, when I was completely self-reliant. I don't know how I did it. I realized it was a lonely existence and spent the past however long now trying to build relationships with people. Only to be let down time and time again. It's made me start to think again, if I'm going to be lonely anyway I'd rather just be alone.

(*The Allure of the Cheshire Cat* 29, II.A)

The specific occasion that led to this post remains entirely opaque. A reader who is not familiar with the author and the context can only infer that the lines deal with the author's disappointment about the behaviour of at least one other person, alluded to rather vaguely by the collective *people*. The only time specification is *today*, which can be interpreted with the help of the timestamp. The post is also marked by a high degree of subjectivity, with the pronouns *I* and *me* being used very frequently. It might, therefore, even be directed at the author herself only, as an *audience of one*. A conceptualised audience encompassing close confidants is also entirely possible.[83]

A certain degree of opacity is, apparently, also deliberately created as a means of privacy protection. In some texts, participants only appear with their initials (see Example 37 above); in others, participants are "labelled" according to their relation to the blogger (for example, *Clog-Wife* in *Clog-Almanac*, II.B and *the Girl* as well as *Grandma* in *Freak Parade*, II.B). This way of referring to participants takes into account that *anyone* could potentially read a post and, for this reason, identities therefore have to be protected. I would therefore like to qualify Puschmann's (2010) statement that

> [i]n addition to this conceptualized audience (what Viégas calls the "core"), a broader actual audience exists that includes overhearers *not anticipated by the blogger*. (Puschmann 2013: 85–86, my emphasis, P.S.)

This may be true for some bloggers but certainly not for those who deliberately protect their texts' participants from *overhearers*,[84] who they well anticipate.

5.7.2 *that excuse is better than 'the dog ate it'*: Bloggers on Duty, Bloggers' Burn Out and the Role of Recognition

In many posts, bloggers voice a feeling of commitment to their readers, which apparently becomes a decisive factor in the production of their posts. Blogger Megan Hourihan explains this by referring to structural characteristics of blogs:

Example 48: Reverse Chronology and Expectations

> Additionally, the newest information at the top (coupled with its time stamps and sense of immediacy) sets the expectation of updates, an expectation reinforced by our return visits to see if there's something new. Weblogs demonstrate that time is important by the very nature in which they present their information. As weblog readers, we respond with frequent visits, and we are rewarded with fresh content.
>
> (Hourihan 2002)

83 Other authors apparently use opacity as a stylistic device. The author of *class (of something)* (II.B) closes one mysterious post stating: "another abstract posting – but that's the road, or style, less taken" The author thereby alludes to Robert Frost's poem *The Road Not Taken*, which underlines the use of opacity as stylistic twist.

84 In Schildhauer (2014: 227, especially fn. 360), I discuss Puschmann's use of the term *overhearer* by drawing on Goffman (1983). In this context, I also point to Hoffmann's (2010: 60) concept *overseer*.

A clear sign of this feeling of commitment is the sorry-post, which is almost generic as early as period I.

Example 49: Excuses of Lack of Postings

I feel a little guilty to be as slow as I have been with updates during the past few weeks, given the amount of attention the site has had lately. I hope any new readers are hanging in there ... I'll have more and better updates one of these days.

(*Windowseat* 17, I)

I'm wayyyy behind in posting. I know, I know.
My only lame excuse is that I haven't had internet access at work for a while. And there just hasn't been a whole lot to write about, because things have been going pretty well, overall.

(*the asylum* 3, II.A)

It is not common for me to be delinquent in my posting, but I have been on vacation. At least that excuse is better than "the dog ate it".

(*Dementia Thoughts* 5, II.B)

Im greatly vexed
I have no comment about how long its been since I last blogged here. I have no excuse except for a zillion of them but no matter.

(*Being Alexus* 2–3, II.C)

The author of *Windowseat* expresses her bad conscience towards her readers. Apparently, regular or even frequent post was part of what readers already expected in period I. Indeed, regular post appears to be a sensible strategy of building a stable circle of readers as Example 48 underlines. From II.A onwards, it has apparently been a convention to go as far as to give solid reasons for the absence of posts. With her statement *that excuse is better than 'the dog ate it'*, the author of *Dementia Thoughts* comments on this situation. In alluding to a stereotypical pupil-teacher situation, she asserts an asymmetrical power relationship with the readers actually taking the role of the demanding and powerful teacher. Lomborg (2014) similarly states:

> Although my analysis does not question that frequent updating is characteristic of the blog genre, it clearly suggests that the updating frequency is a *negotiated convention and expectation*, not a formalized feature. (Lomborg 2014: 66, emphasis in the original)

However, not only post frequency seems to be an important aspect. Many authors literally court their imagined readers by announcing interesting, important and/or entertaining posts to come:

Example 50: Courting the Audience

Stay tuned for a new and important update tomorrow!

(*ModBlog* 19, II.A)

Wait until I post pictures of what happened the rest of the days I was there. Believe me, you will want to see this.

(*E-Housewife* 60–61, II.B)

Striving for both frequency and quality of posts is, therefore, not only intrinsically motivated but also related to the importance of the audience. It is apparently not enough for these authors (the ones cited and others post similar statements) to be just blogging for themselves. They want to be read:

> I feel it is natural for any writer to want readers. None of us would put it on the Web if all we wanted to do was to write. (Blood 2002: 95)

Bloggers know that their way to achieve *recognition*[85] by a circle of readers is to post frequently and to provide high quality content. In her case study, Lomborg (2014: 72–73) is able to show how this leads to negotiations taking place between bloggers and their readers on what constitutes a high quality post. This might vary from blog to blog in terms of, for instance, topics (6.3.4), style (6.4.2) as well as selectivity (5.6.2) and intimacy (5.6.3) of self-disclosure. The readers' means to engage in these negotiation processes are, of course, comments, but also click numbers, shares etc. In this way, both the bloggers' pursuit of recognition and their readers awarding or withdrawing this precious commodity have become decisive factors for the personal weblog and an ongoing, dynamic process of settling central features of the genre.

The high importance of the readership, at least for some bloggers, also bears the danger of blogging becoming a tedious chore, and, finally, of blogging burn-out:

---

85 I use the term *recognition* here following Axel Honneth's theory of recognition (German: *Anerkennung*). Honneth (1994) argues that gaining recognition from others is a central motivation for human action. Humans need others' recognition in order to develop a positive self-concept (see fn. 79, p. 84). One form of recognition that is particularly important in the blogging context is *social recognition* (Honneth 1994: 197): a person is perceived as distinct from everyone else and valued for being special. Also see below: Rosenberg (2009) on *whuffie* – a metaphorical blogging currency apparently based on recognition.

Example 51: Burn-out

> Folks, I'm burned out. I need a break. This just isn't fun anymore. I don't even feel like I'm writing for myself anymore. Even keeping this thing updated has become more of a chore than anything.
>
> (*all the grrrls hate her* 43, II.A)

This expression of "blogging fatigue" (Lomborg 2014: 67) points towards a deep ambivalence in the role of the readership in at least some personal weblogs. The author in Example 51 states that, at first, she intended to write only for herself, but now blogs primarily for her audience. What lies beneath this ambivalence is probably the paradoxical relationship between the private frame of a genre labelled as *personal* and the potential mass audience which is presented with this private and personal content. Waxing nostalgic, the author of *Almost Somewhat Positive* remembers the days when her readership didn't have quite such an impact:

Example 52: Writing as Self-Contained Pleasure vs. Writing for an Audience

> Ahhh, I miss those old days when a blank screen was welcomed and craved. A time before ads and stats, writing for the pure pleasure of hearing my words clacking away (on whatever computer I could get my hands on during Emma's naps). Ultimately for the very pleasure of making myself giggle with the hopes that at least one other person in the cosmos enjoyed reading them as much as I enjoyed sharing.
>
> (*Almost Somewhat positive* 21, II.C)

But even in this memory, the ambivalence mentioned above is present – the author mentions her hope of *at least one other person* reading her lines. Reed sums up this field of tension:

> Although it is known that other people visit the site, journal bloggers insist that they are its main recipient; the popular refrain among them is 'I blog for me'. [...] Indeed, knowing that others visit the weblog is a large part of what motivates the individual to keep posting, when perhaps in the past he or she has failed to sustain privately kept paper journal. (Reed 2005: 231)

Indeed, many DIABLOC texts provide evidence of the fact that authors considered the size of their audience and even took measures to increase it, by, among others, registering on a directory such as *Globe of Blogs* and using tags (4.3):

Example 53: Importance of Readership Numbers

Just signed up my blog at STLBloggers.com, a website for bloggers in the St. Louis area. Maybe I'll get some more people to my journal. Maybe that won't matter since I hardly update. :D

(*A Whirlpool of Dimensional Thought* 196, II.A)

Anyways...since my last weekly welcome we've had a cracking **217** new subscribers join us here at the wonderful world of freyasykes.com...so to each and every one of you welcome...make yourselves at home.

(*Freya Bletsoe's Personal Blog* 11, II.B)

Being read is, again, shown as an important aim of personal bloggers. Particularly, the increase in *followers*, that is, registered readers, seems to be a welcome source of recognition as it makes the presence of readers especially visible. As Reed states, this might have a considerable psychological effect:

> The presence of recipients [...] not only makes bloggers feel the exercise must be worthwhile, it ensures that the person revealed on their weblog [...] is for the first time properly and publicly acknowledged. (Reed 2005: 232)

Rosenberg (2009: 202) uses the term *whuffie* in this respect. Whuffie is the currency of the blog community, based on *recognition* in symbolic forms such as linking, entries on blogrolls, subscriptions, followers etc. and which may have a decisive effect on a blogger's writing motivation.

To sum up, personal weblogs appear to be characterised by the following ambivalence:

- Personal weblogs are usually kept as a leisure activity and for the authors own entertainment (5.2). The genre label alludes to the fact that they should be *personal* in nature, mirroring their authors' interests and likes.
- At the same time, a special incentive for keeping a personal weblog is apparently the presence of an audience and the recognition provided thereby. Building and keeping an audience, however, entails commitment to frequent, high quality post, with the *quality* being subject to negotiations with the audience.

The following sub-chapter will deal with one way out of this paradox, which has been taken by some bloggers.

5.7.3 *If you're like me:* Similarity

It appeared to be a common strategy, even in period I, to explicitly name the target or interest group which a post was written for. These are underlined in the following examples:

Example 54: Stating the Target Group

Web designers (and by that I mean, information architects, interaction designers, graphic designers, etc.), how many of you have said, "users don't [do this thing]" as if the entire audience were one seething mass?

(*Peterme* 1, I, my emphasis, P. S.)

A must read for all fashion fans!!

(*Mysteries of M* 10, II.A, my emphasis, P. S.)

I'll start right off by saying, if you're not using the OPML Editor, you won't get a lot of use out of this.

(*Interalia* 4, II.A, my emphasis, P. S.)

These authors are obviously aware of the possibility that readers may drop by who are not part of the core of their conceptualised audience. Stating the intended target group serves as a signal of exclusion, probably meant to reduce the danger of *audience mismatch* (Puschmann 2010: 74). By specifying the communicative purposes of their post, these authors make a rather precise offer of co-operation (see 1.3.3), which can be rejected easily by uninterested readers. This might have also benefited the writing process, as these bloggers obviously weren't writing for an unspecified mass audience with unknown needs, but for a clearly defined group probably sharing the interests of the author.

This leads to a central point of this chapter: There is some evidence that at least some bloggers assumed a basic *similarity* between themselves and their readers. This similarity might include demographic features such as age and gender, but also extend to political and religious attitudes. For instance, the author of *This is not a fairy tale* presupposes recipients of roughly the same age:

Example 55: Assuming Similarity – Age/Citizenship/Interest

They don't count us young people as likely voters, because they think we're apathetic! Prove them wrong! Go vote! Make a difference!

(*This is not a fairy tale* 195–198, II.A, my emphasis, P. S.)

The choice of pronouns clearly underlines the construction of an in-group (*us*) as opposed to an out-group (*they*). The community constructed that way is marked by common features, with the characteristic *young* being particularly pronounced. This feature is joined by *American citizen* as the post is an appeal to join the presidential election in the US. Finally, the author presupposes some kind of interest in political topics; who else would read a post on the presidential election to the very end and even feel addressed?[86] Similarly, the feminist author of *Bella Vida* addresses female readers only:

Example 56: Assuming Similarity – Gender

> Women in the US have not achieved equality. Do not be fooled. **You** have work to do. The self entitled attitude of thinking that <u>our</u> mothers did enough is not only arrogant but dangerously self defeating. If you want respect, stand up and be respected. If you want rights, stand up and demand them.
>
> (*Bella Vida* 42, II.C, my emphasis, P. S.)
>
> Can you find the similarities between these women and yourself or someone you know? These are the faces of <u>our</u> community. They were elected to represent <u>us</u> and <u>our</u> needs as American citizens.
>
> (*Bella Vida* 68, II.C, my emphasis, P. S.)

The pronouns *us* and *our* again construct a community consisting of the author and her readers, based on similarity, and is addressed explicitly by the phrase *our community*. In *Blonde Nonbeliever*, the author assumes her readers to be atheists, just like her:

Example 57: Assuming Similarity – Religion

> <u>If you're like me</u>, you have probably heard that people think you have actively *chosen* to disbelieve in God. They insinuate that it's just trendy right now.
>
> (*Blonde Nonbeliever* 295–296, II.C, my emphasis, P. S.)

The introductory conditional clause expresses the assumption – or at least the hope – of similarity between the author and her readers in that respect without, however, excluding the possibility of other readers.

By orienting towards an audience concept marked by similarity, the ambivalence between writing for oneself and writing for others addressed in the previous sub-chapter can be solved in the manner of a *both*/and-approach. By adjusting the concept of their audience to their own needs and even explicitly voicing this concept, bloggers could follow topical interests which were simultaneously their own and their readers'.

86 See also Puschmann (2013: 86), who states: "An alternative approach is to rely on the topic in order to get an idea of the audience, since knowledge of and interest in certain topics constrains a blog's potential readership."

5.7.4 *Thanks for listening:* Audience Roles

In this sub-chapter, following Scheidt (2006) as well as Brake (2007), I'd like to focus on what bloggers *expect* from their audiences. In other words: what roles do bloggers assign to their audience? Generally, the available data only allow for plausible *assumptions* about these audience roles which can, additionally, seldom be generalised for all posts on a personal weblog. Sometimes, audience roles appear to vary even within a single entry. What follows is therefore merely a careful approach to audience roles in personal weblogs.[87]

Probably, *the* audience role in personal weblogs is what Scheidt (2006: 198–199) labels the *witness*. In this role, the audience shares the author's experiences and validates them by simply taking note of them. The author of *Alone in Tacoma* (II.B, 61) writes accordingly: "I think the truth is, a part of me writes to say only one thing: *I exist*."[88] In some instances, the conceptualised readers are explicitly asked to look or marvel at something as well as to simply observe experiences:

Example 58: Audience Roles – Witness I

Look what my sweetie had sent me this morning in mail, to make my spirit fly, since I've been a bit under the weather these last few days…

(*reborn by design* 29, II.A, my emphasis, P. S.)

To the journal. A place for us to discover ourselves. And for you to share in our discoveries.

(*At her master's feet* 106, II.A, my emphasis, P. S.)

Witness the return of the early morning drunken phone calls.

(*an insider's view of life* 51, II.A, my emphasis, P. S.)

Here is a video of Charli ripping up paper towels; her Most Favorite Activity of All Time.

(*Beloved Parrot* 13, II.C)

Apparently, it's also important to convince readers that the information given is true. The author of *reborn by design*, for instance, publishes the entire love poem her husband wrote for her after the announcement in Example 58. In Example 59, the author offers evidence (a video clip) for his claim to be able to solve a Rubik's cube in under two minutes:

87 Due to matters of space, I have restricted myself to the most salient roles. Please see Schildhauer (2014: 7.6.6) for a more detailed account.

88 See also Reed (2005: 232) and the discussion above (5.7.2).

Example 59: Audience Roles – Witness II

> For the last few months I had got my time down to around 2 minutes, but I couldn't consistently achieve it. I wouldn't count it as being completed until I could always do it in under 2 minutes.
> Without further ado, here is the evidence.
>
> (*Andy hmmm* 62, II.C, my emphasis, P. S.)

In some cases, the audience is conceptualised as a source of emotional support, which characterises the role that Scheidt (2006: 30) calls *therapist*. In this role, the audience isn't merely a witness but may also be conceptualised as a compassionate listener. In her personal weblog *...Life of L...*, for instance, the author writes about her social hardships at high school. However, what she expects is not a 'real' reaction from the audience; the idea of someone taking their time to 'listen' to her is apparently enough:[89]

Example 60: Audience Roles – Therapist I

> I won't be responding to any "Get help" posts. I won't even bother reading about how I have it so good. It seems like I'm the only person in the world with debilitating shyness. [...] I can't talk to anyone about how I feel, so when I write it here I'm going to be honest and real. I don't want pity or advice...I just want it out of me.
> Thanks for listening...
> .L.
>
> (*...Life of L...* 15, II.A)

In the next example, the audience is also conceptualised as therapists in that rather passive way. Even though the author visualises his audience as true therapists, analysing his behaviour, he does not ask for a 'real' analysis but simply does so on the behalf of his readers:

Example 61: Audience Roles – Therapist II

> So yes, analyze away. I was mad because I'd let my friend go down and just "handled" it by drifting away. I was mad because he died stupidly. I was mad because other people were going to just get on with their lives and so what? And I was unspeakably mad at Ed himself, for not taking advantage of his friends when he must've needed them.
>
> (*Angry Biker Chronicles* 49, II.A)

89 See also Brake (2007: 6–12), who similarly concludes that quite often the mere presence of an audience is enough to motivate bloggers to write and that bloggers often don't expect the audience to react in any way.

Another kind of recognition (5.7.2) is apparently promised by an audience conceptualised as *seeking advice*. In this role, the audience values the expertise of the author in a certain field and intends to benefit from it. In *ACME Baseball*, the author presents himself as baseball expert who analyses statistics and gives advice on how to bet on upcoming matches. Apparently, the author imagines his readers to be very interested and eager to learn:

Example 62: Audience Roles - Seeker of Advice I

What I'm throwing you now is for your edification...CATCH IT!

(*ACME Baseball* 23, II.A)

Similarly to the other roles presented so far, it probably doesn't really matter for this audience role whether there are 'real' readers who ask questions revealing their interest or whether they only exist in the author's mind. Thus, *AskmyPaul* contains posts which answer apparently imaginary audience questions:

Example 63: Audience Roles – Seeker of Advice II

Help! How Do I Email a Large File To My Friend?
How to share a large file with your friend.
Oy! Have you ever tried to email a large picture or file to a friend, only to have it come back rejected with an error message, or worse, have it crash your computer?
Is there a large file that you want to share with someone, but don't have a way to transfer to them? Well fret no more. If you have a computer and an internet connection, you can share any (legal) files with your friends. You don't need to download anything, sign up for anything, or pay for anything (unless you want to make a donatation), and it's really easy to use.

(*AskmyPaul* 40–41, II.A)

The post opens with a question that could have been asked by an authentic reader. The next lines, however, don't contextualize the post as answer to an authentic question, but rather continue with a series of rhetorical questions which stress the relevance for a specific set of readers (see also 5.7.3). In *Deglazed* (II.B), the personal weblog of a star cook, readers apparently asked *authentic* questions in the comments section, addressed comprehensively in subsequent posts.

The audience can also take on the role of a critic who evaluates the personal weblog – layout and style, for example – but also the quality of artistic work or even the blogger's behaviour in a specific situation. In this role, *positive feedback* and support also appear to be essential, in line with what was said on recognition in 5.7.2. This becomes apparent in the following excerpts, where question tags probably aim at eliciting positive comments:

Example 64: Audience Roles – Critic I

> I even pointed out that perhaps other customers were having their cards dropped into a big crevasse someplace by this machine, and didn't they want to at least take the machine out of service? Pretty good there, eh? Thinking of the other fellow, right?
>
> (*Angry Biker Chronicles* 45, II.A, my emphasis, P. S.)
>
> My picture above does have the quality of a photo advertising a vacation resort, doesn't it?
>
> (*ArtLove* 136, II.C, my emphasis, P. S.)

It's probably for that reason that potential criticism is anticipated. By following this strategy, critical comments can, at least potentially, be reduced:

Example 65: Audience Roles – Critic II

> author's note: this was done at the library, and their computers are all screwy, so I can't use spell check, and as all of you know, I can't spell worth a shit, so don't say it, I will for you. "Danny, you spelled like every other word wrong."
>
> (*danny don't go* 61, II.A)

I'd like to subsume Scheidt's (2006: 201–202) role *cultural theorist* under this role of the *critic* as well. In this case, imaginary evaluations are related to the author's opinions, values and attitudes:

Example 66: Audience Roles – Critic III

> Who Wants to Be a Super Model When You Can Be a Super Role Model? Right? Right?
>
> (*Freak Parade* 24, II.B)
>
> So is it wrong to say that I am glad Christmas is over? Is it wrong to want to say it because I want to go buy myself presents?
>
> (*random and odd* 16, II.A)

If the audience is conceptualised that way, its role is often not merely a passive one. In the following examples, the audience is asked to react and take part in the discussion:

Example 67: Audience Roles – Critic IV

> As with all pieces on **peterme.com**, your thoughts are welcome.
>
> (*Peterme* 9, I)
>
> As this is my first review I hope I do well and invite all who stumble upon it to comment and let me know what you think.
>
> (*Maternal Experiment* 18, II.C)

While many of the previously cited examples noticeably indicate an asymmetric relation between (active) author and (passive) reader, these examples allow for the assumption of a symmetric conceptualisation of the audience as conversation partner.

The readers are expected to get even more active way when they appear as *potential source of advice*. In these cases, readers are explicitly addressed with questions voicing an apparently authentic lack of information on the author's side. Readers are obviously expected to react (by commenting, for instance):

Example 68: Audience Roles – Potential Source of Advice

> Quark Publishing System – is this the prototype for a web publishing system implemented in Frontier? Please send email to webmaster@scripting.com if you have experience with QPS. Thanks!
>
> (*Scripting News* 27, I)
>
> So, if you know the book, let me know if I should spend money I don't have on it.
>
> (*'N' is for Neville* 27, II.A)
>
> So that's the dilemma. What do you think? Any thoughts would be appreciated!!
>
> (*Experiencing the Journey* 67, II.B)
>
> If anyone has any suggestions for collections of long form criticism, I'm all ears!
>
> (*dogBoi* 17, II.C)

The authors of these excerpts address an unspecific audience by using the indefinite pronouns *anybody* and *anyone*. Apparently, they assume that the needed experts are among the potential mass audience of the World Wide Web (see also 5.7.1).

A role which is neither addressed by Scheidt (2006) nor by Brake (2007) is the *customer*. However, this concept appears to have spread considerably from some cautious beginnings in period I up to very pronounced forms in II.C. In period I, only Rafe Colburn advertised on his weblog *rc3org*:

Example 69: Audience Roles – Customer I

> Check out the **web site** for my book on CGI programming.
>
> (*rc3org* 3, I)

From period II.A onwards, there were more direct offers. It becomes apparent that authors indeed realised their audience's potential as a sales market and got used to the idea of gaining financial profit from their hobby *personal weblog*. The following example should suffice here (please see 7.2.6 for a more detailed discussion of advertising on blogs):

Example 70: Audience Roles – Customer II

Find out for FREE! That's right! Right now until Sunday night DREAM TRAVELER is absolutely free on Kindle! Get you copy now! http://www.amazon.com/dp/B006F2AGUQ
(*Always Writing* 138, II.C)

The audience is addressed by means of imperatives, additionally emphasised by the use of capitals. Similarly to the roles *cultural critic* and *potential source of advice*, the reader is expected to get actively involved. However, the *customer* role is not linked to recognition in the sense of Honneth (see 5.7.2) and other abstract rewards such as self-validation (Reed 2005: 232). The customer role promises *economic* profit and the non-material rewards of blogging are given less importance. Courting the audience (Example 50) achieves a new significance, then, as rising readership is equal to larger numbers of potential buyers.

Table 19 sums up the audience roles discussed here. Due to matters of space and in order to keep the argument as concise as possible, I haven't discussed the audience roles in period I in detail (see Schildhauer 2014: ch. 7.6.6). Table 19 shows, however, that I could already detect all audience roles with the exception of the *therapist* role already in these first generation weblogs.

Table 19: Audience Roles – Summary

Audience Role	Expectation	Recipient is mainly...	Period I
witness	share and verify experiences	passive	yes
therapist	compassionate listening; psychological analysis	passive	no
seeker of advice	interest in the topic, eager to learn	passive	yes
critic	criticism of contents, behaviour, opinions etc.	passive / active	yes
potential source of advice	provide information sought by the blogger	active	seldom
customer	interest in goods on offer, purchase	active	seldom

Considering Table 19, I'd like to side with Brake (2007) in that the audience is often not conceptualised in an active role, or even as a conversation partner. This rather passive audience concept is shared by the roles *witness*, *therapist* and *seeker of advice*. The role *(cultural) critic* contains some active instances. When readers are imagined as *potential source of advice* and *customer*, however, we can assume that they are also expected to get involved and 'react' in a certain way.

Of course, these audience roles often occur in mixed forms and there are probably various shades in between them. Table 19 might suggest clarity but it should rather be seen as a heuristic tool, highlighting what kinds of audience roles can potentially be of importance for the conceptualised audience of personal weblogs.

5.7.5 Summary

The previous passages have shown that the audience is an important aspect of the communicative situation of the genre *personal weblog*. Here, I'd like to sum up some key aspects.

The audience concept is, apparently, highly variable. It may contain friends and family as well as the potential mass audience of the World Wide Web – sometimes even simultaneously in "concentric circles" (Puschmann 2010: 77) (5.7.1). While some authors appear to write for an audience of one only, namely themselves, others write for a readership from which they expect different kinds of recognition. This prospect of recognition constitutes an important incentive for writing posts. If there is a perceived (or feared) lack of that recognition, frustration and even burn out may follow (5.7.2).

Personal weblogs are characterised by a crucial ambivalence of *personal* (own contents, interests, styles etc.) vs. *public* (desire to be read). One typical way out is to conceptualise the audience as *similar* to the blogger regarding demographic factors, opinions and interests, and so on. Such an audience concept allows authors to write for themselves *and* their readers (5.7.3).

The audience concept assumedly comprises audience roles, that is, what bloggers expect from their audience. These roles range from the rather passive (for example, the *witness*) to more active concepts such as the *customer*. All concepts discussed here apart from the *therapist* could also be detected on period I weblogs (5.7.4).

5.8 Conversational Maxims

In 1.3.3, I've argued that investigating in what way authors orient towards conversational maxims is an important part of genre description – and another step towards reconstructing how authors and their audiences work together in establishing a coherent interaction. When bloggers publish a post, they actually make an *offer of cooperation* to their imagined readers. This offer can be accepted or rejected by *actual* readers, of course. Be that as it may, an offer of cooperation already entails that authors take the conversational maxims, which are derived from the cooperative principle, into account (see 1.3.3). This is also true for posts that are written for an audience of *one*; even if authors write for their future selves they try to be adequately informative, truthful and relevant as well as express their thoughts in an adequate manner.[90,91]

5.8.1 *Publish as fact only what you believe to be true*: Quality

Apparently, this maxim has always had a particularly important role for personal weblogs.[92] It was already codified in very early blogging guides and therefore spread in explicit form. In her influential *weblog handbook*, Blood formulates the following ethical guidelines:

Example 71: Ethical Guidelines of Blogging

1. Publish as fact only what you believe to be true. […]
2. If material exists online, link to it when you reference it. […]
3. Publicly correct every misinformation. […]
4. Write each entry as if it could not be changed; add to, but do not rewrite or delete, any entry. […]
5. Disclose any conflict of interest. […]
6. Note questionable and biased sources.

(Blood 2002: 115–120)

The first of these guidelines reads as if it were a new version of the Gricean quality maxim: *Try to make your contribution one that is true*. But the other five points can also be related to that maxim. (2) and (6) stress the necessity of underlining the truthfulness of posts by referencing, evaluating and linking to external sources (Grice: *Don't say that for which you lack adequate evidence*). (3) and (4) apparently aim at avoiding unintentional deceptions. The same might apply to (5) – if

90 See also van Dijck (2004), who writes: "Writing, even as a form of self-expression, signals the need to connect, either to someone or something else, or to oneself in later life."

91 Interestingly, Puschmann (2009; 2010) argues that the cooperative principle and the conversational maxims are not valid at least for a subgroup of blogs. Particularly ego-blogs are subsumed under "*non-cooperative* behavior (in the Gricean sense)" (Puschmann 2010: 67, original emphasis). I've argued for the contrary in (Schildhauer 2014: 253–255) and will not do so here for reasons of space. However, I'll refer to Puschmann's arguments now and then when discussing the individual maxims one by one in this sub-chapter. I believe that this will illustrate why I consider it more plausible to assume the validity of the maxims for (personal) weblogs.

92 Even though Puschmann (2009; 2010) is quite sceptical concerning the validity of the conversational maxims (at least for some blogs, see fn. 91), he (2010: 71) acknowledges the validity of the quality maxim.

a post is supposed to advertise the blogger's own or third party products, it could be cooperative to a limited extent, with information held back that doesn't serve this purpose well, for example.[93]

Blood's guidelines can be read as formulations of the quality maxim *Be truthful*, which I suggested in Table 3, 1.3.3. Blood (2002) concentrates on efficient information exchange; her main focus seems to be on what she terms *filters* – "the classic weblog" (2002: 7). Indeed, period I weblogs, which typically followed this filtering purpose (7.2.1), already provide evidence for Blood's guidelines being part of the genre. Consider, for instance, the following excerpt:

Example 72: Quality Maxim I – Correcting Inadequate Information in Period I

> Okay, before I ride off into the sunset, a clarification. On the 15th, I called my USB Visor cradle "fragile". [...] As I went about thinking about the issues I had had (flakiness, and a couple of hard locks), I realized that they could all be explained by my thrashing around trying to get things to work. Once I got past a little confusion about when to hit the HotSync button, things settled down, and have been quite stable. I'm explaining all this because I didn't want anyone to read the previous entry and then make a purchase based in part on that information, which has turned out to be incorrect.
>
> (*Genehack* 24, I)

The author characterises the post as *clarification* and states that he wouldn't like incorrect information to circulate or even lead to *purchases*. He thereby stresses how important the quality maxim is to him. The current communicative purpose is obviously the exchange of reliable information. This purpose was also present in some personal weblogs (period II) as the following example underlines:

Example 73: Quality Maxim II – Correcting Inadequate Information in Period II

> Microsoft's Touch Mouse has a fatal flaw that didn't show up when I wrote last month's review: it chews through batteries.
> After six weeks use, I'm now on my sixth pair of AA batteries. That's unacceptable.
>
> (*Bill Bennett* 102–103, II.C)

93 See Lumsden (2008) on limited cooperation, for example in sales conversations.

Apparently, a convention of marking revisions arose. Quite often, authors used *edit* or *update* signs for that purpose:

Example 74: Quality Maxim III – Marking Corrections by using EDIT *and* UPDATE

Why didn't someone tell me linkwatcher hasn't updated in ten days? Better yet, why doesn't my bot tell me that? :/
Update: Oh. Duh. I had my computer unplugged the whole time I was on vacation... And I guess something screwed up the past couple days. Anyway, I rebooted and I think its fixed now.

(*Metalog* 14, I)

Edited to add: The Boy slept like that, on the couch until 3:00 in the afternoon.

(*Freak Parade* 22, II.B)

UPDATE:
The boy found some of these awful pictures. As I mentioned before, he is an art student, so now I am...

(*Biscuits and Buns*, 32–33, II.C)

The quality maxim seems to have been of importance for period II authors even beyond the purpose of conveying correct and current information. As shown in 5.6.1, authors often aimed at displaying authenticity. Additionally, 5.7.4 underlined that authors often imagined their readers in the role of witnesses who observe experiences and who are convinced of the authenticity of the narrated events. Truthfulness played a decisive role in that respect and is explicitly stressed for instance in the following excerpts:

Example 75: Quality Maxim IV – Stressing Truthfulness

Without further ado, <u>here is the evidence</u>.

(*Andy hmmm* 62, II.C, my emphasis, P. S.).

One day after she asked if I masturbated I was done. WHAT? I mean it takes a lot to throw me but REALLY? I told her no, I was lazy and rarely did (<u>that is true</u>) and walked away.

(*And at what place* 18, II.C, my emphasis, P. S.)

Concerning the excerpt from *And at what place*, it's particularly remarkable that it deals with content situated in category 3 on the intimacy scale (5.6.3). Additionally, this example shows that in reality, the quality maxim might be handled quite flexibly: Strictly speaking, the use of the adverb *rarely* turns the answer *no* into a lie. However, in this context, it can hardly be imagined that *No, I rarely do* is perceived as a lie. It's more plausible to assume that the passage is read as a correction of the initial answer *no* and therefore oriented towards the quality maxim.

This flexible way of handling the quality maxim also becomes apparent in the following example from *...Life of L...*, where the author comments on the truthfulness of her post on a metalevel. As she cannot guarantee veracity regarding the current post, she distances herself a bit from this standard:

Example 76: Quality Maxim V – Restricted Truthfulness

Anyway the above is something I needed to get out. The truth of it is rather like a muddled puddle. In other words...writing it was more of the point then [sic!] its truth.
(*...Life of L...* 15, II.A)

Apparently, her *motif for not telling the truth* (see Table 3) is, in that case, the particular communicative purpose of releasing emotional tension, which takes priority over strictly following the quality maxim *Be truthful.*

Other authors deliberately played with the quality maxim. For instance, a post in *Biscuits and Buns* (II.C, 17) is titled *To Hell and Back*, clearly a hyperbole. As readers were probably aware of this, they may have inferred by means of implicature that the author temporarily deviated from the *Be truthful* maxim for the purpose of drawing attention to her post. Another interesting case is *Dandy Darkly* (II.B), which tells a ghost story and blends (1.5.3) the genres personal weblog and ghost story in an interesting way. Apart from some scarce meta comments,[94] the reader – particularly the newbies – had to rely exclusively on the posts to draw that conclusion. Let's consider a particularly illustrative post from that blog:

Example 77: Quality Maxim VI – Fictionality in Dandy Darkly *(II.B)*

An Offer of Optimism
I don't like to think I'm naive. I prefer to consider myself, instead, an optimist. I like to believe my eagerness to find the hidden answer is what sometimes (lately more often) results in my less than favorable situational hardships. Take my shitty apartment for example. There's barely any plumbing. It's beginning to freeze at night. And a week ago, I found a winged rat had chewed through my loaf of bread. [...] This said, I attended the wedding of Sam Hain over the weekend. Sam Hain the Scarecrow Master, the King of Halloween, the Exalted Patriarch of Pumpkins, His Haunted Holiness...
(*Dandy Darkly*, II.B, additional excerpt 02.11.2009)

94 Some posts open with a short summary of the previous plot: "Welcome back to Dandy Darkly's Memoir Macabre! When we last set off, our conflicted protagonist prepared to combat the horrors of the dreaded Soul Eater..." (*Dandy Darkly* 3, II.B).

The first lines resemble a typical post of a personal weblog, seemingly narrating and reflecting personal experiences (7.2.3). However, the discovery of a *winged rat* seems rather unlikely and constitutes a trigger for the implicature that this text obviously doesn't follow the maxim *Be truthful*, instead, has the purpose of creating a fictional world. This becomes even more apparent towards the end of the passage quoted here. Interestingly, the post makes use of blog deixis, for example, *over the weekend*, and the 1st person pronoun, which normally refers to the blog's author but has to be connected to the I-narrator here. Thus, the post creates a blend of the real and the fictional world and strengthens the fusion by playing with the quality maxim. Other than the *To Hell and Back* example mentioned above, this post does not return to the *Be truthful* formulation of the maxim but constantly signals that its other purpose, that of creating a fictional world, is given priority over truthfulness.

5.8.2 *Sunday was my beautiful secret*: Quantity

Above (5.6), I quoted the concerns of some bloggers related to the quantity of information provided in their posts. Other authors such as Amy (*Amy's little life*, II.A), for instance, warned their readers not to disclose information that might be harmful to others – especially to protect children's identities. These considerations can be read against the background of the quantity maxim: *Make your contribution as informative as currently necessary for the jointly established (or established-to-be) purposes of the communicative event in which you are engaged.* In these cases, it is not only an efficient exchange of information that determines what is considered *as informative as currently necessary*, but also the protection of other participants. As a result, authors, particularly in period II, developed protection strategies when they wrote about others:

Example 78: Quantity Maxim I – Strategies of Dealing with Other's Names

Sash took me for dinner last night.

(*Auguries of Innocence* 4, II.A)

So tonight **elayne_7** and I were supposed to go to the LiveJournal MeetUp in St. Louis.

(*A Whirlpool of Dimensional Thought* 46, II.A)

M seems to be out of B's life for a bit ... so she's not acting quite as gay (B). M actually is getting quite hated in her little group of friends. Aww, looks like someone overstayed their welcome. I don't really see or talk to T much anymore...

(*...Life of L...* 11, II.A)

The Boy has been going through a period of severe disregulation with his sleep.

(*Freak Parade* 15, II.B)

While in many cases first names were used, other forms such as pseudonyms, nicknames and initials can also be found. Another strategy, illustrated by *Freak Parade*, was to allude to the relationship between author and participant; *The Boy* thus refers to the author's son.

The strategies probably triggered an implicature based on the quantity of information which is conveyed by an expression. Let's consider the *…Life of L…* example above: Here, the recipient might have felt some sort of information deficit, which probably became even more salient because of the abundance of different initials. The significance of these initials couldn't have been determined by a reader who didn't belong to a circle of trusted friends. This information deficit probably led to the following implicature: *The quantity of information offered by the author is sufficient for the jointly established (or established-to-be) purposes.* Perhaps the reader might have also implicated: *I (the author) could be more informative – but I simply don't want to in this context.* This implicature is even stated explicitly in the personal weblog *Blushes and Shimmy Shakes* and therefore didn't have to be inferred by the reader:

Example 79: Quantity Maxim II – Informativity and Communicative Purposes

For the purposes of this blog, I'll refer to her as B.

(*Blushes and Shimmy Shakes* 7, II.C)

I'd like to agree with Puschmann (2010: 71), who states that it's the author of a blog who determines the quantity of information to be provided. This is also illustrated by these excerpts, which I've analysed above through the lens of *intimacy* (5.6.3, Example 36):

Example 80: Allusions to Intimate Information

Apart from that, its all quiet on the Western front. Apart from amazing and unexpected sex on Saturday <u>Ill leave it to your imagination</u>!

(*andrewf my life* 103–104, II.A, my emphasis, P. S.)

And Sunday? <u>Sunday was my beautiful secret.</u>

(*Hello Stranger* 168, II.B, my emphasis, P. S.)

However, I cannot follow Puschmann in interpreting this as an argument against the validity of the quantity maxim. On the contrary, a post equals an offer of cooperation in which the chosen quantity of information is already included. The reader might accept or decline that offer. If, for instance, background information is not explicitly stated to a subjectively sufficient degree, the reader might conclude not to belong to the core of the conceptualised audience, and could therefore choose to decline the offer of cooperation on the basis of the quantity maxim.[95]

5.8.3 *[back to point]*: Relevance

Concerning this maxim, Puschmann (2010) states the following:

> As noted above, this maxim is affected most drastically by the unique pull situation of the search-driven Internet, where information is offered rather than sent. In its most drastic form, nothing is irrelevant in a search-driven environment, assuming an ideal matching of information and recipient. (Puschmann 2010: 72)

However, the validity of the relevance maxim should be assumed even in such a *pull situation* as described by Puschmann. Search terms, for instance, are chosen by potential recipients because they hope for relevant results according to their current need for information. Thus, they are an explicit statement of the current communicative purposes on the basis of the relevance maxim. Admittedly, search engines are fairly successful in providing only highly relevant results. However, readers still have to check whether what they have found is really relevant to their individual communicative purposes. As far as the authors are concerned, the relevance maxim has a stabilising effect for the production of blog posts. Thus, some authors obviously monitored the relevance of their posts for the global communicative purposes of their personal weblog:

Example 81: Relevance Maxim I – Meta Communicative Evaluation

> Well, I officially graduated on Saturday. I'm now a Real Doctor. Woo-hoo! To celebrate, I went out today and bought a <u>Visor</u>. An orange one. Anybody got any pointers for good PalmOS w4r3z? I found AportisDoc, I got my USB cradle working with Linux (although it's pretty fragile – I need to look into updating my source, I think), now I need some games and stuff.
> <u>Okay, onto the 'bloggin.</u> <u>Here's</u> one more reason why Windows for kisoks is wrong. Imagine the possibilities of Back Orificing one of *those* boxes.
> (*Genehack* 42–43, I, my emphasis, P. S.)

The first part of this post, which reports on novelties in the author's life, is marked by the phrase *onto the blogging* as irrelevant regarding the *actual* communicative purpose of the weblog. The real blogging, in other words: what readers can expect from this weblog, follows afterwards and contains IT-related information. Similarly, the author of *Gently Said* states that

95 See, for instance, Example 46 and Example 47 above.

Example 82: Relevance Maxim II - Communicative Purposes

> This Isn't a Blog Entry
> This is a test message to see if my mind is working. If this were a blog entry I would have a theme, a discourse, a point to make, a desire to convince, actually something to say.
> (*Gently Said* 26–27, II.C)

The term *blog entry* is defined on the basis of the relevance maxim: Only if an utterance is relevant regarding specific communicative purposes (for example, *desire to convince*), can it be labelled *blog entry*.

That authors monitored the production of posts with the relevance maxim in mind also becomes evident when discourse markers are used to mark digressions from the current topic of a post.[96] For instance, the following post from *around my kitchen table* is entitled *The Royal Wedding* and mainly deals with that topic. Right in the middle of the post, however, the author starts complaining about Austrians also having a day off. Only afterwards does she return to the actual topic:

Example 83: Relevance Maxim III - Digression and Discourse Marker

> **The Royal Wedding**
> [...]
> I was pleased to get the day off work – until another niece (sorry, I'm from a HUGE family) who lives in Vienna told me that Austria had also had the day off for the wedding. Why?
> I know we're all in the European family now, even if the UK is the family's grumpy gran, but we have no particular links with Austria, unless you count getting bombed by her most famous son, Hitler.
> I'm putting in a bid in for a bank holiday when Mrs French President Carla Bruni has her baby. Do you think we'll get it? I think the answer will be a resounding, "Non."
> Anyway, back to that wedding.
> I had no intention of watching the proceedings from beginning to end but was sucked in by the strange mixture of order and chaos, chic and tat and dignity and boorishness that accompany most weddings, whether a commoner's or future king's.
> (*around my kitchen table* 53–55, II.C)

96 See, e.g., Giora (1997) on discourse markers.

Brit blogger marks the digression even more abruptly:

Example 84: Relevance Maxim IV – Returning to the Actual Topic

With so much time on my hands yesterday due to the snow storm, I fancied a wee surf in the iTunes Music Store... I was in the market for some new Podcasts. After some fruitless searching for anything that really caught my eye, I noticed a listing for the most popular podcasts pertaining to the number of downloads - the #1 spot was held by The Ricky Gervais Show. If you're British, Ricky won't need an introduction - if you're not, he's the bloke behind the UK version of The Office - that'd be the funny version, not the fucking American rip off, starring Steve "Fudgenugget McAssbandit" Carell.
[back to point]
So I decide to give Ricky's podcast a listen to - and bare in mind, I have a very limited podcast library [...]

(*brit blogger* 24, II.B)

The digressions in these examples can be interpreted as temporary violations of the relevance maxim. By using discourse markers, the authors confirm the validity of the maxim meta communicatively.

Finally, keeping several blogs for distinct topics and/or communicative purposes can be related to the relevance maxim, too. Whereas, for instance, *Jenn's Travel Closeup* (II.B) contains reviews of restaurants and hotels, the author's second blog *Leftover Queen* deals with sustainability. Keeping both topics apart sharpens the communicative purpose of each blog and renders the respective posts relevant to the respective focus.

5.8.4 *~~crap their pants~~ extrude fecal matter*: Manner

Regarding the Gricean maxim of manner, Puschmann (2010: 73) makes a clear distinction between *topic* and *ego blogs*. He argues that the manner maxim is valid for the first group (and for corporate blogs in particular), but does not hold for the second one.[97]

However, I'd like to argue that, especially, the Gricean maxim *Be orderly* achieves a new meaning with regard to blogs in general. In 6.3.4, I'll show that the reverse chronological order of posts is a central feature of personal weblogs. This structural principle triggers an *implicature of sequence*: The order of the posts doesn't only mirror the publishing dates, but also the reverse chronological sequence of the depicted events. Thus, readers might expect that the closeness of events to their current *now* reduces when scrolling further down. This assumption is supported

97 See 7.6.1 for a discussion of this rather problematic typology.

by the fact that some authors use the option to manipulate the time stamp (4.3) in order to fit posts dealing with earlier events into the order of those already published. The personal weblog *it's ok to cry here*, for instance, contains the obviously back-dated post *mostly insignificant blog author is born* (16 April 1978). The following excerpt also illustrates this:

Example 85: Manner Maxim I – Be Orderly – *Reverse Chronological Order of Postings and Actual Order of Events*

> If you search backwards to September of last year, you'll see there are older posts now there, too. I'll continue to catch up with the old photos I have and will let everyone know when that's finished. But in the meantime, feel free to look backwards as well as forward for new posts.
>
> (*Brookston Family Blog*, additional excerpt 05.02.2007)

Even the ghost story in *Dandy Darkly* (see example Example 77, p. 112) follows this principle, although analeptic passages would be entirely possible for the ghost story genre. This is, in my opinion, rather strong evidence for the validity of the maxim *Be orderly* and the implicature of sequence as a feature of the personal weblog genre, into which *Dandy Darkly* embeds ghost story patterns.

The other Gricean manner imperatives (*Be brief, Avoid ambiguity, Avoid obscurity*) seem to be valid for (personal) weblogs as well. This showed especially in some period I weblogs:

Example 86: Manner Maxim II

> The electronic commerce boom may be <u>the best thing that ever happened</u> to manufacturers of delivery vans. [11.18.99]
> According to AltaVista, <u>good decisively triumphs over evil</u>. [11.17.99]
>
> (*Infoshift* 1–2, I)

The weblog *Perfect* stressed brevity and conciseness even more. Similarly to a logbook, the weblog chronicled the websites visited by the author one by one:

Example 87: Manner Maxim III – Be Brief

```
22:37 Sat 21 Jun '97 | www.highfive.com
22:31 Sat 21 Jun '97 | www.52mm.com
15:18 Sat 21 Jun '97 | www.blueberry.co.uk
10:24 Fri 13 Jun '97 | www.anorak.com
```

(*Perfect* 1, I)

In later periods as well, personal weblogs adhered to the Gricean manner imperatives, underlined by the telegram-like style of, for example, the following post:

Example 88: Manner Maxim IV

> Yeah, we're officially together Which is great.. But it sucks that I'm currently hundreds of miles away.. Missing her so much. Can't stop thinking about her [...].
>
> (*Dig your own hole* 26, II.B)

However, the validity of the manner maxim is illustrated even more when authors exploit it. In the following excerpt, two scripts collide in a rather humorous way, namely *taking the dog for a walk* and *taking someone out to a restaurant*:

Example 89: Manner Maxim V – Exploiting the Maxim for Comic Effects

> So, what's on my agenda for the day? Well, I'm going to take Pandora out to celebrate her birthday with a nice piddle against a tree.
>
> (*The EarthaKnittery* 67, II.A)

Of course, it's possible that the author somewhat violated the maxim and created the comic incongruity by accident. It's also entirely possible, however, that the maxim *Avoid ambiguity* is flouted in order to achieve the comic effect. Similarly, this post from *Asleep in the City* plays with the maxims *Be brief* and *Avoid obscurity of expression*:

Example 90: Manner Maxim VI – Exploiting the Maxim for Comic Effect

> Meeting with Brother Chuck to eat some ill fated, extremely unlucky cow who of no fault of its own, possessed a nice chunk of meat which would be most desireable medium rare.
>
> (*Asleep in the City* 68, II.A)

The actual topic of this passage, namely having a steak at a restaurant, is phrased with a ridiculously high number of words.

While the examples discussed so far can be treated neatly by referring to the Gricean imperatives, this doesn't seem to be that easy in the case of others, which also play on the *manner* of articulation. They might be better handled with the rather general phrasing of the manner maxim suggested above (1.3.3): *Express yourself in a way which serves the current jointly established (or established-to-be) purposes of the communicative event in which you are engaged.*

Example 91: Manner Maxim VII – Metalevel

> And all those junior middle managers are going to crap their pants extrude fecal matter in awe of my business acumen.
>
> (*First Person Irregular* 39, II.B)
>
> You MUST FORWARD this bLOg on to ALL of your FRiEnDs and EVERY SINGLE EMAIL ADDRESS YOU CAN GET YOUR HANDS ON. IF you CARE about your [insert favorite subject here: mom, dad, friend, child, earth, country, etc] then you MUST FORWARD THIS BLOG ON, otherwise the CuRsE of the iNteRNet BOOGieMaN will be the stain on your hands forever...
>
> (*AskmyPaul* 6, II.A)

Crossing out one expression in *First Person Irregular* in order to choose another one is a way of dealing with the manner maxim on a metalevel. It draws attention to both the graphic and the stylistic form of the utterance. On a stylistic level, a rather ironic tension arises between a vulgar phrasing (*crap their pants*) and the formal equivalent (*extrude fecal matter*). Crossing out the vulgar phrase, instead of just erasing it, makes this comic tension possible. The example from *Askmy-Paul* draws the reader's attention to its graphic form in particular. Apparently, the author uses the mixture of capitals and lowercase letters in order to mimic the graphic form of some e-mail hoaxes (see, e.g., Heyd 2008: 37). Therefore, this is an instance of pattern quotation (1.5.3).

5.8.5 Summary

In sum, this sub-chapter showed that conversational maxims as formulated in Table 3 are of high relevance for the personal weblog genre. I'd like to highlight the quality maxim in particular as it appears to constitute a very salient, and probably prototypical, feature of the genre in all periods. It was codified very early in guides such as Blood's *weblog handbook* and also appears in more recent guides, e.g., White and Briggs (2011). Regarding that maxim, period I weblogs focused on transferring correct and reliable information. Personal weblogs, on the other hand, have apparently foregrounded the ideal of authentic and truthful self-disclosure. Additionally, I've discussed the maxims of quantity, relevance and manner and pointed out in what way they underlie the production and reception of (personal) weblog posts. Finally, I've made a point of highlighting the flexibility and creativity that bloggers show in handling these maxims, for instance, when they play with the quality maxim to raise attention or exploit the quantity and manner maxim for comic effect.

5.9 Summary and Conclusions

Apparently, typical (personal) weblogs were a leisure activity, even though the boundary with professional blogging grew increasingly blurry (5.2). Furthermore, immediacy was a key feature of personal weblogs in all periods, and in some cases, was even creatively staged. In this respect, the timestamp of blog posts played a central role as it acted as deictic centre from which the reference of deictic expressions could be determined. Particularly, proximal deictic expressions were highly frequent in all periods and underline the centrality of immediacy for personal weblogs, and also weblogs, although to a lesser degree (5.3).

While early weblogs were kept by male IT-aficionados, the demographic profile broadened concerning both gender and profession in period II (5.5). Even though the communication form allowed for multiple authorship, notably period II personal weblogs were typically kept by one author only (5.4). Personal weblogs were a means of self-disclosure, first and foremost characterised by authenticity or at least the presentation of a close link between offline- and blog self (5.6.1). Authors varied in how selectively (5.6.2) and intimately (5.6.3) they self-disclosed. A medium level of intimacy, however, appears to have been typical of personal weblogs.

The conceptualised audience was another crucial aspect. It was particularly important for blog authors as a source of various forms of recognition (5.7.2, 5.7.4). The audience concept was variable and might have been as complex as to include both family and friends, plus a potential, and largely anonymous, mass audience. This could be shown from examining forms of address as well as the management of background knowledge (5.7.1). While some authors got frustrated by the feeling of having to satisfy the needs of a demanding audience only (5.7.2), others imagined their audience to be similar to themselves. Consequently, these authors could write according to their own interests *and* have the impression of fulfilling the expectations of a like-minded audience (5.7.3). The audience can be envisioned in various roles. Apparently, a 'real reaction' was not important or even desired in every case, particularly for the roles *witness*, *therapist* and *seeker of advice*. In other roles such as *customer*, *cultural critic* and *potential source of advice*, the audience was, however, expected to get actively involved.

In 5.8, I've argued that the conversational maxims of quality, quantity, relevance and manner played a decisive role for the production and reception of posts on (personal) weblogs. I've highlighted the role of the quality maxim and pointed out that the imperative of truthfulness and reliability of information was codified in various blogging guides. Meta comments in DIABLOC texts of all periods also underline its importance. I've also pointed out that the maxims are used flexibly and creatively. After all, personal weblogs have much more to offer than effective transfer of information.

6 Language, Image and More: Structural Characteristics

The most obvious thing to do when looking at a genre is to describe what the individual texts actually look like, that is, their structural characteristics. In doing so, I'll use the internal differentiation of the structural dimension introduced in 1.3.2: macro-, meso- and microlevel.

6.1 What I Did | What I Read

Of course, there's an abundance of studies dealing with structural characteristics of blogs. Table 20 and Table 21 provide an overview; this isn't exhaustive, of course. However, most of these studies don't focus specifically on the personal weblog genre but rather on blogs in general.[98] This doesn't mean that these studies are of no value for current purposes, but that we have to be cautious as to how their results compare to an analysis focussed on the personal weblog alone. Period I weblogs don't feature in any study, which is surprising as they are regularly referred to (e.g., Mauranen 2013; Miller & Shepherd 2009). There are some figures concerning the extent to which images are embedded but detailed analyses on language-image-links on personal weblogs are still missing. The same is true for the topics: Usually, broad types are postulated (Grieve et al. 2011; Puschmann 2010) that don't provide much insight into what it actually is that bloggers talk about. All in all, there's still a lot to be done. This chapter is a humble contribution, which can't, of course, address everything that could be done, but which will answer some old and open up some new questions.

As there's such a wealth of phenomena in this dimension that could be analysed, I had to draw on a wide range of methods. I followed a corpus linguistic approach, using the *WordSmith 6.0* software, to gather data on word and sentence length, type-token-ratio, word frequency and keywords.[99] I used a thousand-word-sample

98 The sampling is either conducted in a randomised way (Herring et al.), aims at maximum topical variation (Gerdes 2005; Grieve et al. 2011), follows a top-down approach with many presumptions (Hoffmann 2010) or remains rather opaque, as for example Puschmann's (2010: 109) "sufficiently large corpus of private weblogs".

99 A keyword analysis compares the frequency counts of the research corpus and compares them to a reference corpus – here: the British National Corpus (BNC). The resulting list contains those words which are significantly more or significantly less frequent than in the reference corpus and which can, therefore, be assumed to be

of each DIABLOC blog for these analyses – and all the words available on shorter blogs – to ensure that very long blogs didn't distort the results.

Features like, for example, layout (including font types and sizes, colours etc.), language-image-links and types of images were analysed by combining two other approaches. Schmitz (2010; 2011) proposes using the perceptible surface of a text as a basis for analysis. Similarly, Androutsopoulos (2010: 426) employs a monitor-based approach.[100] The strength of these two approaches lies in the fact that researchers describe everything that can be perceived on a surface, no matter whether this is language, image or some other mode. One problem of the monitor-based approach, namely that scrolling makes the perceptible surface dynamic, can be cured by adding screenshots or – as in this book – hyperlinks to the original websites under analysis when documenting the results. Another problem is harder to tackle: *How* the surface is perceived may *vary* according to the employed hardware (Pentzold et al. 2013: 88). On top of that, not only hardware is "responsible" for how a website can be perceived, but also software; most importantly, the browser. Just consider the abundance of forum discussions on why *Chrome* displays a site differently from *Firefox* and *Internet Explorer*. Additionally, a user's default settings come into play: If, for instance, a particularly sophisticated font is used on a website but not installed on my computer, my browser will just use Times New Roman, 12 pt. How can I make assumptions about how the author *intended* the site to be displayed, then? Another problem arises with classifying colours: Just try to decide for, say, five randomly chosen *WordPress* blogs in a row to decide whether the background is white or rather light grey…

I therefore analysed the *source code* of the DIABLOC blogs. It can be displayed easily; a right click on the website and then on *display source code* or similar provides information on fonts, colours, image sizes etc. The source code alone, of course, was also not sufficient for my analyses, as, for instance, image types couldn't be deduced from <img>-tags alone. Therefore, a combination of both the monitor- and the source code-based approaches, complemented by corpus linguistic analyses, provides the methodological basis of this chapter.

---

characteristic of a certain period of the research corpus (and consequently allows cautious assumptions about the genre *(personal) weblog* in a specific period).

100 In German: *bildschirm-basierter Ansatz.*

Table 20: Studies on Structural Characteristics of Blogs I

Level	Studies	Key Words / Observations
Macro	-	-
Meso	Balakina (2011), Crystal (2011), Grieve et al. (2011), Herring et al. (2003, 2004, 2005, 2006), Herring & Paolillo (2006), Hoffmann (2010) Hodkinson (2006), Huffaker & Calvert (2005), Mauranen (2013a), Miller & Shepherd (2004, 2009), Myers (2010), Nilsson [Hendrick] (2002), Puschmann (2010), Schlobinski & Siever (2005c), Schlobinski & Siever (2005a), Schlobinski & Siever (2005b), Gerdes (2005)	• several layout types can be differentiated according to how header, sidebar(s) and footer are arranged (Schlobinski & Siever 2005b: 59) • dominance of sidebar-left layout (Gerdes 2005: 99), or layout types with *one* sidebar, respectively (Balakina 2011: 43) • interactive elements such as search box, opinion polls, blogrolls, guestbooks and calendars • whether interactive elements are used or not is related to the communication form, which is also responsible for reverse chronological order (Herring et al. 2005: 145, 153).
Micro I		**General Remarks** • typical blog post: approx. 200 words, mainly language-based, only few hyperlinks; considerably more links to other sites than blog-internal links (Herring et al. 2005: 153–156); but consider Myers (2010: 28): "[B]logs vary enormously in the number and type of links" • Herring & Paolillo (2006): correlation between linguistic markers and post types *filter* and *diary* • common typology of *personal* vs. *thematic* blogs (or similar, here: Grieve et al. 2011: 320); Lomborg (2014: 77) highlights the importance of topical variability of posts **Language** • Nilsson [Hendrick] (2002: 25): "jargon specific to blogging" – lexemes such as "*blog, blogger, blogging, memes, post, posting, trackback*, etc." • Puschmann (2010: 111): "subjective human perspective present in prototypical ego blog" – high frequency of 1st person pronouns; high degree of stylistic variability (Puschmann 2010: 61) • Hofmann (2010: 217): "high clausal complexity as well as lexical variety" • cohesion mostly within posts, seldom between several posts • Crystal (2011: 72–73): search engine-optimised posts with specific stylistic characteristics

Table 21: Studies on Structural Characteristics of Blogs II

Level	Studies	Key Words / Observations
Micro II	Balakina (2011), Crystal (2011), Herring et al. (2005), Hoffmann (2010) Nilsson [Hendrick] (2002), Puschmann (2010), Schlobinski & Siever (2005c), Schlobinski & Siever (2005a), Schlobinski & Siever (2005b), Gerdes (2005)	**Hybridisation Hypothesis** – Schlobinski & Siever (2005b: 82) characterise blogs as a communication form in which orality and literality blend into a specific hybrid practice – similarly Crystal (2011: 68), who describes the syntax of blog posts as "sequence of units of thought which simply do not correspond to the kinds of sentence division we expect to see in print" – Balakina (2011: 39–41) supports this thesis, too, and detects a number of CMC features which are usually interpreted as serving a purpose of emulating orality in a written medium: clippings, capitalisations, reduplications etc. (Balakina 2011: 44–51) – Nilsson [Hendrick] (2002: 28–37) argues for a variety *Blogspeak*, which she also conceptualises as hybrid of orality and literality – However, Gerdes (2005: 110) states that asterisk constructions such as **cuddle** as another CMC feature are rather marginal in blogs and characterises blog language globally as "*standard English* writing" (Gerdes 2005: 118, original emphasis) – apparently against the hybridisation hypothesis. Similarly Hoffmann (2010: 222): "I consider personal weblogs as written monologues, which exhibit only few features of prototypical spoken dialogues." Hoffmann (2010: 224) also mentions "narrative and argumentative text types which can equally be found in written monologues […] as well" **Language-image-links** – Quantitative analyses on embedding images on blogs in Herring et al. (2005), Schlobinski & Siever (2005c: 63–64) and other studies in Schlobinski & Siever (2005b) – so far, to my knowledge, no detailed analysis of language-image-links / image types on blogs

6.2 Macrolevel – Personal Weblogs as Part of a Website

Figure 10: The Blog-Page (B) as Central Node within a Network of Perma-Sites (P) and Earlier Blog-Pages (simplification: I neglected hyperlinks among the perma-sites)

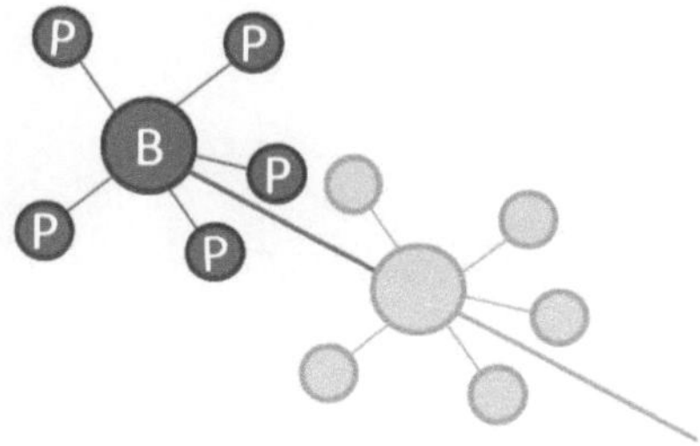

In this sub-chapter, I'll turn to the blog-page as part of a whole network of sites within a domain. Let me make a preliminary remark: Since the invention of the permalink (4.5.3), each blog-page[101] created with a blog-system has been embedded into a network of perma-sites for each entry on that page. These perma-sites can be reached via the permalink, which is part of the metalinks of each post. Additionally, the blog-page is usually linked to pages displaying earlier entries by hyperlinks at the bottom of the page. This was already true for many period I weblogs. A blog-page is therefore, strictly speaking, a central node of a bundle of pages which are tightly linked with each other. Here, however, I'd like to focus on the blog-page alone for the sake of simplicity.

The most important feature for navigating within the blog-domain is the navigation bar. It contains hyperlinks for intra-domain navigation, usually in horizontal order somewhere close to the header, but sometimes also in vertical order in the sidebar.[102]

---

101 See 1.3.2, Table 2 for a definition of the term *blog-page* as I'm using it here.

102 Some period I weblogs, e.g., *Bump*, also place their navigation bars in the footer.

Example 92: Some Forms of the Navigation Bar (rc3.org, *I* | 2bitstudios, *II.A* | Pukeko Flat, *II.C)*

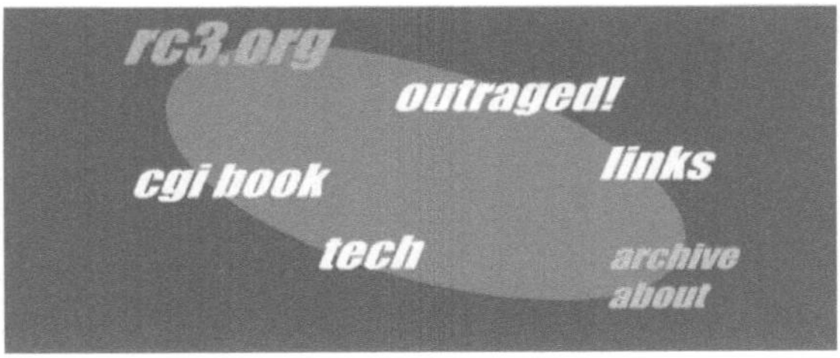

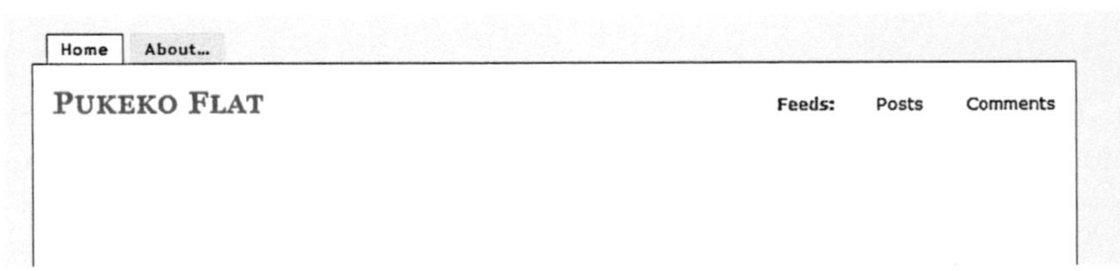

As the navigation bar is so important for the intra-domain navigation, I've quantified its occurrence to provide a basis for the following considerations:

Table 22: Macrolevel I – Navigation Bar as Indicator for the Domain-Internal Structure

Period	Navigation Bar				Total (valid cases)	
	yes		No			
I	86.7%	(26)	13.3%	(4)	100%	(30)
II.A	38.0%	(38)	62.0%	(62)	100%	(100)
II.B	52.0%	(52)	48.0%	(48)	100%	(100)
II.C	60.0%	(60)	40.0%	(40)	100%	(100)
$\varphi_c = 0.274$ | $p < 0.0001$						

The development is interesting: While the navigation bar was obviously a typical element of period I weblogs, it was only marginal in II.A. Its use increased until II.C, where, again, more than half of the blogs featured a navigation bar. This development was probably connected to the possibilities of creating static pages[103] offered

103 This feature of blog-software hasn't been discussed here; but see Schildhauer (2014: 162–163).

by blog-systems. We can, in the light of Table 22, assume that, indeed, a considerable fraction of blog-pages was part of a more complex domain-internal network.

Figure 11: Domain-internal Hierarchy - Type I

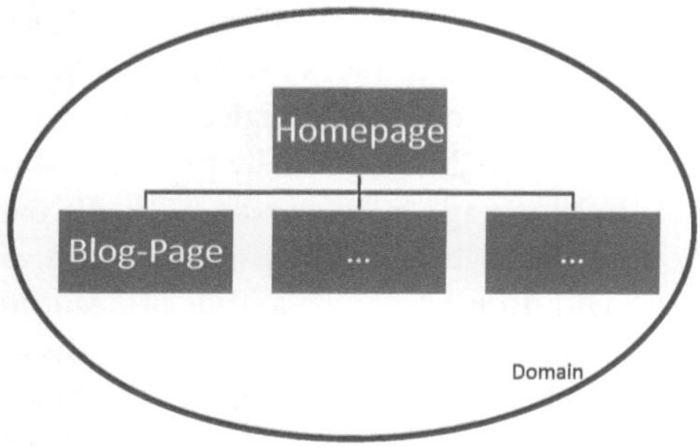

Within such a network, hierarchical relations emerge. There are, apparently, two types of hierarchies regarding the position of the blog-page in a network. In type I, the blog-page is a subordinate part of a domain which users enter via a homepage or an index-site. From there, visitors can reach the blog by clicking on the blog-link in the navigation bar. Type I blogs are, therefore, not accessed directly via the URL of the domain (as for instance *www.bump.net*, I) but via a sub-folder of the domain. The weblog *Honeyguide* (I), for instance, was part of the domain *www.chaparraltree.com* and could be reached via the URL *www.chaparraltree.com/honeyguide/*. For type I, the other pages of the domain are usually independent from the blog, content wise. Raphael Carter's (*Honeyguide*, I) navigation bar, for instance, listed the items *Homepage, Fiction, Vending Machines, Robots* and *Games* next to the weblog.

Figure 12: Domain-Internal Hierarchy – Type II

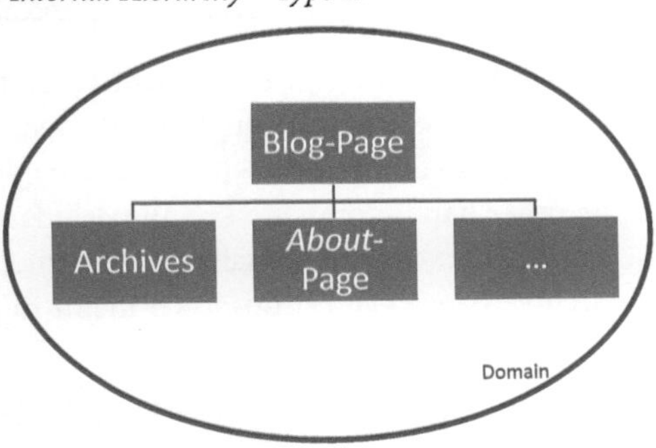

In type II, the blog takes another position. In this case, the blog itself is the gateway through which the domain is entered and is, therefore, accessed via the domain-URL (for example, *www.bump.net*). This type also comprises blogs like *My Right Hip*, whose URL is *www.myrighthip.wordpress.com*. *My Right Hip* was actually located in a sub-domain of the WordPress site because the author didn't purchase his own domain. However, blogs like this one behave like other type II blogs in every respect, so we can safely neglect this aspect. As illustrated in Figure 12, the other sites of the domain usually perform subordinate functions which are related to the blog-page in some way.[104] This is particularly obvious when authors introduce themselves on *about*-pages; but it also holds true for other kinds of additional information. The author of *Beautiful Dreamer* (II.C), for example, tried to enhance the understanding of her posts by providing a sub-page introducing all the characters of her dreams. The blog-page of *Maternal Experiment* (II.C) linked sub-pages entitled *About the Dependent Variable (me)* and *Pictures With My Independent Variables (the fam)*. From a structural point of view, this blog was quite close to a traditional family website. However, its dominating element was the blog-page.

The types are distributed in the corpus as follows:

Table 23: Macrolevel II – Domain-Internal Hierarchy Types

Period	**Domain-Internal Hierarchy**						**Total (valid cases)**	
	Type I		**Type II**		**No structure detectable**			
I	26.7%	(8)	60.0%	(18)	13.3%	(4)	100%	(30)
II.A	5.0%	(5)	33.0%	(33)	62.0%	(62)	100%	(100)
II.B	1.0%	(1)	51.0%	(51)	48.0%	(48)	100%	(100)
II.C	2.0%	(2)	58.0%	(58)	40.0%	(40)	100%	(100)
$\varphi_c = 0.289$ | $p < 0.0001$								

Next to type I and II, Table 23 contains those blogs which don't feature a navigation bar and for which, therefore, no type could be detected. Obviously, type I was a marginal phenomenon in all periods, with a bit more prominence in period I. Type II, on the other hand, dominated in all periods. Considering that even blogs without a navigation bar can contain domain-internal links (for instance, links to the archive pages via a drop-down menu in the sidebar), the

104 The dominance of the blog-page is also underlined by navigation bar designs as in *Pukeko Flat* (Example 92), where the blog-link "lies" above the about-link.

third column could be treated as special case of type II. If we follow this line of thinking, type II displays a fraction constantly above 90%.

The data in Table 23 indicates a rapid emancipation process of the (personal) weblog, which was probably already underway in period I. The blog-page as subordinate part of a domain was almost exclusively displaced by a blog-dominated macrostructure. This dominance was reflected formally (direct access via domain-URL) and content wise (other pages provided information dependent on the blog).

Possibly, this process is also connected to the weblog, as a genre, splitting off from the personal website (for example, *MacRonin*, I) and the e-zine (*Need to Know*, I; see Blood 2004: 54). In period II, *Reborn by Design* (II.A) and *Evan4sh* (II.B) apparently still mirrored the older, website-like macrostructure. As Rosenberg (2009: 8) outlines how weblogs split off from personal websites because of a need for a dynamic display of information,[105] it seems quite plausible to assume such a macrostructural trace of the root genre in weblogs (period I) and even some later personal weblogs.

This assumption is also supported when guestbooks, a typical feature of personal websites, are taken into account. I could only detect these in the DIABLOC in period I (6.7%) and II.A (14.0%). Gerdes (2005: 104) argues convincingly that the guestbook, the place to leave greetings after visiting a page, was displaced by the comment function and its much higher interactive potential.

The personal weblog *Pop Goes the Artist* (additional excerpt 2007) illustrates this transition from personal website to personal weblog impressively: The first archived version (23.06.2006) can still be recognised as a personal website – including *What's New* labels. The blog could be reached via a link in the navigation bar and there was also a guestbook link. From 2007 onwards, the domain could be entered via the blog-page. This blog-page also contained a navigation bar, including a guestbook link. By 2008, the guestbook had disappeared.

In summary, we can assume that from period II.A at the latest, a domain was set up for the sake of the blog itself. Certainly, the communication form played a role here as well. However, we should not neglect that in WordPress (II.C), for example, a static page could be made homepage of a domain and, therefore, a type I hierarchy would have been possible. Despite this, type II dominance of the blog-page appears to have become typical of the personal weblog genre.

105 See also Rehm (2006: 246).

6.3 Mesolevel – Design and Layout

In this sub-chapter, I'll address some design features first and then move on to discuss some elements of the blog-page and their constituents.

6.3.1 Design

Schlobinski & Siever (2005a: 59) proposed a typology of basic layout types for blogs (Figure 13), to which I added two more types in order to adjust it to my analysis. Type 5 describes a layout with two sidebars on the right. Type 6 is the "odd" category, comprising all those blogs which don't fit into any of the others. The distribution of these types is displayed in Table 24 below. Statistically, there is a clear relation between layout and period. We can assume that there was some sort of development from period I to II.C; indeed, (personal) weblogs type 1 (sidebar left and right) disappeared over time: While almost half the period I weblogs followed this pattern, no personal weblog did so in II.C. The development of type 2 (sidebar left) was fairly similar.

Figure 13: Blog Layout Types (Schlobinski & Siever 2005a: 59)

Table 24: Mesolevel I – Layout Types

Period	Layout												Total (valid cases)	
	Type 1		Type 2		Type 3		Type 4		Type 5		Type 6			
I	46.7%	(14)	36.7%	(11)	13.3%	(4)	3.3%	(1)	0.0%	(0)	0.0%	(0)	100%	(30)
II.A	9.0%	(9)	27.0%	(27)	48.0%	(48)	14.0%	(14)	1.0%	(1)	1.0%	(1)	100%	(100)
II.B	1.0%	(1)	17.0%	(17)	56.0%	(56)	14.0%	(14)	10.0%	(10)	2.0%	(2)	100%	(100)
II.C	0.0%	(0)	9.0%	(9)	69.0%	(69)	15.0%	(15)	6.0%	(6)	1.0%	(1)	100%	(100)
$\varphi_c = 0.351 \mid p < 0.0001$														

In addition to these developments, we can find a pronounced increase of type 3 (sidebar right).[106] Type 3 was joined by type 5 (two sidebars right), which resulted in a clear preference for a text-to-sidebar reading-path as opposed to sidebar-to-text. Hussey (2011) explains this development from blogger perspective:

Example 93: On Sidebars

Early on in web design, the left column was for navigation because we knew that what was on the left would definitely be on people's screens. The farther to the right we went, the less sure we were. This idea stuck with us in early blog designs until we learned that our sites would be indexed more efficiently if we had sidebars on the right so that search bots would hit content first, not sidebar. Today, with better CSS layouts, SEO isn't the reason we do it. I think we're doing it for A) style and B) to maximize reading efficiency on a page. With words going left to right across the pages, I want people's eyes to return to my content and not get distracted by the sidebars. At least that's the theory.

(Hussey 2011: 188)

According to Hussey, then, period I layout was mainly influenced by the infrastructure of the communication form. Later, the impact of this factor decreased in favour of considerations of "reading efficiency". Schlobinski & Siever (2005b: 61) additionally assume an influence of journalistic genres. Whereas I cannot make general statements about that possible impact here, the personal weblog *Mind the Gap* (II.C) indeed clearly exhibited such an influence concerning its three-column-layout and typographical design (black and red font colour, headline in serif font). The author Shaaz Nasir is, in fact, a journalist, which might explain this particular orientation to journalistic patterns.

106 This result contrasts with both Gerdes (2005) and Schlobinski & Siever (2005b), whose data suggest a dominance of type 2.

Another composition increasingly typical of personal weblogs was already present in *Genehack* (period I), where the elements sidebar, header, body and navigation bar constituted individual layers on a green background. This layer-like design was accentuated by the use of different background colours for these elements and by having a distinctive 3D frame for each element. In period I, this pattern was marginal (26.7%); in later periods, approximately 50% of the blogs used it (II.C even 60%). In II.C, a dynamic variant of this layer-composition gained importance (8% in II.C; 1% in II.A and B): In personal weblogs such as *Maternal Experiment* (II.C), scrolling moved only the posts while the other elements of the page remained in place. This created the illusion of a transparent post layer gliding over a layer beneath containing the other elements. In summary, 68% of the personal weblogs in II.C implemented a layer-composition (60% static, 8% dynamic). This kind of layout can be considered typical in II.C.[107]

A similarly pronounced preference concerning background colours developed as shown in Table 25:

Table 25: Mesolevel II – Background Colour (Posts)

Period	Background Colour (Posts)										Total (valid cases)	
	White		Black		Coloured		Grey		Other1[108]			
I	56.7%	(17)	3.3%	(1)	16.7%	(8)	13.3%	(4)	0.0%	(0)	100%	(30)
II.A	49.0%	(49)	11.0%	(11)	40.0%	(40)	0.0%	(0)	0.0%	(0)	100%	(100)
II.B	62.0%	(62)	9.0%	(9)	24.0%	(24)	3.0%	(3)	2.0%	(2)	100%	(100)
II.C	61.0%	(61)	6.0%	(6)	31.0%	(31)	1.0%	(1)	1.0%	(1)	100%	(100)
$\varphi_c = 0.172$ | $p = 0.0004$												

In all periods, white was by far the preferred background colour for posts.[109] This is probably due, again, to considerations of legibility. Interestingly, II.A showed a particular preference for black and coloured backgrounds (together: 51%), which was very likely linked to the particular prominence of the blog-system *Blogger* in

107 With $\varphi_c = 0.215$ and $p < 0.0001$, there is a statistically significant relation between period and layer-layout so that we can assume an evolutionary change of the genre towards that feature.

108 For example, images as background.

109 Due to the layer-composition mentioned above, a different colour might have been for the layer underneath the posts in some cases.

that period;[110] Blogger offered templates with black and coloured backgrounds, as shown in Example 94:

Example 94: Mesolevel III – Blogger *Templates*

As far as the font colour of posts[111] is concerned, black could be expected to have been the preferred option. However, the use of black decreased in favour of grey and coloured variants:

Table 26: Mesolevel IV – Font Colour

Period	Font Colour (Posts Main Part)								Total (valid cases)	
	White		Black		Colour		Grey			
I	6.7%	(2)	76.7%	(23)	6.7%	(2)	10.0%	(3)	100%	(30)
II.A	7.0%	(7)	41.0%	(41)	12.0%	(12)	40.0%	(40)	100%	(100)
II.B	5.0%	(5)	26.0%	(26)	14.0%	(14)	55.0%	(55)	100%	(100)
II.C	2.0%	(2)	20.0%	(20)	30.0%	(30)	48.0%	(48)	100%	(100)
$\varphi_c = 0.231 \mid p < 0.0001$										

Consequently, period I showed a pronounced preference for black font on white background (46.7%), followed by black on colour (16.7%) and black on

110 With $\varphi_c = 0.214$ and $p = 0.002$, there is a statistically significant relation between the variables *blog-system* and *background colour*. In total, 59.3% of black and 44.7% of coloured backgrounds can be attributed to *Blogger*.

111 I am referring to the main text here. As Example 94 shows, the headlines of posts can be different in colour from the main text.

grey (13.3%). In the following periods, the black-on-white preference decreased (from 29% in II.A to 15.0% in II.C) and gave way to grey-on-white in particular (6.7% in I, 17% II.A, 37% II.B, 30% II.C). This could have been influenced by aesthetic considerations: For grey-on-white, the contrast between font and background isn't that sharp; at the same time it provides high legibility (Żebrowska 2013: 179). Additionally, it can be assumed that the communication form played a role, as well. For instance, the blog-systems MovableType and WordPress apparently prefer grey-on white, with 50% of the MovableType blogs and 45.7% of the WordPress blogs featuring grey-on-white. Apparently, some blog-systems impose colour preferences by means of their default settings (see also Example 94 for Blogger templates).

As far as font types are concerned, I resorted to a basic distinction between serif and sans-serif fonts. As Table 27 shows, bloggers in all periods preferred sans-serif fonts, probably again due to their higher legibility on screens (Żebrowska 2013: 180).

Table 27: Mesolevel V – Font Type

Period	Font Type				Total (valid cases)	
	sans serif		*serif*			
I	88.2%	(15)	11.8%	(2)	100%	(17)
II.A	93.3%	(83)	6.7%	(6)	100%	(89)
II.B	94.8%	(91)	5.2%	(5)	100%	(96)
II.C	75.5%	(74)	24.5%	(24)	100%	(98)
$\varphi_c = 0.261 \mid p = 0.0001$						

In sum, there are patterns in the field of design that established themselves as typical of personal weblogs. As the communication form allowed for alternative options, these patterns can be attributed to evolving genre conventions.

6.3.2 Designing Headers

Well above 90% of the (personal) weblogs in each period contained a header. Sometimes, authors placed an additional, descriptive slogan below the header, briefly elucidating the respective blog; for example, "The Misadventures of a Somewhat Whiny Geek" (*DogBoi*, II.C). Such a slogan could be found on 56.7% of period I weblogs, and from II.A (44%) with an increasing tendency (up to 63% in II.C).[112]

112 $\varphi_c = 0.134$, $p = 0.065$ – statistically not significant.

While some authors used standard headers (*My Right Hip* in Example 95 below), others creatively designed this element:

Example 95: Mesolevel VI – Headers

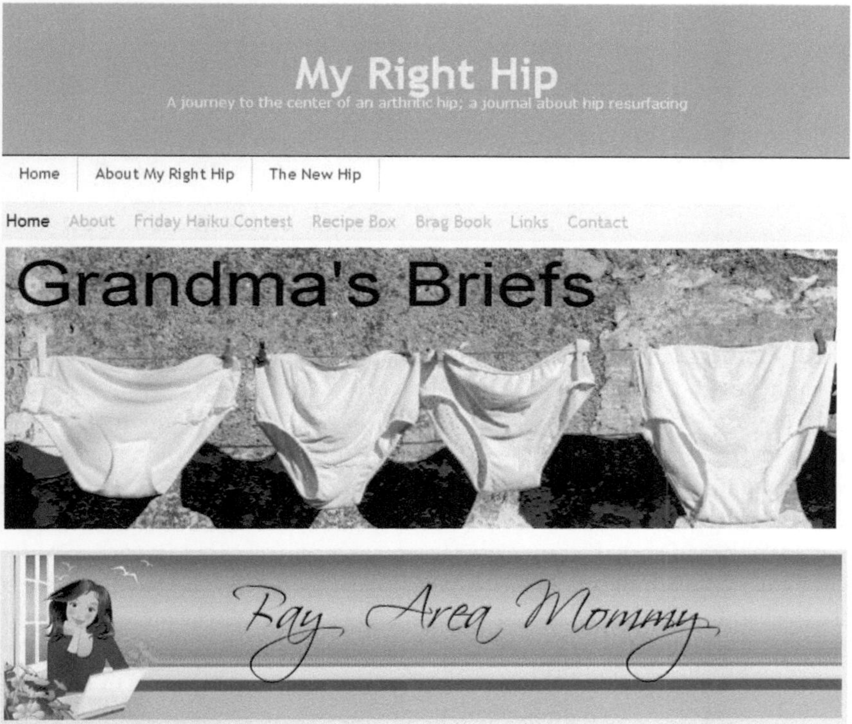

In general, a header could merely present the blog's headline (*My Right Hip*), additionally implement a photograph (*Grandma's Briefs*) or exhibit some other, even artistic language-image-combination (*Bay Area Mommy*). Most period I headers were particularly plain; quite often they merely contained a headline that barley contrasted with the design of posts:

*Example 96: Mesolevel VII – Period I Header (*Flutterby*)*

Surely, this is linked to infrastructural restrictions such as storage space and bandwidth. Using images in that period was basically a matter of resources, (4.4). Particularly outstanding was, therefore, the header of *Infoshift*:[113]

Example 97: Mesolevel VIII – Header Infoshift *(Period I)*

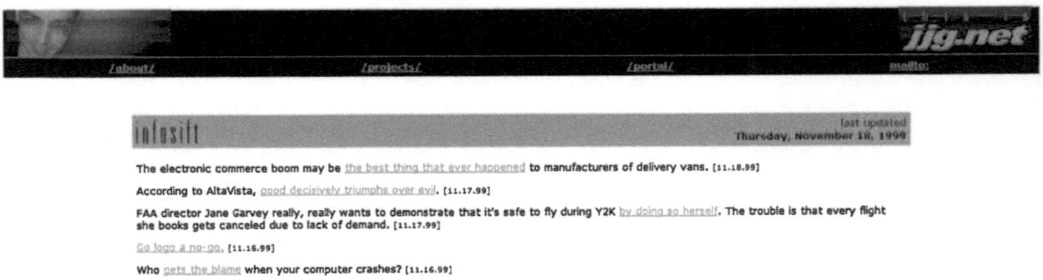

Embedded in a sophisticated overall design, the header most strikingly shows the author's face. I'm only speculating here, but this might be related to notions of authenticity and reliability of the contents of this blog (5.6.1; 5.8.1). Probably, the connotations evoked by this header design go beyond my suggestions. However, the example might serve as a case in point to show the importance which the header design might have had: The header influences or, at least, has the power to influence the way recipients read and make sense of the posts of a particular blog. Due to the principle of reverse chronology, there is even a spatial contiguity between header and first posts as in Example 97; a reader focussing on the most recent posts also simultaneously perceives the header. This might increase the header's influence on how these posts are read, namely coloured by the header's connotations.[114] I would like to assume that authors, as in Example 95 and Example 97, drew on this function of the header, in particular when they didn't use standard headers provided by the blog-system.

---

113 Jessie James Garrett only implemented this header design from April to November 1999. I can only speculate whether infrastructural restrictions of the communication form were the reason for him deciding against that design.

114 See Jäger (2002) and particularly Holly (2009) on that issue. The connotations described here for the header resemble what Holly (2009) writes about several camera angles in talk shows, whose connotations might strongly influence how a particular speaker's part is perceived.

6.3.3 Typical Elements of the Sidebar

Along with the header, the sidebar also provided scope for individual design. For instance, authors could make use of various widgets (4.9.2), or embed images in the sidebar; the sidebar of *Gentle Apocalypse*, II.C, consisted entirely of a seemingly endless series of images! In addition, the use of widgets wasn't limited to those offered by the blog-system software by default and depended on, among others, the author's skills.

As early as period I, the sidebar served two main functions. On the one hand, it could contain navigation elements such as links to earlier posts or a vertical navigation bar (for example, *The Obscure Store and Reading Room*). On the other hand, Blood (2000) remarks that Cameron Barrett used his sidebar for listing other weblogs (2.2.1), and therefore suggests a community-oriented function.

An important navigation element of the sidebar was to enable access to the blog's archives, which could, for instance, appear as list of hyperlinks or as a drop-down menu. Providing access to the archive has its origins in period I but increasingly gained importance from II.A onwards:[115]

Table 28: Mesolevel IX – Access to Archives via Sidebar

Period	Archives				Total (valid cases)	
	No access via sidebar		Access via sidebar			
I	80.0%	(24)	20.0%	(6)	100%	(30)
II.A	35.0%	(35)	65.0%	(65)	100%	(100)
II.B	20.0%	(20)	80.0%	(80)	100%	(100)
II.C	26.0%	(26)	74.0%	(74)	100%	(100)
$\varphi_c = 0.351 \mid p < 0.0001$						

This dramatic increase was probably connected to the communication form: First, managing archives was a tedious business in period I, and this only eased in period II when blog-systems started relieving the bloggers of this burden. Second, adding some sort of archive access point to the sidebar was not only easy in blog-systems but even part of the default settings.

115 In period I, a link to an *archives* page included in the navigation bar (instead of the sidebar) was actually more frequent. As I used blog archives as an important indicator to test the validity of blogs for the DIABLOC (2.3.2), nearly all blogs of my corpus contain archives. That means that even blogs listed under "no access via sidebar" quite probably contain archives, then accessed via the footer, the navigation bar or similar.

Further important navigation elements were tags, categories and labels shown in the sidebar, enabling the navigation of blog posts via topic-related criteria. In period II.C, 55% of personal weblogs offered at least one of these options.[116] A search box was also integrated to an increasing extent and use spread from 10% in period I to 45% in II.C.[117] The search box element could be easily added, particularly in II.C, as it was a default widget (4.9.2, 4.9.3). Apparently, it was on the way to becoming a typical feature of the personal weblog. A calendar function, however, was only offered by a decreasing minority (24% in II.A, 15% II.B and 12% II.C).[118]

As far as the community-oriented function of the sidebar is concerned, let's look at the blogroll first, which Blood (2000) goes so far as to consider the *conditio sine qua non* for the emergence of the sidebar.[119] The blogroll might have had its origin in *Camworld's* list of other weblogs (2.2.1). At least, this is, to my knowledge, the first blogroll ever attested. The element worked like a meta-filter which selected a few blogs from the growing mass of available blogs and recommended them to the audience (Nilsson [Hendrick] 2002: 8). Additionally, the blogroll as a "statement of social affiliation" (Marlow 2004) quite likely served a contact function (1.3.4). Consequently, its importance as an expression of *recognition* (5.7.2) cannot be underestimated (Rosenberg 2009: 211).

Table 29: Mesolevel X – Blogroll

Period	Blogroll						Total (valid cases)	
	No		Yes		Undecided			
I	73.3%	(22)	26.7%	(8)	0.0%	(0)	100%	(30)
II.A	43.0%	(43)	55.0%	(55)	2.0%	(2)	100%	(100)
II.B	36.0%	(36)	53.0%	(53)	11.0%	(11)	100%	(100)
II.C	52.0%	(52)	42.0%	(42)	6.0%	(6)	100%	(100)
$\varphi_c = 0.183$ | $p = 0.001$								

116 See 4.3 for further information on tags, labels and categories. This point also tells you about the fact that *labels* are, in fact, *categories*, only that they are offered by *Blogger* (instead of, for example, WordPress).

117 In statistical terms, this development is significant, with $\phi_c = 0.243$ and $p = 0.001$.

118 This development, too, is statistically significant, with $\phi_c = 0.172$ and $p = 0.021$.

119 Even though it is definitely true that the blogroll is an important element and even contributed to the emergence of the weblog genre (2.2.1), I don't find it plausible to think of it as the only reason for the emergence of the sidebar as a blog element. Just consider the navigation functions performed by sidebars (also in period I), which can even be traced back to those personal websites which contained a vertical navigation bar (my own from 1997 was made exactly that way).

The data in Table 29, however, clearly indicates that the presence of blogrolls decreased after a peak in II.A. Reflecting on his own blogging practice, Hussey (2011: 204) also suggests that blogrolls were getting out of date. According to him, the vast number of recommendable blogs made keeping a blogroll – one that, above all, didn't forget to include any blogger-friend – rather impossible. Indeed, Hussey states that blogrolls rather transformed into lists of websites with interesting content, partly in order to get away from the social stress involved in keeping a blogroll. This trend might be reflected in the column *undecided* in Table 29. Under this label, I've counted link lists which weren't explicitly labelled *blogroll* or which didn't contain only blog-related links. Assumedly, the rapid spread of the *follower*-widget in II.C also played a role here (from 1% in II.B to 37% in II.C – statistically very significant with $\varphi_c = 0.527$ and $p < 0.0001$). This widget is related to Twitter's follower feature: Members of the audience can use their own blog or a social network account, for example, Facebook, to subscribe as a follower of a certain blog. From a functional point of view, the follower widget entailed a shift of focus as it was no longer the bloggers who stated their affiliation with others as with the blogroll, but recognition was, in contrast, awarded the other way round. The follower widget revealed, to some extent, the community of readers emerging around a certain blog.

Two other community-related elements also show an interesting development: One option was that (personal) weblogs could contain a form field which readers used to subscribe to a mailing list, providing their e-mail address, in order to receive notifications about new posts or even receive their contents via e-mail. Alternatively, bloggers could include a link leading to the blog's RSS feed, which basically served the same functions: New posts, or their blurbs at least, were sent to the audience. Readers used special software (RSS reader) to compile the feeds of several sources and thus get a neat feed of news that they were interested in. Both elements can be framed as embeddings on the communication form layer (1.5.3) and show a significant increase:

Table 30: Mesolevel XI – Mailing List and RSS Feed

Period	Mailing List				RSS Feed				Total (valid cases, both separately)	
	No		Yes		No		Yes			
I	70.0%	(21)	30.0%	(9)	96.7%	(29)	3.3%	(1)	100%	(30)
II.A	95.0%	(95)	5.0%	(5)	77.0%	(77)	23.0%	(23)	100%	(100)
II.B	79.0%	(79)	21.0%	(21)	40.0%	(40)	60.0%	(60)	100%	(100)
II.C	58.0%	(58)	42.0%	(42)	16.0%	(16)	84.0%	(84)	100%	(100)
$\varphi_c = 0.345 \mid p < 0.0001$					$\varphi_c = 0.565 \mid p < 0.0001$					

Within the blogging context, both elements are associated with Dave Winer's name. Indeed, a mailing list called *DaveNet*, which Winer used from 1994 onwards to inform subscribers about technical developments and personal thoughts, was the predecessor of Winer's famous *Scripting News* weblog. Starting from the mailing list, Winer first designed a *News Page* (similar to Berners-Lee's, see 4.3) and then *Scripting News* (Rosenberg 2009: 46–60). From the very beginning, therefore, the communication forms *blog* and *e-mail* can be considered to be linked. In period II, blog-systems apparently revived this connection – but only in II.B. In II.C, the mailing list was established as an important feature. The development of RSS technology started around the millennium and was promoted substantially by Winer (Hayder 2006: 156–157; Stauffer 2008: 221–227). In II.C, offering an RSS feed was a typical feature of the personal weblog.

Both features provided bloggers with an opportunity of gaining and *keeping* regular readers who were relieved of the tedious burden of regularly checking the blog for new posts. Assumedly, then, this convergence of the pull communication form *blog* (Efimova 2009: 86) with the push communication forms *e-mail* and *RSS* was mainly motivated by the fact that bloggers strove to attract regular readers, possibly as a source of recognition.

A need for social belonging and recognition is, possibly, also what drove some bloggers to display awards and buttons in their sidebar. Awards were, in this context, trophies of recognition of a particular sub-community of the blogosphere. The author of *E-Housewife* (II.B), for instance, showed that she was part of the *mommy blog* community by displaying buttons from several directories such as *The Mom Blogs*. Additionally, one part of her sidebar contained the proud exclamation "I'm a Top Momma!" awarded by the mommy blog site *www.topmomma.com*. If bloggers wanted their site to be displayed on that directory, which entailed the right of displaying the award in their sidebar, they had to meet a number of competitive criteria such as image quality and readership numbers.

Another element of the sidebar, which can also be subsumed under *community-related*, is the author's short profile, where authors introduced themselves as well as topics and purposes of their blog in a number of short, sometimes even elliptical sentences. Usually, authors also embedded an image here. In II.C, a *Facebook* badge fulfilled the same function on some personal weblogs. The profile feature spread considerably from 6.7% in period I to 45.0% in II.C. Like the search box, the profile established itself step by step as a typical element of the sidebar of personal weblogs.

6.3.4 Posts from a Mesolevel-Perspective

In 1.3.2, I defined posts as a formal unit, marked, most importantly, by a timestamp at the beginning or the end. From period I onwards, such a timestamp can be found on nearly every blog in the DIABLOC.[120]

From II.A onwards, timestamps were accompanied by metalinks as elements formally separating posts from one another. Without any exception, from II.B, all personal weblogs in the DIABLOC contained these kinds of links. In general, blog-systems generated these links automatically. One of these metalinks is the permalink (4.5.3), which linked to the individual page of a certain post and which could also occur more than once (if heading and timestamp were used to display this link, for instance). Additionally, comment links and links to the author's profile page may have been part of these metalinks.[121] From their first appearance in II.A, the mean number of metalinks rose steadily, although not in a statistically significant way[122] (from 1.74 in II.A to 2.82 in II.C).

The comment function, which is often accessed via a metalink, was established as a key feature of personal weblogs right after the spread of blog-systems:

Table 31: Mesolevel XII – Comment Function

Period	Comment Function				Total (valid cases)	
	No		Yes			
I	100.0%	(30)	0.0%	(0)	100%	(30)
II.A	31.0%	(31)	69.0%	(69)	100%	(100)
II.B	6.0%	(6)	94.0%	(94)	100%	(100)
II.C	11.0%	(11)	89.0%	(89)	100%	(100)
$\varphi_c = 0.618 \mid p < 0.0001$						

Most interestingly, there was a slight decline from II.B to II.C. What could have been the reason? In 7.6.2, I'll dwell a little on the idea that blogs competed with social network sites in II.B; for example, status updates on *Facebook* and personal

120 Indeed, there are only three personal weblogs in the corpus whose entries do not contain a timestamp: *Inter alia* (II.A), *House Renovation on a Budget* (II.B), and *Bella Vida* (II.C).

121 As well as the metalinks, labels, tags and categories can appear as hyperlinks on the top or bottom of posts. Categories already appeared occasionally already in period I; labels and tags from II.B onwards.

122 I applied the T-Test, comparing the mean values of the separate periods (3.3).

weblog posts fulfil similar functions. My idea is that a process of functional differentiation took place in which social network sites took over shorter types of posts from personal weblogs, whereas personal weblogs won out on longer and more reflective posts. Assumedly, this differentiation process is also mirrored in the development of comment function implementation – social network sites might have been seen as far more suitable for quick-and-easy exchanges of opinions.

A key feature is also the reverse chronological order of posts:

Table 32: Mesolevel XIII – Reverse Chronology

Period	Reverse Chronology				Total (valid cases)[123]	
	No		Yes			
I	20.0%	(6)	80.0%	(24)	100%	(30)
II.A	1.1%	(1)	98.9%	(92)	100%	(93)
II.B	0.0%	(0)	100.0%	(97)	100%	(97)
II.C	0.0%	(0)	100.0%	(98)	100%	(98)
$\varphi_c = 0.393$ | $p < 0.0001$						

Table 32 shows that, indeed, this structural principle was present almost without exception. In II.A, *august dreams* was such an exceptional case, publishing a new page for every post, instead of displaying all posts on one page. This personal weblog was run by *Diaryland* and also contained the label *diary* in the navigation bar. These indicators suggest that *august dreams* exhibited features of the online diary genre and, therefore, was situated in the transition zone between the genres *online diary* and *personal weblog*.

The picture in period I was not that straightforward. A considerable fraction of authors in this period didn't implement reverse chronological order but rather followed some other principle. The weblogs *Need to Know* and *Linky & Dinky*, for example, published one new page every week and in that rather resembled e-zines. Apparently, there were two competing solutions for the basic problem that all weblog authors were faced with; namely how to display rapidly-updated content without losing older information and drowning in *what's new* buttons. Authors either published all posts on one page in reverse chronological order, or one new page for each post, with the navigation bar providing access to every entry-page (for example, *Windowseat*). Bausch et al. (2002) label these two approaches *post*

123 Naturally, I had to exclude personal weblogs with only one post as well as blogs without timestamp from this survey.

and *page paradigm* and point out that the page paradigm dominated in the early years of the WWW. It obviously constitutes a link to offline writing traditions. They also underline the effort involved if authors adhered to that paradigm while constantly updating the contents of their sites. I'd like to conclude that authors, in adjusting to their new needs, successively took the step from thinking in pages to thinking in posts. While online diaries and other early WWW genres such as the personal website still exhibited rather strong links to offline writing, (personal) weblog authors generally took this step. In period II.A, they were assisted by blog-systems and their default settings.

A cursory glance at the length of posts also yields interesting results:

Table 33: Mesolevel XIV – Post Length (Word Forms)

Period	Post Length (Word Forms)				N (of total)
	Min.	Max.	Mean	σ	
I	7.00	1796.00	208.40	403.05	30 (30)
II.A	1.00	916.00	239.40	190.76	100 (100)
II.B	39.71	929.70	269.50	182.30	100 (100)
II.C	9.00	1965.00	433.67	375.85	100 (100)

Table 33 shows that the mean post length increased from period I onwards. The transition from II.B to II.C is especially remarkable. This dramatic increase in mean post length might also be connected to the process of functional differentiation between personal weblogs and social network sites outlined above. While shorter post genres such as update (7.2.2) and filter posts (7.2.1) were highly suitable for status updates on, say, Facebook, personal weblogs obviously featured longer posts, for instance narrating and reflecting on personal experiences (7.2.3). Additionally, Table 33 mirrors a widening of the variation scope of the genre (1.5.1) in the increase of standard deviation. In other words: As well as blogs with fairly long posts, there were also, apparently blogs with rather short ones. In II.C, one personal weblog exhibited a mere nine-word average only. It appears that not all bloggers joined in the trend.[124]

124 There may also be a connection to a rather contrary trend, namely relying on embedding images instead of typing long posts (see 6.4.4).

At the end of this sub-chapter, I'd like to consider the *topics* (personal) weblogs usually dealt with. Table 34 displays the results of a *WordSmith* keyword analysis (up to 25[125] words with the highest keyness):

Table 34: Mesolevel XV – Keywords

I	II.A	II.B	II.C
WEB	GUYS	MOVIE	FACEBOOK
HTML	LINK	LINK	TWITTER
INTERNET	INTERNET	LOVE	GOOGLE
NETSCAPE	STUFF	WEBSITE	MOM
EMAIL	ASS	CHRISTMAS	LOVE
NEWS	MOVIE	ASS	WEBSITE
(WEB)SITE	FOLKS	INTERNET	LINK
PAGE	UPDATE	DAY	DAY
JAVA	NIGHT	NIGHT	PHOTO
SOURCE	FUN	FUN	UPDATE
FRONTIER	THING	WEEKEND	VIDEO
AOL	HELL	VIDEO	FRIENDS
UPDATE	WEEKEND	FOOD	KIDS
HUMOR	TIME	THING(S)	THINGS
BROWSER	SHIT	UPDATE	STORE
PERL	MOOD	KIDS	GIFT
REDESIGN	DAY	SHIT	FUN
LINUX	SITE	WEEK	LIFE
SUBJECT	LOVE	FRIEND(S)	BOOK(S)
CGI	WEB	STUFF	LINK
APPLE	FRIENDS	MORNING	TIME
SALON	PICTURES	WINDOW	WEEK
MAC	KIDS	MUSIC	BAR
TECH	CRAP	LIFE	
VERSION		GUY	

125 I limited the *WordSmith* results list to 100 entries. Subsequently, I cleared the lists. I only kept nouns (or bases for conversion that couldn't be identified as verb) that were most likely not part of metalinks, timestamps and other standardised blog elements. Singular and plural instances of one lexeme were treated as one (with the plural given in brackets). The same is true for *website* and *site* – subsumed under *(web)site*. In II.A and II.C, less than 25 keywords remained after that procedure. *Folks* and *guys* in II.A are, apparently, rather ways of addressing the audience than indicators for topics.

It's rather striking that the period I keywords are almost exclusively IT-related. This observation neatly relates to my statistics of overall topic orientation:[126] I coded 43.3% of the period I weblogs with the category *technology / software.*[127] In later periods, there were still traces of this rather tech-savvy period I orientation; for instance in lexemes such as *Internet, website* and *link.* The increasing importance of social network sites is reflected by the high-prominence position of *Facebook* and *Twitter* in II.C.

Other lexemes such as *day, night, morning, time, mood, weekend, week, life* and *fun* are rather part of the field of everyday processes and experiences. They're complemented by lexemes from the field of social relations: *friends, love, mom* and *kids.* Interestingly, the fraction of personal weblogs focussing exclusively on everyday events decreased over the periods from 35.0% in II.A to 19.0% in II.C. *Mom* and *kids* could also relate to *mommy* blogs such as *Maternal Experiment* (II.C), whose entries deal with childcare, issues related to the role of mothers and similar. However, only 2% in II.B and 3% in II.C were coded with this category.[128] A slightly higher fraction was taken by the category *diet and cooking* (7% in II.B, 4% in II.C), to which apparently the lexemes *food* and *bar* are related. The lexemes *store* and *gift* in II.C probably reflected the increasing importance of the category *e-commerce* (7% in II.C).[129]

Both the keyword analysis and coding the overall topic orientation suggest a high degree of subject variability. On the one hand, a high fraction in each period could be assigned to the *variable* category; for example, 52% in II.A and 39% in II.C. These blogs are, apparently, internally heterogeneous in terms of theme. On the other hand, those blogs exhibiting a clear thematic focus show, by contrast, a broad variety of different topics. It's hard, therefore, to describe general trends. However, it's remarkable that the category *variable* declines, which might suggest a tendency to a more pronounced thematic focus for individual blogs, and, possibly, to keeping separate blogs for separate topics (see 5.8.3).

---

126 This overall orientation was coded on the basis of qualitative content analysis of all posts on a blog-page and by taking categories, labels and tags into account. If the individual posts dealt with different topics, the blog was coded *variable.*

127 Of course, there are also other topical fields such as *film and TV* (*Windowseat*), *politics* (*Flutterby*) and *economy* (*Geoffs Gems*) in period I.

128 *E-Housewife* (II.B) calls itself a *mommy blog* but in fact all posts on the DIABLOC page deal with travelling, which is why this personal weblog was not assigned to the category *mommy blog* but *travel* instead.

129 This is most likely connected to the spread of the post genre *advertisement* (7.3.2) and the growing importance of the role concept *customer* (5.7.4).

6.3.5 Interim Summary

For some features of the mesolevel, bloggers apparently developed pronounced preferences. This is true for design features such as layout, background and font colour (6.3.1). Similar statements can be made concerning some elements of the sidebar, especially concerning the short profile and search function. The blogroll, however, which was particularly important for connecting blogs with one another and also as a source of recognition, was replaced by follower widgets (6.3.3). I also conducted a detailed analysis of some headers (6.3.2) in order to highlight the importance of this typical element and to exemplify some basics of how language-image-links will be tackled in the next sub-chapter. The glance at the centrepiece of every blog, the posts, also yielded interesting results (6.3.4): I've traced the emergence of reverse chronology in a situation of two competing solutions to the same problem (dynamic content). Additionally, I've used observations on post length and topics to anticipate some considerations on post genres to be dealt with in chapter 7. I've characterised the personal weblog as highly variable in terms of topic and highlighted some general trends nevertheless.

6.4 Microlevel – Posts as Language-Image-Clusters

6.4.1 Weblogs are about Links: *Hyperlinks in Posts*

Some years after the spread of blog-systems and the take-off of the blogging phenomenon, Blood (2004: 54) summarised the perspective of some first-generation authors on the new blogs: "These are diaries, not Weblogs; Weblogs are about links." Thereby, Blood highlighted the key role of hyperlinks for first-generation weblogs and voiced her doubts that this feature was still important for later blogs. A first glance at the total number of hyperlinks in Table 35, however, seems to contradict her:

Table 35: Microlevel I – Total Number of Hyperlinks per Post and Blog-Page

Period	Hyperlinks: Total Number per Post and Blog-Page				N (of total)
	Min.	Max.	Mean	σ	
I	0.45	29.00	4.87	6.65	30 (30)
II.A	0.00	9.33	3.32	1.91	99 (100)[130]
II.B	1.00	33.00	6.77	4.73	100 (100)
II.C	1.00	57.00	10.92	8.12	100 (100)

130 I excluded *Astronaut Ambition* from this survey as it's generally a homepage with hyperlinks to certain entries. The number of hyperlinks per post and blog-page could, therefore, not be calculated.

Indeed, there was a slight decrease from I to II.A, which is, however, not significant[131] and which was reversed by an increase towards II.C. Period II.C, then, significantly differs from II.B.[132] The relatively high standard deviations in I and II.C additionally suggest a wide variation scope for the genre. This data, however, only seemingly contradicts Blood. This becomes apparent when a more differentiated approach is taken:

Table 36: Microlevel II – External Hyperlinks per Post and Blog-Page

Period	External Hyperlinks per Post per Blog-Page				N (of total)[133]
	Min.	Max.	Mean	σ	
I	0.00	23.00	3.91	5.64	30 (30)
II.A	0.00	4.00	0.73	0.82	99 (100)
II.B	0.00	5.43	0.93	1.21	99 (100)
II.C	0.00	6.25	1.01	1.27	99 (100)

In Table 36, I only counted external hyperlinks, that is, links leading away from the blog's domain such as links to other blogs, news sites etc. There is a significant drop from period I to II.A according to T-test, and even though there is a slight increase towards period II.C, the mean by far does not reach its period I value again. Consequently, the implementation of external hyperlinks was typical of period I and considerably less important for the personal weblogs of period II.[134]

But how, then, can the increase of the total number of hyperlinks per post be explained? A plausible candidate would be the use of domain-internal hyperlinks, pointing to pages within the blog's domain. However, they can be discarded as their mean value rises only slightly from period I (0.43) to II.C (0.65). Apparently, pointing to pages on their own blog is something that all authors do to a similar extent in all periods. What is more important are apparently the category, tag and label hyperlinks usually to be found at the bottom of a post:

131 T-test gives $p = 0.219$.

132 Here, t-test gives $p < 0.0001$.

133 I excluded *Astronaut Ambition* (II.A) for the reasons mentioned in fn. 130 and one personal weblog from II.B and II.C each because of their highly exceptional use of external hyperlinks (*Booklooker*, II.C, for instance, lists hyperlinks to 155 books in one entry). See Schildhauer (2014: fn. 473) for statistics including these cases.

134 This is quite likely to be connected to the centrality of the post genre *filter* in period I, which I'll focus on in 7.2.1.

Table 37: Microlevel III – Category-, Label- and Tag-Hyperlinks

Period	Category-Hyperlinks per Post and Blog-Page				Tag-Hyperlinks per Post and Blog-Page				Label-Hyperlinks per Post and Blog-Page				N
	Min.	Max.	Mean	σ	Min.	Max.	Mean	Σ	Min.	Max.	Mean	σ	
I	0.00	2.93	0.17	0.58	0.00	0.00	0.00	0.00	0.00	0.00	0.00	0.00	30
II.A	0.00	2.67	0.17	0.49	0.00	0.00	0.00	0.00	0.00	0.00	0.00	0.00	100
II.B	0.00	12.70	0.97	1.87	0.00	7.50	0.34	1.22	0.00	9.60	0.58	1.74	100
II.C	0.00	5.20	0.54	0.99	0.00	22.80	1.49	3.75	0.00	11.86	1.13	2.55	100

Hyperlinks of this kind show a considerable (and statistically significant) increase especially towards period II.B. While category-hyperlinks already appeared on 10% of the period I weblogs, labels and tags only appeared in period II.B. Labels were offered by Blogger, tags and categories by WordPress and other blog-systems. All three kinds of hyperlinks can be used to build semantic networks of posts on a certain blog (see 4.3).[135] They differ in the way they were used: Categories were usually situated on a higher level of abstraction and provided hyperonyms to key words in the respective post; on average one to two per post. Tags are, rather, keywords taken from the entry – usually four to five per post – and labels take an intermediate position; about 3 per post on average.[136] In II.C, at least one kind of these hyperlinks could be found on 75% of the personal weblogs (20% in II.A, 71% in II.B). From this data, it can be concluded that use of these hyperlinks not only developed into a typical personal weblog feature but was also mainly responsible for the puzzling results in Table 35. In sum, while posts contained similarly high numbers of hyperlinks in every period, the focus appears to have shifted from external hyperlinks to links building networks of blog posts. Apparently, *external* content lost significance for bloggers and blog-internal contents gained importance simultaneously.[137]

135 In Schildhauer (2014: 305–306), I also show that tags are originally used to link posts on several blogs and that a decreasing number of DIABLOC blogs contained these external tags (46.2% in II.B, 38–1% in II.C). Categories, too, were used in this external way (13.7% in II.B, 10.5% in II.C). Interestingly, categories could also be used in both ways at the same time – in that case, category-hyperlinks at the end of posts usually pointed outwards, categories in the sidebar inwards. In II.C, the internal structuring, however, was much more important than external uses for both categories and tags.

136 See Schildhauer (2014: 304–305) for detailed statistics.

137 I made similar statements about the development of the blogroll and the follower widget in 6.3.3.

6.4.2 The Language of Blog Posts

Evidently, it's hard to pinpoint something like *the language of personal weblogs*, which is also the shared credo of the studies cited in Table 20 and Table 21. In this sub-chapter, I'll therefore only highlight certain aspects related to the hybridisation thesis (see also 6.1).

First of all, *WordSmith* frequency analysis shows that personal pronouns, particularly of the 1st person, are far more frequent in every DIABLOC period than in the BNC:

Table 38: Microlevel IV – WordSmith *Frequency Analysis*

	BNC	DIABLOC			
		I	II.A	II.B	II.C
1	the	the	the	the	the
2	of	to	**I**	**I**	To
3	and	of	to	to	**I**
4	to	a	and	and	and
5	a	and	a	a	a
6	in	in	of	of	of
7	that	**I**	in	in	in
8	is	is	that	it	it
9	it	that	it	that	that
10	for	<u>com</u>	is	is	**my**
11	was	this	**you**	for	**you**
12	**I**	at	for	**my**	is
13	on	with	**my**	**you**	for
14	with	www	on	on	on
15	as	be	was	was	was

There's a clear caesura between I and II.A as *I* moved from rank 7 to rank 2. It was accompanied by *you* and *my*, which were not among the 15 most frequent words in period I. Additionally, there are parts of URLs in the period I list (*www*, *com*). Even though this is actually a *WordSmith* problem (due to the dots in URLs, the elements are counted as tokens), this result mirrors the importance of external hyperlinks mentioned above (6.4.1). Later periods seem to have been focussed more on the bloggers themselves.

Biber (1988: 19, my emphasis) states that "first person pronouns share a *colloquial, informal flavor*." These attributes can also be used for at least part of the DIABLOC, which is underlined by the fact that emphatics like *fuck* or *super-pissed* can be found in about 10% of the blogs from II.A to II.C. Colloquial or slang expressions (*screw around* in *Camworld* 41, I and *give one's two cents* in *Alone in Tacoma* 18, II.B) can be found in every period (16.7 % of period I weblogs, between 10 and 15% in later periods). Derivations such as *newsy* (*A stranger here myself* 2, II.A), *cheery* (*Rebelle Fleur* 7, II.C) and *Ok'ish* (*David Parkinson* 65, II.B)[138] also point in that direction. This similarly holds for clitics (*I'm* instead of *I am*), which can be found in the vast majority of (personal) weblogs (80% in I, 85% in II.A, 71% in II.B, 77% in II.C).[139] The mean word length of 4.6 (I), 4.2 (II.A and II.B) and 4.3 (II.C) is also more similar to genres such as personal letters (3.9) or even face-to-face conversations (4.1) instead of, for instance, academic prose (4.8).[140]

These features can also count as an indicator of a rather spontaneous way of writing, including little editing. Interjections (period I and II.C in 10%, II.B 18% and II.A 23% of the texts) and references to mental processes confirm this impression:

Example 98: Microlevel V – Spontaneity

That's the T-shirt I made on Tuesday which is brown not black (looks better anyway). Um... something complexity... Distinctive complexity.

(*Atomic Raygun* 40, II.A)

So... I have a couple of things to post tonight and remember, these are things which don't belong on my other blog - things which concern those who read my other blog specifically.
The first is a really odd dream I had last night... or perhaps this morning. One of those dreams where you remember every little detail. So here's what I remember from it [...]

(*Dig your own hole* 17–18, II.B)

In both excerpts, the particles *um* and *so* in connection to the punctuation ... suggest phases of thinking-while-writing – similar to fillers and short pauses in face-to-face conversations. The corrections of *complexity* to *distinctive complexity* as well as *last night* to *this morning* also suggest a somewhat spontaneous writing process. This connects neatly to the observations concerning *immediacy* in 5.3.

These similarities to face-to-face conversations have been termed instances of *emulated orality* by Schlobinski & Siever (2005b: 81). Other examples can also be interpreted in such a way:

---

138 On *ish* and its development, see Pentrel 2013).

139 Gerdes (2005: 110) reports similarly high values.

140 The values are taken from Biber (1988: 255, 262, 264).

Example 99: Microlevel VI – Emulated Orality

lemme tell ya

(*Andrena's Ankh* 12, II.A)

A real just doin' it kinda Nike advertisement.

(*Botton Your Lip* 9, II.A)

i guess my question to yall is would you participate in this type of relationship?

(*aquababie's world* 70, II.B)

Bob was a regular at the Copper Mug where Carol works, is knowledge of music was phenomenal [...] they played some of is best moments on the radio [...]

(*Bert Gilbert* 9, II.B

The examples contain imitations of phonological processes typical of rapid speech, for example, reduction of unstressed pronouns (*you* > *ya*), enclitics (*kind of* > *kinda, let me* > *lemme* where additionally the plosive /p/ is assimilated to /m/) and H-dropping (*his* > *is*).

Some graphostylistic elements are probably motivated in a similar way. Reduplications of graphemes such as *grrrrrrrr yayayayaay* (*Bound and Gagged* 17, II.A) could be used to mark emphasis and even emulate intonation (Dittmann 2001: 87). However, reduplication has apparently also moved away from merely imitating spoken language as examples such as *AIIRIRGGRGGRGRGGGHHHHH* (*Bosquet's Land* 22, II.A) suggest.

Emoticons are a rather marginal phenomenon in the DIABLOC, even though they can be found in every period (10% in period I, 24% in II.A, 12% in II.B and II.C). They usually occur at the end of posts and express the author's attitude towards the contents of a post. The following example illustrates this function very clearly:

Example 100: Microlevel VII – Emoticons and Evaluation

:(
My Uncle Benny(my godfather) is in the hospital bleeding from his lungs unable to breath. he is on a respirator and has a feeding tube in him :(:(:(
eek :(

(*angrybit* 43, II.A)

Asterisk-constructions[141] such as **sigh** are usually interpreted as a strategy to compensate for the lack of non-verbal cues (Storrer 2001: 448). While

141 Schlobinski (2001) uses the term *Inflektiv* for these constructions. I refrain from this term here as it is tailored to the German grammatical system (including inflectional endings for infinitives) and does not really fit the English version.

this phenomenon appears to be rather typical of chat conversations (Henn-Memmesheimer & Eggers 2010; Schlobinski 2001), it can be found on only a few (personal) weblogs (6.7% in period I, 16% in II.A, 12% in II.B, 11% in II.C). *If* a blog contains *one* instance, however, it is quite likely that it also contains others. This obviously, then, is a matter of individual bloggers' preference. The most common asterisk-construction is **sigh** (15 of 61 in total) but nouns such as **kisses** (*Ask Temptress* 18, II.C) can also be found in the DIABLOC. Asterisk-constructions can also be used creatively (Beißwenger 2002):

Example 101: Microlevel VIII – Creative Use of Asterisk-Constructions

> But don't say anything...that's right if we all ignore it we can't be accused of any crazy talk...they can't drag us off to the asylum if we all comply and stay quiet eh? All us crazy's together...crazy crazy crazy's...
> *wanders off jabbering to herself, muttering out loud to the walls and any random passing dog.*
>
> (*Freya Bletsoe's Personal Blog* 64, II.B)

Regarding the sentence level, there also appears to be a broad scope of variation. While some personal weblogs contain paratactic and elliptical sentences (*Anela Palekaiko* below), others display quite the opposite preference (*Historical Digression* below):

Example 102: Microlevel IX – Parataxis and Hypotaxis

> theres a surf contest at hb and one of the surfers who aparently won first place today came by my work and he gave me his autograph... hes only 13 and hes gone pro... check him out here christian wach otherwise ive been working alot.. too much almost.. been ummm yea im tired... alrighty... gonna go to sleep... oh but before i do... ive been thinking alot about a certain person and like... i miss this person so much... and i keep thinking abou thow much i feel for them and how much i want to be around them and near them adn a part of their life and have them be a part of my own... and its tough bc i dont know if its possible for us to coexist in a loving relationship... so yea...
>
> (*Anela Palekaiko* 3, II.A)
>
> The bombardment of Fort Sumter, April 12, 1861
> Mary Chesnut of Charleston, South Carolina, aristocratic wife of lawyer and former U.S. Senator James Chesnut, did not need any newspapers to tell her of the firing on Fort Sumter. Her husband, serving now as a colonel with the South Carolina militia, had been actively involved in the negotiations with Federal troops in the fort out in Charleston harbor. In the dark hours before dawn on April 12, 1861, Mary Chesnut lay in bed, fully aware that Confederate forces would commence a bombardment at 4:30 if the Federals did not abandon the fort.
>
> (*Historical Digression* 5–6, II.C

Historical Digression is particularly marked by the use of appositions (*aristocratic wife [...] Chesnut*) and participle constructions (*serving now as a colonel [...]*). I've chosen these two examples because they are so illustrative. This scope of variation is present in every period, however, that is, there is no change from parataxis to hypotaxis, or similar.

The syntactic patterns in both examples correspond to their choice of words: While *Anela Palekaiko* contains colloquialisms such as *alrighty*, *Historical Digression* uses words with poetic connotation (*bemoaning*, *plight my troth*). In general, the standardised type-token ratio (STTR) suggests a high degree of lexical variety for all periods:

Table 39: Microlevel X – Standardised Type-Token-Ratio

Period	STTR				N (of total)[142]
	Min.	Max.	Mean	σ	
I	25.29	84.00	73.94	10.30	29 (30)
II.A	53.50	77.20	71.51	4.07	95 (100)
II.B	61.81	77.75	72.01	3.24	100 (100)
II.C	41.29	79.50	71.52	4.45	99 (100)

These results are way above the values Biber (1988) reports for various genres (for example, 55.2 for science fiction), although this might be due to *WordSmith*[143] tokenisation errors. This potential source of error is the same for all periods. As the standard deviations are fairly low, I'd like to conclude that the STTR is indeed similar for all periods. Consequently, it can be assumed that rather literary examples, such as *Historical Digression*, do not differ much from other blogs in their degree of lexical variety but only in terms of connotation. Period I stands out with its standard deviation of 10.3. The extremes of this continuum are marked by *Perfect* (an uncommented list of hyperlinks, STTR = 25.00) and *DanDot* (84.00) with a high density of IT-related terms.

All the phenomena discussed so far nicely fit into the debate on the hybridisation hypothesis: In short, blog-posts cover all shades from emulated orality to

142 The STTR value was not assigned to blog-pages with a token count below 100 as the measure was calculated in 100-word steps.

143 See the discussion on Table 34 above.

prototypical literality.[144] There are also, however, examples that apparently don't fit this categorisation model:

Example 103: Microlevel XI – SEO-Post

> [...] A great way to build anticipation while thwarting expectations is to put the ring box in a mini Christmas stocking. The mini Christmas stocking should easily fit in a bigger box that is placed in the special lady's traditional stocking. The surprise will be great and you have managed to hide the tell-tale ring box within the mini Christmas stocking.
> Other jewelry can be presented in the same way. Why not make the gift-giving experience a little fun by using a mini Christmas stocking to provide some flavor and character? [...]
>
> (*Dressed in Style* 7–8, II.B)

The frequency of the keyword *mini Christmas stocking* in this example is remarkable, especially as it's never replaced by a pronoun. It's very likely that this interesting style is motivated by the aim of search engine optimisation (SEO). As keywords of the post are intended to serve as search terms for search engines, they are repeated as frequently as possible because search engine algorithms will then rate the post very relevant for a search term and assign the blog a higher rank on the results page. Posts that follow SEO principles can be found from period II.B onwards. *Bay Area Mommy* (II.C) even employed a plugin, which left traces in the source code, to help optimise headlines, the main bodies of posts and other aspects of SEO.

6.4.3 Image Types

In this sub-chapter, I'll discuss several image types which I consider typical of the personal weblog. First of all, I'd like to introduce a basic distinction. On the one hand, there are images which are most likely self-made, that is, created by the blog authors themselves, their friends etc. On the other hand, blogs also contain images from other sources; mostly, of course, from other websites.

The most typical proponent of the self-made branch is, undoubtedly, the *snapshot*. Let's consider three examples of this type:

144 In the terminology introduced by Koch & Oesterreicher (1985; 1994) blog posts range on a continuum between the poles of conceptual orality and literacy. However, see my discussion of these terms (using the example of a webchat) in Grube (2011).

Example 104: Microlevel XII – Self-Made Images – Snapshots (Her Heart, My Hands, *II.B* | Ravenwood Ranch, *II.C* | In a Silent Way, *II.C*)

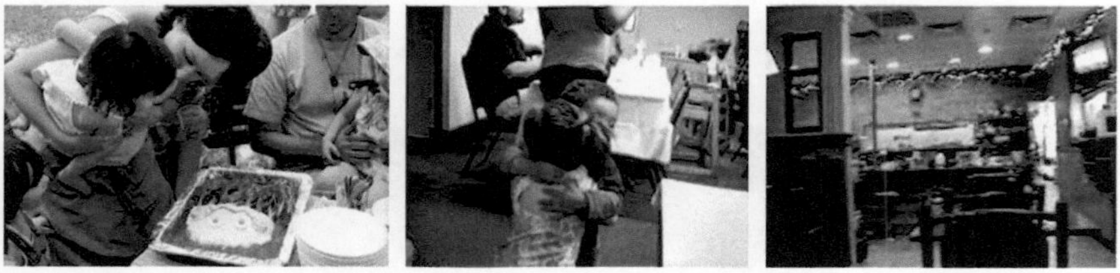

The images in Example 104 have probably been taken with a digital camera. For the images from *Her Heart, My Hands* and *Ravenwood Ranch* in particular, it can be assumed that they were produced spontaneously and are, consequently, not staged. This is also suggested by the fact that the people in the pictures aren't looking into the camera but are engaged in some interaction. The rather unfavourable angle of the *Ravenwood Ranch* image and the blurriness of the rightmost image also underline the impression of spontaneity. The fact that snapshots often show important objects only in part (for example, the embracing children in the middle) might be connected to spontaneous production, too.

Snapshots are, presumably, meant to refer to concrete objects, events or people rather than carrying a generic reading. The image on the right-hand side, for example, refers to a specific restaurant and not to empty bars in general, which is also obvious from the wording of the post.[145] There's probably a whole range of things that can be captured by snapshots; most probably they all share the feature *visible like that* (Stöckl 2004a: 136) as opposed to pictures showing, for instance, tremendously enlarged insects taken with special cameras or even microscopes. In addition to people, meals appear to be depicted rather frequently as in Example 105. Like other snapshots, they're usually taken from a medium distance and exhibit a frontal view. Images such as Example 105 give us the impression that we're sitting at the table instead of the author. Normally, snapshots are meant to illustrate what's written in the respective post, and probably to give proof of authenticity (Holly 2009: 399; Steinseifer 2011: 184). It seems that they're motivated in a mainly pragmatic way, which is probably why they often lack the sophisticated post-editing more typical of the *photo art* images of the self-made branch. A third self-made type is the *product image* – photographs that usually

145 See Pflaeging (2013: 55) on denotation vs. reference and Stöckl (2004a: 248) on singular vs. multiple denotation.

accompany review posts. Both the *photo art* and the *product image* type are, however, rather marginal in my corpus as compared to snapshots.

Example 105: Microlevel XIII – Self-Made Images II – Snapshot of a Meal (Jenn's Travel Closeup, *II.B*)

On the other branch – imported images – there are, essentially, no limits to the variety of image types. Here, too, there are product images such as the following:

Example 106: Microlevel XIV – Imported Images I – Product Images (Bay Area Mommy, *II.C* | Blushes and Shimmy Shakes, *II.C* | Horses & Heels, *II.C*)

As opposed to self-made product images, which show the product in an everyday setting, imported images usually depict the product only in front of a white background and also often suggest sophisticated lighting and post-editing (see, especially, the left- and right-hand images above). Cover-images such as the one from *Blushes and Shimmy Shakes* are very commonplace in review posts.

Another typical group of imported images are language-image-compositions. Example 107 shows one example of this category, which constitutes a fairly established type in itself. It combines images and headings in complementary relation under a common topic (*I am a mother).* The background is black, combined with a white sans-serif font in capitals. The image captions of the second line are subject-related (*What I...*) and work towards a climax: *I think – I really do – I really want to do.* The complementary language-image-link often results in hyperbole (*What I really do*) or incongruity (*What I think I do*) with a comic effect.

Example 107: Microlevel XV – Imported Images II – Language-Image-Composition (Bella Vida, *II.C*)

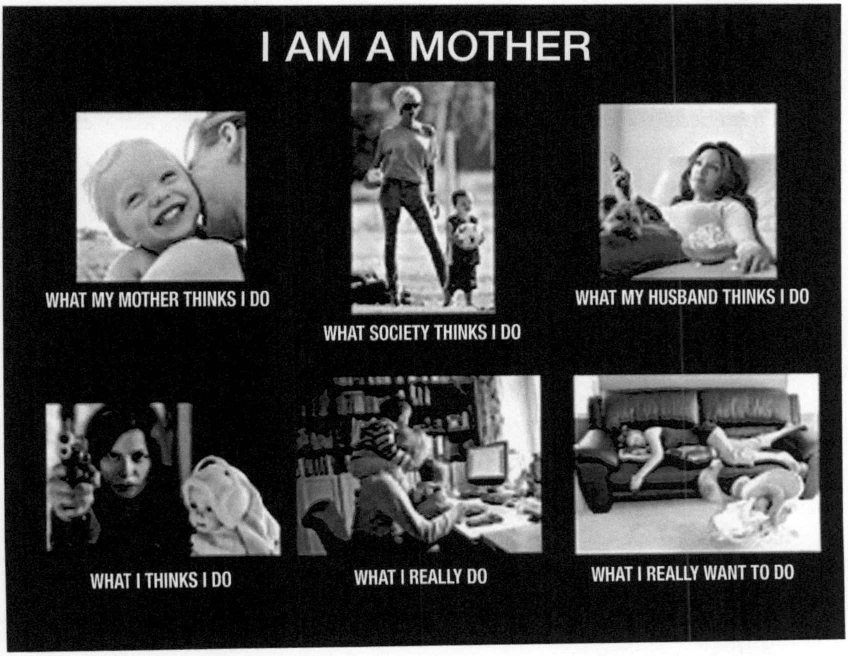

6.4.4 Language-Image-Links

Apparently, and surely connected to the increasing ease with which images could be created, uploaded and embedded, the number of images per post grew considerably.[146]

Table 40: Microlevel XVI – Number of Images and Image Size

Period	Images per Posting and Blog-Page					Scaled Size of JPEG-Images in 100 Pixel²				
	Min.	Max.	Mean	σ	N (of total)	Min.	Max.	Mean	σ	N (of total)[147]
I	0.00	1.00	0.06	0.21	30 (30)	0.00	261.85	18.75	54.12	30 (30)
II.A	0.00	2.22	0.33	0.51	100 (100)	0.00	8568.30	367.55	917.27	100 (100)
II.B	0.00	10.67	1.05	1.78	100 (100)	0.00	6727.57	564.09	818.86	100 (100)
II.C	0.00	12.00	1.95	2.12	100 (100)	0.00	4989.47	809.83	776.12	98 (100)

Interestingly, there are blogs in each period whose posts don't contain any images at all. Therefore, the standard deviation increases and suggests a growing variation scope of the genre category from exclusively language-based blogs to exemplars very rich in images. At the same time, the exemplary survey of the scaled size of JPEG-images[148] (including those displayed in headers and sidebars) indicates that images in general took up an increasing amount of space on personal weblogs.[149] This data suggests a preliminary differentiation of language-image-links on personal weblogs from the perspective of information value (Nöth 2000b: 484, Stöckl 2004a: 254, 2004b: 15):[150]

146 The difference between the mean values of all periods is statistically significant according to the t-test.

147 I could not determine the scaled size for two personal weblogs in II.C as the images on these blogs are embedded in a way that does not allow for displaying these attributes.

148 JPEG is one of the main image formats on the Internet. The exemplary focus on this file type originates from another study in which I also looked at file size (in kB) and number of the JPEG files of every DIABLOC site. For this study, I used the file lists displayed in the *Windows Explorer*. The scaled size, which takes into account that bloggers might modify the original size of an image when embedding it on their blog, was determined by using a special display option offered by *Firefox*. See Grube (2013) for preliminary results of that study, which I cannot discuss here in detail.

149 According to the t-test, the differences between I and II.A as well as II.B and II.C are statistically significant.

150 Stöckl (2004b: 15) adds a perspective of perception and saliency to the category of information value: "In textual practice one mode is often made salient while others recede into the background – both in perception and production. Genres or text

- Personal weblogs whose entries are exclusively language-based and which consequently do not exhibit language-image-links in posts (excluded from this sub-chapter)
- Posts in which language and image both contribute, to varying degrees, to establishing the overall meaning
- Posts in which language almost recedes to the background in favour of the use of images[151]

Posts of the third kind, which is probably close to Stöckl's (2004a: 280–282) *image only* category, could only be found from period II.B onwards, and then only sporadically. Language is often limited to headings and, sometimes, a brief comment announcing the image(s) in the posts. Example 109 provides access to an image-series, which can be viewed by clicking on a *continue* hyperlink below the image. The beginning of the post on the blog-page only makes use of language for giving the date and the headline *One Dreary Day*. From a semantic point of view, the language-image-link can be described as complementary (Stöckl 2006: 28): Without the image, the linguistic message would not be coherent as its reference can only be deduced from the grey weather in which the images were obviously taken.[152]

The second information value category mentioned above mainly assembles clusters in which images are used in an illustrative way as they depict objects which are named in the verbal text (Stöckl 2004a: 254). In this relation, the language-based part of the message can be received coherently without any need of the image (Holly 2011a: 250; Steinseifer 2011: 182–183). From a syntactic point of view, there are three variants of this illustrative language-image-link: First, images may be embedded in the text as shown in Example 108. Second, a sequence of language in the order image → language. And third, a sequence of language → image.

---

types differ a great deal in how they foreground and background modes and submodes."

151 The boundaries between the second and third category mentioned here are certainly fuzzy. This list is only meant as a heuristic for the following observations, not a clear-cut typology.

152 Additionally, there is a particular tension between language and image in this example as the heading does not relate to the main content of the image(s) (woman wearing latest fashion).

Example 108: Illustrative Language-Image-Link (50 Years of Angst, II.C)

Choking the Chicken.

Back view of Sa Casa Nova, chicken house on upper terrace.

We bought our house in Mallorca 12 years ago. The owner said it dated back five generations, making the finca over 200 years old. Like many subsistence farms on valuable real estate, it was subdivided a number of times before we purchased it. We own a little less than two acres.

Stone houses may last forever, but the building was abandoned and in ruins. A steel support post prevented the front archway from falling down and killing someone.

Example 109: Image Only Post (Beneath the glass, *II.C, additional excerpt 12.03.2012*)

MARCH 18, 2012

One Dreary Day

Example 110: Illustrative Language-Image-Link, Announcement of Image (Bhutan Diary, *II.C*)

The current temple was built on the site of Asoka's temple in the 6th century and fell into decline in the 12th century when Muslims invaded the region. Although some repairs were attempted, the largest and last renovation occurred in the 1880s. The temple is built of brick and rises to an impressive height of 55 meters. Words really can't do it justice, so here's a picture:

Example 111: Illustrative Language-Image-Link, Delayed Anchoring (In a Silent Way, II.C)

Some people look forward to March because it means Madness –basketball that is, others await the seminal seedlings of spring, but for me it's a harbinger to the eight days of masticating matzoh. It gets stale. Although the days begin to lengthen, it is at this time that I find myself most susceptible to Seasonal Affective Disorder. In early March the Manischewitz items begin to cluster at the fringes of aisles. But this year, I may not be so dour. If Zaidy's truly is, as the owner quotes on his website, "the best deli/restaurant in town?" maybe my spirits have reason to rise while my bread remains

Example 112: Language-Image-Chain with Illustrative Language-Image Relations (E-Housewife, *II.B*)

The *Procession* happens in the morning, and in the afternoon, for three days there is a huge *Corral*, where there is bullfighting, but not the kind that there is in Spain. This type of bullfighting is much less elegant, but it's so entertaining. *Many people get drunk* and go inside the *Corral* to try and mount the bull. There was this guy that dresses as Zorro, who got on the bull a few times.

and here is a girl that mounted the bull better than all the guys who tried before her.

Another part of the entertainment, is when the planes pass by the corral. They pass by so low that sometimes it's scary because of the noise.

After the corral, everyone goes to *los corpos* to have some drinks and dance. There met

Example 113: Ekphrastic Language-Image-Link (Barefoot Travelers, *II.C*)

Steamship Graveyard

Posted on October 28, 2010

Paddle wheel from graveyard beside Dawson City - Look at the size!

In all three variants, the anchoring of the image in the verbal text plays an important role. In this context, *anchoring* refers to the point at which the verbal text explicitly names those objects depicted in the image which are relevant to the overall message. In Example 108, the image is anchored already in the first sentence. The nominal phrase *our house* can be related to the image on the left-hand side. Recipients were probably quick to interpret the photograph as depicting the house described in the verbal text.

In Example 111, the author chose a sequential pattern of the image → language type. The anchoring in this example takes place at a much later point. It is only in line 7 that the author refers to *Zaidy's* for the first time – the restaurant whose entry is depicted by the photograph. I'd like to assume that recipients are fairly patient in their process of working towards coherence. Even though, or perhaps even because the image is seen first and the relation between verbal text (opening with remarks on the author's mental illness) and image is not clear at all, recipients assumedly continue reading and immediately match language and image when coming across the anchoring point.

Both Example 108 and Example 111 also illustrate the important function of the verbal text of reducing the inherent ambiguity of the image: Example 108 could possibly refer to Italian landscapes but the verbal text tells the viewer that it's about a *finca* with signs of decay. Similarly, Example 111 depicts a certain restaurant and not some random nightclub. Probably, both examples follow a pattern which Holly (2006) has termed "mit Worten sehen" – *seeing with words*. The decay of the finca is only brought to attention when pointed out by the verbal text. The same holds for the name of the restaurant, which would probably not be deciphered.

Besides anchoring the image – or, more precisely, its contents – in the verbal text, there is another way of sequencing language and image: The verbal text provides an elaborate description of an event or object, which is then followed by an explicit announcement of the following images. These images are, then, brought into an illustrative relation to the verbal text. The verbal text in Example 110 first informs about the characteristics of a temple. It closes by stating that words couldn't do the monument justice and announces the image. This also sheds light on the role images probably play in illustrative relations: In this case, probably exemplary for others, the author clearly includes the image to compensate for the shortcomings of the mode of language.

Apart from complementary and illustrative relations, personal weblogs also contain ekphrastic clusters which usually consist of images and their captions. In these constellations, the verbal text names and highlights certain objects depicted in the image which are relevant to the wider context of the post. In Example 113, the verbal text focuses on the size of the paddle wheel. The person in front of the wheel mainly serves as a way for the recipient to estimate the wheel's height. In the wider context of the post, this language-image-cluster is used in an illustrative relation, when the verbal text describes a cemetery for paddle steamers. This shows how language-image-links can be established simultaneously on several layers in complex language-image-clusters.

Finally, let's broaden the view from single language-image-clusters to larger cluster sequences. Modelled after Holly (e.g., 2009), I'd like to use the label *language-image-chain* for sequences such as the one in Example 112, where language and image alternate so that recipients oscillate from language to image and back again. Language-image chains may contain both illustrative and complementary relations. In this example, the author uses a language-image chain to convey travel experiences and mainly uses illustrative relations. The first image is anchored by the noun phrase *this guy that dresses as Zorro*, the third by *planes pass by the corral.* The second image is introduced by *here is a girl.*

6.4.5 Summary

In this sub-chapter, I've identified several typical features and tendencies on the microlevel. Hyperlinks were an important feature in all periods. However, the focus shifted from external hyperlinks in period I weblogs to hyperlinks mainly establishing blog-internal semantic structures (6.4.1). The language use in (personal) weblog posts was highly variable; blog posts covered the whole language use continuum from emulated orality to distinctly literary (6.4.2). Image inclusion was marginal in period I but quickly gained importance later on. Among others, self-made snapshots were apparently typical of personal weblogs (6.4.3). I've identified illustrative, complementary and ekphrastic language-image-links and also discussed more complex language-image-clusters (6.4.4).

6.5 Summary and Conclusion

Based on a monitor- and source code-based approach (6.1), this chapter looked at structural characteristics of (personal) weblogs. I narrowed the perspective successively from the macrolevel (blog-page as part of a domain) and the mesolevel (design and elements of the blog-page) to the microlevel of language-image-clusters.

On the macrolevel, the blog-page was typically both formally and content-wise the central element of a moderately-complex website. This feature was already dominant in period I and was further consolidated in the following periods (6.2).

On the mesolevel, a typical personal weblog contained a header (6.3.2), a sidebar on the right-hand side, white background and grey sans-serif font (6.3.1). It is very likely that a randomly-chosen personal weblog would have displayed a blogroll in II.B, and in II.C, a follower widget. It was also increasingly likely that the sidebar contained a short profile, a list of tags, categories or labels as well as a search box (6.3.3). In II.C, posts were considerably longer than in previous periods, which is probably connected to developments in the set of post genres (see next chapter). From II.A onwards, posts were arranged almost exclusively in reverse chronology. In period I, audiences could also come across weblogs following the page-paradigm (6.3.4). In this respect, this chapter (complementing 4.3) traced the origins of *the* key features of blogs in general (see, e.g., Blood 2000).

Despite a wide scope of variation, the typical personal weblog probably tended to show various features of emulated orality in all periods (6.4.2). While hyperlinks in period I primarily pointed to external sites, this had changed profoundly by II.C, when hyperlinks were mainly used to structure blog-internal contents. While period I weblogs were almost exclusively language-based, in the following periods, images gained increasing importance. Among the typical image types were self-made snapshots, self-made or imported product images and language-image-compositions (6.4.3). These images were used in various relations with the verbal text, for instance in illustrative and in complementary ways. More complex clusters may, for instance, have taken the shape of language-image-chains.

7 Purposes of Personal Weblogs: An Analysis of Post Genres

7.1 What I Did | What I Read

Considerations about the purposes of blogging – what do bloggers actually do when they blog – date back to the first essays on blogging that originated in the context of the first blogging community. Rebecca Blood's (2000) "Weblogs: A History and Perspective" has come to play a particularly important role in this respect, accompanied later by her "weblog handbook" (2002). Blood attempts to define her own blogging practices as well as other "original weblogs" in contrast to what she perceives as new practices of a "post-Blogger explosion". She develops the following typology:

Table 41: Blood's Functional Weblog-Typology (Blood 2002: 6–9)

blog	reporting and reflecting on everyday life in short entries (short-form journal)
notebook	elaborate reflections on specifc topics
filter	presentation and evaluation of web-based information sources

Blood's (2002) typology has become particularly influential for research on blogs because it has been taken up by Susan Herring and her team in BROG (Blog Research on Genre Project), who used it as a basis for quantitative content analysis (Herring 2003; Herring et al. 2004, 2005, 2006; Herring & Paolillo 2006) and developed the following category system:

Table 42: Functional Blog-Typology Developed by BROG (Herring 2003; Herring et al. 2004–2006; Herring & Paolillo 2006)

filter	presenting and commenting on web-based sources
journal (*diary* in Herring & Paolillo 2006)	reporting and reflecting on the everyday, on feelings and thoughts
k-log (not in Herring & Paolillo 2006)	information/observations concerning a specific topic, project, product

While the earlier BROG publications view these types as *blog* types, Herring & Paolillo (2006: 7) state that "a single blog may contain posts of more than one genre". From the perspective of the Rhetorical School, Miller & Shepherd (2004) aim at setting blogging within to a broader cultural context. They identify *self-expression, self-clarification, self-validation* as well as *relationship development* as key purposes of blogging. Finally, interviews, surveys and other rather more ethnographic studies have been conducted on the purposes of blogging. These are summarised in Table 43.

Table 43: Primarily Ethnogaphic Studies on Blogging Purposes and Their Results (Overview)

<table>
<tr><th></th><th>Studies</th><th>Key Words / Observations</th><th></th><th></th></tr>
<tr><td rowspan="2">Interview</td><td rowspan="2">(Nardi et al. 2004a), (Nardi et al. 2004b), (Schiano et al. 2004), Reed (2005), Brake (2007), Baumer et al. (2008), Rosenberg (2009)</td><td>updating others on activities and whereabouts, documenting life, information, expressing point of view, expressing advice, sharing experience, filtering, informing people on field of expertise</td><td>primarily informative</td><td>7.2</td></tr>
<tr><td rowspan="2">influencing others, seeking others' opinion and feedback, boasting, achieve public acknowledgement, making money, entertainment</td><td rowspan="2">primarily appellative</td><td rowspan="2">7.3</td></tr>
<tr><td rowspan="2">Participant Observation</td><td rowspan="2">Efimova (2009)</td></tr>
<tr><td rowspan="2">community building, community forum</td><td rowspan="2">primarily contact-oriented</td><td rowspan="2">7.4</td></tr>
<tr><td rowspan="2">Survey</td><td rowspan="2">Lenhart & Fox (2006), Baumer et al. (2008), Schmidt (2009)</td></tr>
<tr><td>therapy, confession, thinking by writing, releasing emotional tension, self-validation, research and knowledge work, self-revelation, creative self-expression, catharsis, outlet for thoughts and feelings, blog as muse, provide evidence of autonomy and self-distinction, entertainment, democratic self-expression, personal reflection</td><td>primarily focussed on writing process as such and its benefits</td><td>7.5</td></tr>
</table>

From a methodological point of view, analysing both communicative and non-communicative purposes is probably the most challenging part of a genre description. The adjustments made during the BROG mentioned above have shown that it's almost impossible to characterise the purpose of one specific blog in a few words because bloggers apparently have a tendency to think in posts rather than whole blogs (6.3.4). In other words, bloggers use several *types of posts*, depending on their current needs. Herring & Paolillo already speak of "genre" in relation to these types of posts and this is the approach that I took in the analyses presented in this chapter: I assumed that the personal weblog is, in fact, a super-genre (Luginbühl 2014a) comprising several post genres (see 1.4 above). As these genres are more clearly defined in terms of structure and, most importantly, *function*, their analysis provides a sound basis for statements about the purposes of personal weblogs. These general statements can be made by drawing on the genre profile concept outlined in 1.4, especially the *repertoire* and *frequency* of post genres, as this will tell us which post genres are typically used on personal weblogs.

Still, determining the repertoire of post genres is not a trivial issue. In 3.2, Figure 6, I've already outlined a framework for the analysis of post genres: Step I triangulated insights from previous studies (Table 41, Table 42, Table 43) and the meta discourse of the blogging community (see 11.3.3) to generate preliminary ideas about the genres. In step II, I proceeded to posts in the DIABLOC blogs with explicit comments on the genre of a certain post, for example, labelling a post as *review*. This step is in line with the premise outlined in 1.1 that genres achieve labels within a given community. The analysis of post genres, therefore, also took an ethno-category based approach. These posts were analysed linguistically (for example, topic, pronouns, deictic elements, cohesive devices, use of hyperlinks but also image use) to set up first genre descriptions. Step III then took all the posts in the DIABLOC into account. By constant comparison of posts with each other (particularly in deviant cases), the genre repertoire was refined until saturation was reached.

This framework results in differentiated descriptions of post genres. Like genres in general, they can be thought of as prototypical categories with more and less typical examples. Consequently, there are also fluid boundaries between the categories, for example, between the genres *sharing experience* (7.2.3), *update* (7.2.2) and *giving advice* (7.2.6). An elaborate update, for instance, can, at least in some passages, closely resemble a sharing experience post. Sharing experience posts, in turn, can be very similar to giving advice posts in their reflection passages. In general, it's only a small step from reporting on some experience (*This is how I resolved issue xy.*) to instructing others (*I suggest you resolve issue xy like I did*). This doesn't only have theoretical implications but also impacts how to determine frequencies of post genres: Whenever a post appeared to be a boundary case between two genres, or even a hybrid, I coded both genres. In order to reduce the impact of coding errors or inconsistencies, I measured the frequency in terms of blog-pages in which at least one post exhibited a certain genre. So, when at least one post was coded with a genre category, this counted as *exhibited*. The frequency measure applied here therefore highlights the spread of a post genre over several blogs, that is, how many blogs make use of the genre.

This measure also proved very useful in highlighting the heterogeneity of blogs in terms of the number of different post genres they usually make use of (7.6.1).

In what follows, I first provide descriptions of key post genres. These descriptions also make transparent which structural characteristics I consider typical of these genres and therefore used in the coding process described above. I'll move from primarily informative post genres to appellative and contact-oriented genres. Finally, I'll address frequency issues in order to make general statements about *which* genres are typical in which corpus period.

7.2 Primarily Informative Post Genres

7.2.1 *Who gets the blame when your computer crashes:* Filtering the Web

Filter posts are apparently *the* post genre of period I (7.6.2). Rebecca Blood (2002: 7) defines the "classic weblog" on the basis of this practice, as do other period I authors:

Example 114: Characterising Weblogs in Terms of the Filter Practice

> Weblogs are often-updated sites that point to articles elsewhere on the web, often with comments, and to on-site articles. A weblog is kind of a continual tour, with a human guide who you get to know.
>
> (Winer 2001)
>
> This is a Weblog. Here's the deal with a Weblog. Whenever I find something I think is interesting or cool, I'll link to it here.
>
> (*Research Buzz* 2, I)

Rebecca Blood's label[153] *filter* captures the essence of this practice: The growing World Wide Web is filtered through the perception of the respective author;[154] valuable sources are presented on the blog. Other descriptions of this practice draw on the verbs *share* and *point* (for example, Winer above). Example 115 illustrates several ways of presenting the filtered content:

153 As Barrett (1999a/b) shows, this label was in use even before Blood's influential texts.

154 Sometimes, for instance in *LTSeek* (period I), *offline* sources are also 'filtered'.

Example 115: Filter Posts I – Presenting Filtered Content

New Frontier sites: Calvary Presbyterian Church, Barreau du Québec, The Pixel Pen.
It seems like I'm pointing to HotWired's Packet channel every day. Today's piece by Simson Garfinkel is an invaluble explanation of how MAE West works. Our ISP, Conxion, is linked into MAE West, which means that DaveNet and Scripting News come thru the MAE system (I think...).
ZipIt is a Macintosh program that zips and unzips archives in a format fully compatible with PKZip for the IBM and zip implementations on other systems. It's vastly easier to use than the Windows equivalent program, WinZip, which is a dauntingly complex maze of wizards and vacuous help files.
ZipMagic – use zip files without unzipping them. (Windows)

(*Scripting News* 32–34, I)

5/9/00
In E-World, Capital Is Where It's @
New York Times (free registration required)
Young New Yorkers without neckties or profits were on stage pleading for money for their startups.

(*GeoffsGems* 1–2, I)

Week of 8 October 1999
subject: biology - arthropods
source: Nature Science Update
Myrmeco-topiary: an African ant prunes its host tree to prevent invasion by other ant species. (A BBC News story describes the experimental method.) [...]

(*Honeyguide* 1–3, I)

The excerpt from *ScriptingNews* begins with an uncommented list of links. However, it seems to be more common to accompany the sources with brief commentary, which usually comprises a short synopsis of the source's content (particularly in *Honeyguide*) and/or some sort of evaluation concerning its quality. For instance, one source on *Scripting News* is characterised as *invaluable explanation of how MAE West works* and thereby both summarised and evaluated.

Scripting News shows a tendency to *incorporate* the three aspects *presenting a source, giving a summary* and *providing an evaluation.* Hyperlinks are integrated into the sentences and evaluations linked to the summary, as in the *MAE West* example above. *GeoffsGems*, on the other hand, tends to separate these moves and presents the hyperlink, its source (for example, *New York Times*) and a synopsis in a template-like structure. The synopsis is usually (as in the excerpt above) a mixture of paraphrase and direct quotation. *Honeyguide*, eventually, uses both strategies. The structural setup of the individual content units resembles *GeoffsGems*. At the same time, hyperlink and synopsis are incorporated. This also becomes obvious from the fact that it is not the headlines which serve as links but syntactically prominent elements of the synopsis, for example, the subject as in *A BBC News story describes…*).

Generally, the topics in Example 115 are treated in a rather descriptive manner, with stance varying between neutral-epistemic (*GeoffsGems*, *Honeyguide*) and evaluative (*Scripting News*). In *Honeyguide*, we find a topical classification which reveals a preference for natural science topics but also shows that, generally, rather disparate topical fields are dealt with. *Scripting News*, too, incorporates very different sub-topics, in this case, from an IT-related field. The excerpts above also illustrate that filter posts tend to appear as lists of topical units which are not linked with each other, employing, for instance, markers such as *on another note* and *what is also interesting*.

Therefore, there is no *topical* coherence between the passages. It can rather be assumed that users need to know about this practice of filtering the web in order to render the posts coherent, that is, answer the question *What's that supposed to tell me?*. It can be imagined that recipients might have drawn appropriate inferences on the basis of the relevance maxim (see 1.3.3, 5.8.3), leading them to link all the passages of a filter post to the overall communicative function: *this author obviously tries to provide me with interesting links*.

In some filter posts and in contrast to the ones in Example 115, incoherence arises on a propositional level:

Example 116: Filter Posts – Propositional Incoherence

Could this be why WebTV (ahem, Microsoft) dropped support for Java?
(*Camworld* 11, I)

The discourse deictic element *this* refers to the contents of the linked source, which is, however, not summarised on the weblog. Rather, the post is based on a presupposition, namely that *Microsoft* is no longer willing to support the development of the script language *Java*. The causal subjunction *why* allows for the assumption that the linked website will provide reasons for this state of affairs. To a recipient who does not know the linked source, *this* remains underspecified from a semantic perspective. Thereby, a tension arises which is grounded in the resulting incoherence of this line. This might be a strategy consciously employed by Cameron Barrett (the author of *Camworld*) in order to appeal to prospective readers to follow the link. From this perspective, Example 116 is an exploitation of the quantity maxim, which skilfully uses the possibilities of a filter post.

Stylistically, many filter posts tend to concision, as is also illustrated by the following excerpts:

Example 117: Filter Posts III – Tendency to Concision

The electronic commerce boom may be the best thing that ever happened to manufacturers of delivery vans. [11.18.99]
According to AltaVista, good decisively triumphs over evil. [11.17.99]

(*Infoshift* 1–5, I)

[03 Nov 2004|04:56pm]
Link from matchboy... www.anotherfouryears.com
They have an RSS feed too so you can put it on your friends page...
www.livejournal.com/users/another4years
4 comments|post comment

(*This is not a fairy tale* 124–129, II.A)

In the *Infoshift* excerpt, the individual topical units are marked as independent posts with their own timestamps. Each of these posts is no longer than two sentences, which is also true for *This is not a fairy tale*. All the posts cited so far are written in the present tense, marked by a matter-of-fact style and deal with *external* topics; that is, topics that do not deal with the author's immediate everyday experiences. There are only few directive speech acts, for example, in *Research Buzz* where readers are urged to follow certain links by the use of imperatives. Assumedly, this directive speech act is also part of the hyperlinks themselves as their interactive potential is an invitation to click in itself.

The following excerpts show that there are also more author-centric posts apart from the matter-of-fact posts mentioned above, leading attention away from their authors:

Example 118: Filter Posts IV – Author-Centric Type

A font that's like me: Periodically Coherent.

(*Hack the Planet* 16, I)

This article ran last week in Wired, bemoaning the current state of academic genomics. I think it's pretty far off base – not everybody wants to work in a business environment, and those who stay in academentia aren't necessary going to be any less inventive or daring than those making the industry plunge. People don't go into academics for money, so trying to understand them by looking solely at that is a good way to be wrong. Consider, for example, that (broadly speaking) industry scientists don't publish nearly as much as their academic colleagues, and that status (quite important to some) is closely tied to publication record – then you'll begin to understand what's going on.

(*Genehack* 46, I)

In *Hack the Planet*, a font type is related to the author's personality. Most likely, this allusion can only be understood by drawing on adequate background knowledge that most likely only regular readers possess. Thereby, this analogy also strengthens this weblog's community.

In contrast to the other excerpts cited so far, the *Genehack* example above deals with the contents of the source in an argumentative way. A thesis (marked by *I think*) is followed by an argument (*People don't go into academics for money*), which is supported by an example (*consider, for example*). The imperative *consider* furthermore allows for the assumption that readers are not only supposed to follow the argument but also to subscribe to the author's position. This way of linking filtering and voicing opinions is apparently typical of period II (see 7.6.1).

Finally, there are filter posts which accentuate an entertainment aspect. In period I, *Linky & Dinky* presents hyperlinks in an entertaining, fictitious dialogue between the protagonists *Linky* and *Dinky*. The following excerpt from period II also seems to pursue entertainment purposes:

Example 119: Filter Posts V – Entertainment

> The last couple of days have been adventures through, around, inside and out of spime, and I will end my gravity with a levity of the impossible. Atlantis: No way, No how, No where Thus spake Kevin Christopher.
> "Atlantis continues to captivate people's imaginations because it offers the hope that lost ideals or some untapped human potential will someday be uncovered, not the masonry blocks of a dead civilization. Scrying for crumbled roads in Bimini or poring over the outline of some terra incognita on a forged map ignore the real Atlantis, the undiscovered country of human ideals."
>
> (*abuddhas memes* 30–31, II.A)

Abuddhas memes presents hyperlinks in a clear structure (*source*, *synopsis*, *quotation*), which resembles some excerpts presented in Example 115. Language use in the introductory passage (*end my gravity*, *Thus spake Kevin Christopher*), however, clearly plays with the manner maxim and creates a comic effect while actually presenting a sober source. This way of filtering is probably aimed at gaining attention by sticking out against the background of 'traditional' filter posts.

Alongside the growing potentials of using multimodal elements (4.4.2), the scope of variation of filter posts widens as well. In period II, especially from II.B onwards, authors also filter images. *Rebelle Fleur* (II.C), for instance, contains a post which comprises a series of tattoo pictures filtered from other web sources, announced only by *Love them*. Due to the constraints of the communication form, authors in earlier periods would have posted links to the respective images.

7.2.2 *Working at main office today. STOP*: Updating Friends and Family

Updates are mentioned both by some ethnographic studies cited in Table 43 and by DIABLOC posts. Alternatively, authors use terms like *news* (in a personal sense), *minutiae* and *report*. As the term *update* appears to be the most frequent way of referring to these posts and is already established in previous research, I have adopted it here as well.[155] The common denominator of all update posts is the practice of summarising the latest happenings in the author's everyday life:

Example 120: Update I – Summary of Happenings

Ok, I'll stop quoting Jefferson Airplane (or Starship or what have you) and move on to updates. Angish can be delt with later...
Well, I've been going to the gym pretty much religiously lately. I don't know if I've lost any weight, but now I worry that I'm putting on bulky muscle..again.
I've been out and about, having a fairly good time. Looks like the test of me will be reveiling itself when school starts...hopefully I'll pass.
I jus finished Michael Moore's book, "Stupid White Men". It was quite witty and refreshing, considering the Repulican Convention has prevented a lot of Repulican jokes from being run through late night TV. [...]
Saw the MTV Video Awards. They were MUCH better then last year's publicity stunt fest.
Well, having that all summed up, I must be off to get ready. I'm getting my hair done today. Good thing, since my roots are looking pretty trailer by now. Oh, and by the way I got Windows XP (yay) so I'll be....happy.

(...*Life of L*... 19, II.A)

In Example 120, the author announces *updates* (see fn. 155) and specifies the function of the post in the last paragraph by using the verb *summed up*. The post takes the form of a list, with the list entries dealing with different sub-topics: sports, going out, books, TV, software. Similarly to filter posts, the list entries are

155 The term appears both as noun and as verb (for example, *(to) update friends and family*). The noun is not only used in its singular form to refer to one post of that type but also in plural to denote a collection of personal news. In addition to this purpose-oriented meaning, three other senses can be detected: First, the verb *to update* denotes writing and publishing posts in general (e.g., *Alumimnum Lunch*, add. Excerpt 18 June 2006: "I will take great pains to update more often.") Second, the verb can be used to point to modifications of the blog-site: "I was bored so I updated my site a little bit. [...] Updated interests. [...] Added links [...]" (*AllieKat* 42–52, II.A). Third, there is a nominal use which marks posts that were edited (e.g., corrected) after their release (see 5.8.1, Example 74).

not linked by linguistic means. However, it is possible to render the post topically coherent as all list entries relate to the global topic *news in the author's life*.

A closer look at the topical sections reveals a common pattern: Every section comprises a key piece of information conveyed by assertive speech acts and, sometimes, accompanied by additional information. The sections close with some evaluation in the form of an expressive speech act, revealing the authors stance and feelings about the key information. In Example 121, I have selected some topical units from Example 120; key information is underlined, evaluations are in bold:

Example 121: Update II – Microstructure

Well, I've been going to the gym pretty much religiously lately. I don't know if I've lost any weight, **but now I worry that I'm putting on bulky muscle..again.**
I've been out and about, having a fairly good time. Looks like the test of me will be reveiling itself when school starts...hopefully I'll pass. [...]
Oh, and by the way I got Windows XP **(yay)** so **I'll be....happy**.

(*...Life of L...* 19, II.A, my emphasis, P. S.)

Example 122 similarly orients towards this structural pattern. In this case, the topical units are indeed marked by bullet points. Again, each unit comprises key information and its evaluation. Additionally, the structure is extended by occasional invitations and/or requests.

Example 122: Update III – Macro and Microstructure

Thursday: February 26, 2004
I have about 2 minutes to write this post so a quick overview of what I've been doing... again in the form of a list!

- Eating toasties - mmm Crunchie toasties are v v v nice - try it before u dismiss the idea!
- Watching Friends - I've decided to watch Friends from the beginning - ie. starting Series 1 Episode 1... I'm now on S1E16... Chandler in episode 7:... (hee hee) [...]
- buying wrapping paper from tesco - guess how much for a tesco value 2m roll..... 44p i tell you! what a bargain! [...]
- Playing tictactoe - a lot... it's part of my coursework... go ahead challenge me to a game (you can do it on msn) but you'll never win
- Sleeping
- nothing much exciting sorry... [...]

Clearly 2 mins has passed and now I have 20mins in which I can do some constructive work before lunch...

(*amy's little life* 63–72, II.A, my emphasis P. S.)

From a stylistic perspective, both Example 120 and Example 122 are marked by a tendency to concision that resembles filter posts.[156] While Example 120 tends to use elliptical constructions dropping subjects (for example, *Saw the MTV Video Awards*), Example 122 employs participle constructions. The following example obviously plays with this standard of concision:

Example 123: Update IV – Telegram

Working at main office today. STOP. Going very well. STOP. Had Mexican food *and* Starbucks. STOP.
Big smiles all around. STOP.

(*an insider's view of life* 105–106, II.A)

The post imitates a telegram-like style, underlined by the participle constructions and the characteristic *STOP*. This case can be classified as pattern embedding (1.5.3) because clearly, and probably on purpose, typical features of the telegram are embedded in a personal weblog post. The pronounced focus on concision in telegrams is strongly influenced by constraints of the communication form which are not relevant to the personal weblog. In this case, playful and/or entertainment motifs can be assumed to be the underlying reason for the pattern embedding.

In general, the apparent tendency to concision is probably motivated differently. The examples cited so far refer to a rather restricted time frame available for writing the respective post. The author of *…Life of L…* (Example 120) states that she *must be off and get ready*. In Example 122, the author sets a limit of *2 minutes* from the very beginning – and comments on that time frame again at the end of the post: *Clearly 2 mins has [sic!] passed…* The beginning of Example 123 can probably be read as a present tense reference to the immediate circumstances; most likely, then, this post was composed in a hurry at work.[157]

There are also some cues related to the conceptionalised audience of update posts. The authors of *Amy's little life* (Example 122) and *The Core* (II.B), for instance, are college students updating their friends and families at home. The author of *Whirlpool of Dimensional Thought* also mainly addresses his family. A specific audience concept of friends and family is therefore entirely possible for

156 Additionally, presenting list items as well as the structural pattern *information – evaluation* are features to be found in filter posts, too.

157 See also 5.3 on the "ethos of immediacy" and 5.2 on personal weblogs as workplace distraction.

update posts; however, as *...Life of L...* illustrates, rather unspecific conceptualisations are also possible.[158]

7.2.3 *I like electricity and beer keeps colder with it*: Sharing Experience

The practice *sharing experience* is mentioned in numerous ethnographic studies (Table 43) as well as DIABLOC posts and is usually characterised as follows:

Example 124: Characterising Sharing Experience *Posts*

> I'm all I have to work on, so if I write "I I I I I" it's not because I think I'm great, but just because I don't have any other way to talk about my experiences and figure out what they mean.
>
> (*Atomic Raygun* 50, II.A)

This passage mentions three aspects: Reporting on the author's experiences, reflecting on them and, related to this, personal improvement. There are only few competing labels for this practice. Occasionally, the same or very similar practice is described as *musing*, which possibly accentuates the reflection aspect.

Sharing experience posts contrast with the filter and update posts discussed in 7.2.1 and 7.2.2 in that they depict *one* event coherently and reflect on it, often in an elaborate way. Thereby, sharing experience posts are marked by a pronounced topical coherence. The following examples mention the topic in their opening sentences. They also show that hyperlinks – a structurally highly relevant feature of filter posts – are missing almost entirely. *If* they occur (as in the second excerpt below), they are used to provide additional background knowledge to render the post coherent (see also 5.7.1, Example 41).

158 See, for instance, Example 60 where the author thanks an unspecific audience: "Thanks for listening..."

Example 125: Sharing Experience Posts I

2.28.00

some more musing about living online. i was in the salon on saturday waiting for my sister to get done with a client (so she could dye my hair purple), and sat talking to my step-mom, who was also waiting for my sister to get done with the paying client. anyway, she mentioned that it was surprising that it hadn't rained that much today, i responded with "oh, is there supposed be a storm coming in?". when she said yes, it hit me that other people tune in to the weather and get a forecast of what the weather will be like for the next couple days. i just walk out my door and see what it's like. the weather doesn't matter online. 22:14

(*EatonWeb* 19, I, my emphasis, P. S.)

June 24, 2006

BOOM!

I was sitting at home Friday evening and then a suprise power outage occured. This is weird because NES never loses power. The power came back on for a few minutes and then went out again. This time it didn't come back on again. Well I'm bored. What to do without TV? I know, I'll vacuum. That was dumb since there was no power. I thought, MAN!, I have to blog about how dumb I was for trying to vacuum without power. I go up to the computer to blog and......no power. Slap a stupid sticker on me.

Everybody in the neighborhood is walking outside asking if they had power and exchanging what nots. As my neighbors were leaving to have drinks elsewhere I saw this huge explosion on the other side of the interstate. I'm talking about a fireball with a mushroom cloud that went big time with a huge boom a couple of seconds later. I'm talking with my neighbor asking if he just saw that and he was like yeah. I thought the Race Way exploded cause they're this crack head minded gas station just waiting for something wrong to happen but it wasn't.

A couple of minutes go by and I'm thinking that I watch way too much TV. This was a real explosion that happened and there could be people injured. I call 911 to report what I saw and it turns out that a utility pole that caught fire and the transformer on top blew up. That was one hell of a transformer (more than meets the eye, robots in disguise)! The power was out for only an hour and a half and then it came back on. I realized a couple of things during this power outage. I like electricity and beer keeps colder with it.

(*Chris Loyd* 2–5, II.B, my emphasis, P. S.)

The topical coherence of both posts is also reflected in the use of cohesive devices as, for instance, (partial) recurrences (for example, *power*, *(surprise) power outage*, *(living) online* etc.), proforms (*she*, *it*) and subjunctions (*when*, *since* etc.) highlighted in the excerpts. The underlined elements are part of a network of semantic relations, which, particularly in *Chris Loyd*, is centred on topical key words such as *power (outage)* and *explosion*. Most strikingly, both posts exhibit a cohesive frame which is established by the (partial) recurrence of a key word from the opening sentence: *living online: online* (*EatonWeb*) and *surprise power outage: this power outage* (*Chris Loyd*).

As mentioned by Example 124, the excerpts are very author-centred, which becomes apparent from the frequent use of the 1st person pronoun *I* (see also 6.4.2). The feature of topical coherence can therefore be specified: Sharing experience posts typically focus on a subjectively-important event experienced by the author.[159]

Particularly, the excerpt from *EatonWeb* above shows a dual structure; a reporting section is followed by a reflective passage:[160]

Example 126: Sharing Experience Posts II – Dual Structure

> 2.28.00
>
> some more musing about living online. i **was** in the salon on saturday waiting for my sister to get done with a client (so she **could** dye my hair purple), and **sat** talking to my step-mom, who **was also waiting** for my sister to get done with the paying client. anyway, she **mentioned** that it **was** surprising that it **hadn't rained** that much today, i **responded** with "oh, is there supposed be a storm coming in?". when she **said** yes,
>
> **reporting section**
>
> it **hit** me that other people tune in to the weather and get a forecast of what the weather will be like for the next couple days. i just walk out my door and see what it's like. the weather doesn't matter online. 22:14
>
> **reflective section**
>
> (*EatonWeb* 19, I, my emphasis, P. S.)

The caesura between reporting and reflection is accompanied by a change in the use of tenses. The reporting section is dominated by past tense (bold in Example 126), while the final section employs present and future tenses (underlined). The excerpt from *Chris Loyd* also follows this dual structure. The author formulates his personal moral, which he introduces by *I realized a couple of things*. However, the reflective passage is less elaborate than in the *EatonWeb* post and apparently takes a comic twist, highlighting the author's dependence on electricity already mentioned throughout the post.

In both posts, the dominance of assertive speech acts allows for assuming a primarily informative function. Other posts, however, additionally follow an appellative function, aiming at influencing the readers' behaviour.

---

159 I am well aware of the several facets of the term *experience* both in everyday life and in sciences and humanities. I am referring to an everyday understanding of the term here – in line with my approach of describing genres as *ethno*categories.

160 In Schildhauer (i.pr.), I have shown that the reflective passage can be further differentiated into personal and general reflections.

Example 127: Sharing Experience Posts III – Appellative Function

Thursday, March 8, 2012 **A warning** Okay, I admit it. I made a boo boo. I posted on the U.K. Amazon readers site by mistake. [...] I got so many vicious replies, people accusing me of trying to sneak in self promotion (as if that's punishable by death), people reading the book samples and then saying how much they sucked, people posting on the forum calling me all kinds of horrible things. [...]	**reporting section**
My warning to all authors out there is to stay away from the Amazon forums altogether. It's not worth the little promotion you get with all the jerks surfing them who have nothing better to do than rip apart your self-esteem. [...] (*Always Writing* 85, II.C)	**reflective section**

The post is introduced as *a warning* and this indicator of the post's central illocution can be found again at the beginning of the final paragraph. Out of a negative experience, the author thereby develops not only his personal lesson but also urgent advice for his readers.

In this example, the audience is conceptualised as *authors* according to the principle of similarity (5.7.3). In contrast to update posts, however, it is hard to make general statements about the role of the target audience of sharing experience posts as this may range across all levels of specificity discussed in 5.7.1. It can be assumed that the readers are envisaged in the role of a witness (5.7.4). A special case appears to be *I am the Man Letters* (II.C), which consistently blends the genres personal weblog and private letter. The individual letter-posts (sharing experience) are addressed to the author's father.

As far as the reporting section is concerned, it can also be noted that, besides the purely language-based examples in Example 125 to Example 127, there are several multimodal variants (particularly from II.B onwards). Example 108 and Example 112 (6.4.4) may serve to illustrate this.

In the examples cited so far, the topic is unfolded according to a narrative pattern. A pronouncedly descriptive way of dealing with the topic can be found in the following example, which depicts, in detail, several aspects of the experience *when your period is late*.

Example 128: Sharing Experience Posts IV – Descriptive Treatment of Topic

Today is Thursday. My period should have begun on Wednesday. Thus, I am nervous. There is a particular sensation that you experience when your period is late. Your fingers and toes become tingly, your bowels clench on their own, and you find yourself misusing words. You are unable to concentrate on anything except interrogating your body. "Seriously, what is this shit? Is this because I exercised more than usual? Or because I stressed out for two straight days? Could driving in a car for a long period of time do this? I spent a lot of time with new girls; maybe they threw me off my cycle? Speak, bitch." But your body, she is not talking.
Then you try to close your eyes, to breathe slowly, to commune with your uterus. "Uterus?" you ask, "I need to know. Is there a fertilized egg in there?" But then, just as you feel it's about to answer, your emotions rush at you, overtake you, and tell you either what you fear or want to hear. The only thing you know for sure is the absence of blood. [...]
After work, I take the test. Unless I bleed first. Come on, blood.

(*'N' is for Neville* 2–6, II.A)

Example 128 ends with the author's decision to take a pregnancy test after work. I would like to assume that this decision is the result of a reflective process which took place *while* the author was writing the post. Therefore, this post illustrates that the writing process in itself may serve important functions for the author (see 1.3.4). Indeed, the conceptualisation of the sharing experience pattern cited in Example 124 already points to a quest for meaning in the authors' experiences as a fixed feature of the production of these posts. Apart from this rather cognitive striving for meaning, some sharing experience posts apparently aim at releasing emotional tension as a benefit of the writing process. In these cases, the reader is probably conceptualised as therapist (5.7.4).

7.2.4 *So back off, Mr. Governor*: Voicing Opinions

Example 129: Characterising Voicing Opinions *Posts*

It is a great article. blog provides a space for people to share their opinions and things.

(Comment on Meg Hourihan: *What we are doing when we blog*, 2002)

But at the end of the day each of us are simply digital pamphleteers voicing our opinions and hoping to sway public opinion for what we perceive to be the good of our nation.

(*Indie Castle* in Benton 2006b)

The comment on Meg Hourihan's essay above accentuates the aspect of informing about the author's opinions. Kevin's (*Indie Castle*) statement, on the other hand, does not only focus on the political aspect of voicing opinions but also foregrounds the appellative function aiming at influencing the readers' point of view. We could conclude, then, that there is a continuum ranging from merely informative to rather appellative in this practice of voicing opinions. However, the DIABLOC texts show a pronounced tendency to the *voicing* pole of that continuum rather than the *influencing* one. This is also underlined by the community's labels *expressing point of view* and *sharing / voicing opinions*, which I have chosen as the representative term here.[161] Example 130 illustrates the informative pole of the continuum:

Example 130: Voicing Opinions I – Informative Post

Connections
I was thinking about the positives and the negatives of the Internet.
And I believe there are a lot more positives than negatives.
Think about all the connections you make - how much it can broaden your mind.
In these past years I have had the opportunity to speak to people who come from such diverse backgrounds, going through experiences and situations I would never even thought of. We have spoken about about subjects that never crossed my mind before and I have learned so much I would have completely ignored if I had never met these people.
It's priceless.
To be able to speak to someone so candidly and so intimately about your life, and have the other person do the same. In real life you might *know* someone, but you would not know *them*, you might not know their internal struggles, you might not know they are alcoholics... [...] People open up to you. You connect. Personaly suffering becomes **shared**, and the pain somehow diminishes.
Without the Internet I would probably never had spoken to the daughter of an alcoholic, a victim of domestic violence, and heard about their epxeriences. [...]
It makes me feel so human.
It make me feel so human to read those words, written by someone else's hands, yet so similar to the thoughts running through my head.
Now I feel like I have the **right**, like I have **permission** to feel the way I do. Knowing there are people out there who feel the same way as I do, who **truly** understand, is just amazing. It is totally different from a friend telling you *everything will be alright*, or giving you a hug and letting you cry, hoping it will all be better. That helps. But a person who has not been through a similar experience cannot **know** how I feel, cannot *expect* to know. They can only give a different kind of help.
So I am grateful for everything I have gained and am still gaining from the Internet. So much more than we would ever have hoped for...

(*A la Coque Wonderland* 41–46, II.A)

161 In period II, the term *rant / ranting* is also rather wide-spread; apparently a label for a related practice. Reed (2005: 28), however, characterises ranting as a "a kind of therapy, a means for clearing the mind [...] an unstructured outpouring of personal feelings or passing rage [...] an outlet for everyday frustrations." I will therefore refer to *ranting* later, in 7.5, when focussing on the writing process itself.

The opening sentence mentions *positives and negatives of the Internet* and, thereby, mirrors patterns of a pro / contra argument. Indeed, it is followed by a thesis (*there are lot more positives*), which is supported by a key argument (*all the connections you make*). Numerous examples from the author's experience underline the argument and, at the same time, show that the point of the post is to share a personal point of view. The text predominantly uses assertive speech acts; the only directive speech act is realised by the imperative *Think of all the connections you make*. The pronouns *you* and *your* can be read both as personal and indefinite pronouns; the personal pronoun underlines the imperative, which can be interpreted as an appeal to take the author's position even though, on the surface, it is a mere appeal to think about the issue. The following passages, however, are entirely focussed on the author. They inform about her point of view and do not ask the reader to subscribe to it.[162]

The following example shows a stronger inclination to the appellative pole:

Example 131: Voicing Opinions II – Appellative Pole

Too much too soon?
Today Gov. Rick Perry of Texas signed a law requiring girls entering the sixth grade to have the new HPV vaccination.
I have nothing against vaccinations. When it comes to mumps, measles, chicken pox, I'm all for them, sign me up. And I completely understand why certain ones are required to enter school. An entire class of five year olds coming down with red spots isn't a pleasant thought. I am not against the idea of an HPV vaccine, either – on the contrary, I think it has the potential to do a lot of good - but the idea of a state requiring this particular vaccine at this point in time rubs me the wrong way.
First, while it must have passed clinical trials and been deemed safe for humans since it is on the market, it was just approved last year, for goodness sake! What if five years from now some horrendous side effect is discovered and thousands of young women suffer because they were required to get it? Far fetched, perhaps, but that's my gut reaction.
Second, does it really need to be required at all? Measles, mumps and chicken pox can spread like wildfire in a closed in space such as a classroom, but HPV is an STD. I am not in the mood to discuss today whether teenagers should or shouldn't be sexually active, but I can state that usually kids aren't having sex in algebra class. A teenager with HPV is not putting her classmates at risk by her presence in the room. That alone should remove the discussion from the hands of lawmakers and place it into those of the girl and her parents.
But what really, really makes me boil is the knowledge that lawmakers are being assisted in this decision by Merck's use of lobbyists and campaign contributions. I haven't looked up the data on this, but I am not naïve enough to believe it isn't happening.
So, back off, Mr. Governor. The sexual health of my (as yet non-existent) daughter is my purview, not yours.

(*Excessively Diverted* 71–77, II.B)

162 For further strategies of voicing opinions, see Myers (2010: 95–113).

The post opens by presenting a hyperlink and resembles a filter post in this respect. It becomes apparent, however, that the linked article only serves as the starting point of the argument and supplies important background knowledge for the recipient. While the argumentative structure of Example 131 is similar to Example 130, there are differences on a stylistic level. The central arguments – the side effects of versus actual need for vaccination – are phrased as rhetorical questions and have a more appellative effect than the assertives in Example 130. The differences between these two examples become particularly obvious when the concluding passages are compared. While the conclusion in Example 130 is focussed on the author, the final passage of Example 131 is an explicit appeal to a politician – revealing a very specific audience concept in that respect.

A similar, partly appellative orientation towards a very specific audience concept is also shown by *Aunti Craker* (II.A). Here, the argumentative posts are part of a blog-conversation. The author repeatedly replies to comments by another blogger (Concerned Citizen, CC):

Example 132: Voicing Opinions III – Blog Conversation

Once again BLAH BLAH BLAH FROM CC. IF YOU CAN NOT SAY ANYTHING WORTH HEARING DON;T SAY ANYTHING AT ALL.
THANKS FOR STOPPING BY NOW GO AWAY.

(*Aunti Craker* 47, II.A)

In conclusion, I would like to point out that benefits of the writing process also play a role in this post genre. In Example 131Example 132, exclamations or references to emotions (*What really makes me boil*) support the assumption that the release of emotional tension is also part of the function of this text. The same holds for Example 132. Example 130, on the other hand, starts with a reference to cognitive processes (*I was thinking*). Possibly, the writing process in this case helped the author to become aware of her point of view and the reasoning behind it.

7.2.5 *My rating: 4 of 5 stars*: Review

The post genre *review* is related both to sharing experience and voicing opinions as it comprises reporting on the author's experience of a certain item, mostly from the fields of film, TV, literature and gastronomy. The personal weblog *Jenn's Travel Closeup* is almost entirely devoted to this practice. The author defines the purpose of her blog as follows:

Example 133: Characterising Review *Posts*

Why I Blog....
The goal of this blog is to inspire the traveler. Its goal is not foremost for "tourists", but for people who are really looking for personal experiences in their journeys. <u>This blog will offer up close and personal reviews of various travel destinations, in order to give a flavour to the places that are written about here</u>. [...]
I will also write about foods from other places. One of the best ways to travel, when you don't have a lot of money is through food. [...]
I hope this blog will become an <u>informative place for all different kinds of travelers to get information about what this world has to offer</u> and how we all have so much to teach each other. Thanks and Enjoy!
(*Jenn's Travel Close Up*, II.C, additional excerpt *about*-site, my emphasis P. S.)

The *Why I Blog* passage also points to the primarily informative purpose of the post genre *review*.

Example 134: Review I

<u>Mother's Day at La Pentola: Saint Augustine, Florida</u>
May 20th, 2008 by <u>Jenn</u>
We have walked past La Pentola (which is Italian for The Cooking Pan) many times on our evening walks and it always looks so romantic and inviting with their tiled courtyard filled with greenery. So a few weeks ago when I was looking for a place we could take my mom to Mother's Day Brunch, I decided to check out La Pentola. [...]
We got there a few minutes early, but they showed us to our table straightaway. It was a really hot day that day, so we were happy to see that our table was under the roof. We were still able to enjoy the courtyard without burning to a crisp.
Brunch at La Pentola is a la carte. [...]. As always, I looked for the dish with the most interesting combination of flavors. I found it in their fried egg selection which was served over corn tortillas with roasted red peppers, peas and a tomatillo sauce. I am a big fan of Huevos Rancheros, so I decided to give it a go. [...] Our server was very polite, and nice, but seemed really frazzled. In fact, it seemed that they were short staffed for a Mother's Day brunch. There were about 10–15 tables outside and at least as many as 20 inside - and the servers were individually working tables both in and out.
Soon the meals came. My eggs were cooked to perfection and the tomatillo sauce was delicious. I liked the addition of red peppers, although they seemed to be from out of a jar, rather than roasted at the restaurant. [...] But all in all, I really liked my meal - it was a large portion and served with a side of tasty home fries, very filling and had that unique flavor combination I was craving. [...]
My assessment is that La Pentola is the kind of place you go to enjoy the small plates, appetizers and salads which are all reasonably priced, and inventive, but avoid the entrees which are pricey and small of portion.
(*Jenn's Travel Closeup* 127–138, II.B)

Similarity to the sharing experience genre mentioned above also becomes apparent from the dual structure exhibited by this excerpt. In the reporting passage, the author talks about her experiences in a restaurant. As in Example 126, this passage is marked by the use of past tense. The concluding paragraph is similar to the reflective passage in sharing experience posts and contains the author's evaluation of her time in that restaurant. Instead of a personal moral, however, the passage voices the author's opinion, introduced by *My assessment.* This dual structure is employed rather flexibly the reporting passages also contain occasional assessments.

The post from *Jenn's Travel Closeup* apparently contains a high number of images, which are, however, not accessible via the Internet Archive. Instead, the browser displays placeholders with the rather telling names of the image files: *la-pentola-egg-with-tomatillo-sauce.jpg*, for example. These names allow for the assumption that the images were intended to serve as illustration of the verbal text (see 6.4.4).[163] In other review posts, images are used in a similar way:

Example 135: Review II

My Brief Review of Jonathan Franzen's Freedom (slight spoiler under cut)

Sep. 26th, 2010 at 1:04 PM

Freedom by Jonathan Franzen

My rating: 4 of 5 stars

This book would have earned five stars, but the end felt entirely disconnected from the rest of the book. It was inauthentic, and felt like it was designed to appeal to a movie going audience.

The rest of the book is brilliant, though I found the entire mountain top renewal section to be superfluous. It felt like it was crammed into the book so Franzen could expound upon his environmental issues; in particular, his devotion to songbird ecology. Personally, I'm a lover of birds, and especially songbirds, but even I found no value in the constant discussion of feral and outdoor cats, the populations decimated by our technology, and the destruction of habitats. This is a book about family, and when he sticks to that, Franzen delivers a virtuoso performance.

(Slight Spoiler Below This Point)

Leave a comment | Add to Memories | Share | Link

163 In Schildhauer (2014: 322–323), I also argued for the metonymic nature of language-image links in reviews.

The heading of this post contains the genre label *review*. Most interestingly, the post opens with the concluding assessment (*My rating: 4 of 5 stars*). This rating is taken up in the first paragraph; apparently the author's opinion takes centre stage in this review. This is also underlined by the evaluative stance expressed by adjectives such as *inauthentic*, *brilliant* and *superfluous* and author-centred expressions as *It felt like* and *I found*.

What is shown in Example 135 is actually a *blurb*, which means that the rest of the post can only be viewed by clicking on the hyperlink *Slight Spoiler Below This Point*. This passage is not archived and can therefore not be taken into account here. I would assume, though, that the rather evaluative part shown in the blurb is accompanied by a more elaborate report on the author's opinion of the book. Therefore, we can at least assume that this post, too, exhibits the dual structure mentioned above, but in reverse order, though.[164]

Reviews can occur in connection with the advertising genre (see 7.3.2 below). Blood (2002: 120) suggested already that some authors received products in exchange for reviews. The DIABLOC contains various examples of this practice, as for instance, the following:

Example 136: Review III – Products for Blog Posts

The other day I received a purse to review. It came from an online army navy store called PX Supply. They sell everything from combat boots to souvenirs. And they have free shipping on all domestic orders.
I've had the purse for awhile now and I really like it. It's a soft canvas with embroidered pockets on the front. There is a large zippered pocket on the back, a large snap closed compartment inside and 2 narrow pockets on each side of the purse. The strap is adjustable and has swivel hooks to hold it on so the strap doesn't get twisted.
It's very well made and holds a lot of stuff. There is plenty of room in one of the front pockets to easily hold a cell phone. I smoke so the second front pocket easily holds my cigarettes and lighter. You could also use the pocket for your keys.
There are embroidered stars along the top edge of the purse along each side of the zippered closure. It's easy to find things in the purse and it measures 12" X 8" X 2". It's the perfect size for me. It's not too big or too small. I think I'll be using this purse as my everyday purse.
I showed it to my 16 year old grand daughter and she loved it so it's good for a young person too.

(*Army Mom* 3–7, II.C)

164 The reverse order and the blurb are probably strategies to not *spoil* the book for those interested in buying the book.

The post explicitly points out that the author received the product for review. Obviously, it is part of the agreement between the author and the company that the review should contain a hyperlink to the company website and a brief introduction of the company. In that respect, this post differs from the examples discussed so far. The highly positive tone and evaluative stance taken throughout, further emphasised by evaluative verbs such as *like* and *love*, might raise doubts about the authenticity of the opinions; I will come back to this issue when discussing the advertisement genre in 7.3.2.

7.2.6 *When in doubt, cut it out:* Giving Advice

As a final point in this section, I would like to turn to the post genre *giving advice*, which also shows overlaps with the sharing experience genre. Furthermore, it can be situated in the transition zone between primarily informative and appellative genres:

> Bloggers used their blogs to express opinions and advice, often with a clear statement of particular actions they wished their readers to take. (Nardi et al. 2004a: 226)

This practice is not only labelled *giving advice* but also *tip*, *guide* and *warning*.

The overlap between giving advice and sharing experience is illustrated by Example 127 above. This post is entitled *A warning* and exhibits the typical dual structure of sharing experience posts. However, it does not primarily formulate a personal moral but an explicit warning to the readers. On their about site, the authors of *Daily Home Renovation Tips* (II.B) state their purpose "to add a tip […] every day, based on our own personal experiences," also underlining the relatedness of the *giving advice* and *sharing experience* genres. There are also other authors who define their blog primarily by referring to the giving advice practice:

Example 137: Giving Advice I

My First Blog :)
OK. So now I have my blog all setup and nowhere to go. I guess I'll have to start posting stuff here.
So welcome to my little place on the net. I guess I'll start sharing my thoughts and insights on all things like computers, shopping, cars and gadgets. […]
So if you're here and reading this, hopefully I'll be adding more. Feel free to ask me about something, and I'll try to provide you with some free advice :)
Paul

(*AskmyPaul*, II.A, additional excerpt 06 May 2005, my emphasis, P. S.)

Welcome To Ask Temptress
Sunday, September 18th, 2011, by Temptress, Personal Message, No Comments
Wow, so, this is the first post! *smiles* Welcome to Ask Temptress!
I'm sure you're probably wondering what it's all about… Well, to sum it all up, my name is Temptress and this is my advice column and the place where you'll see me posting tidbits about my personal life and what not. For a more detailed description and to send me your e-mails, I encourage you to click on the "About" tab, which can be found at the top of the page.
I'm very excited about the opening of Ask Temptress! So far, everything is coming together better than I planned it out to be. *smiles* Don't you just love it when that happens?!
Kisses
-Temptress

(*Ask Temptress* 147–153, II.C, my emphasis, P. S.)

This orientation is also mirrored in the titles of both personal weblogs, which contain the verb *ask*. In relation to this, the authors conceptualise their readers as seekers of advice (see 5.7.4) and present themselves as experts in their respective fields. The two examples also indicate the topical variety possible for giving advice posts. While *AskmyPaul* defines its field as comprising "computers, shopping, cars and gadgets," *AskTemptress* contains categories labelled *Relationship Advice* and *Sex Advice*.

Considering the stylistic level, I have already mentioned the strategy of using fictitious reader questions to gain attention and set the topical focus of an individual post (5.7.4, Example 63). The following excerpts illustrate this strategy again as it appears to be typical of giving advice posts.

Example 138: Giving Advice II – Fictitious Reader Questions

Help! How Do I Email a Large File To My Friend?
How to share a large file with your friend.

(*AskmyPaul* 40, II.A)

Cheap Books, Textbooks, Videogames, CDs and DVDs for Frugal People.
Looking to buy books for your kids' summer reading lists? Do you love to read books? Do you like owning your own copy of DVD's? Would you rather have your own copy of a music CD instead of just a downloaded file?

(*AskmyPaul* 69–70, II.A)

Want to synchronize from the menu instead?
Here you go!
Adding right-click synchronization to the OPML Editor

(*Interalia* 1–3, II.A)

Show Me the Money: Where Is My Money?
Many of you who filed taxes this year may have already noticed that the tax refund checks and electronic deposits sent rather quickly by the IRSthis year. But for those who should receive a rebate and have not as of yet, where are the rebate checks?

(*Cheré takes on the world* 35–36, II,B)

How Often Should I Train Abs?
24 July 2008
A question many people ask is "**How often should you train abs?**". And this question gets a wide range of replies.[...]

(*Eat Train Sleep,* 13–15, II.B)

Apart from staged reader questions, giving advice posts show other typical characteristics:

Example 139: Giving Advice III

Today's Round Up
Never use emoticons, it makes you look like an arse. Learn some deep breathing or a martial meditation, don't read blogs about writing, go and write.

(*Comedy Writer* 12, II.B, my emphasis, P. S.)

Maybe it's True, But Maybe it's a Virus
Don't take a chance. Many times you'll receive an email that "might" be legitimate, so you decide to forward it to all your friends "just in case it's true", but it's better to hit the delete key.
"When in doubt, cut it out"
There is always the possibility that the email message is carrying a virus or trojan, so it's safer to delete it than to infect all your friends. Keep in mind that it clogs up the internet mail servers and wastes people's time in having to download then delete the emails. An estimated 90 % of email internet traffic is junk spam, and someone ends up paying for all that bandwidth and time; and that someone is you and me.

(*AskmyPaul* 18–19, II.A, my emphasis, P. S.)

Both excerpts – and particularly the one taken from *Comedy Writer* – make frequent use of directive speech acts realised by imperative verbs (underlined above) such as *go and write*. In some instances, the imperatives occur in connection with negations and thus resemble prohibitions: *don't read*, *never use*, for example. In *AskmyPaul*, the central piece of advice is put in bold and formulated as a rhyme: *When in doubt, cut it out*. What follows are arguments supporting the slogan. Similarly, *Comedy Writer* supports individual instances of advice with arguments: *Never use emoticons, it makes you look like an arse* being one example. Comparatives like *better* and *safer* additionally express the authors' preferences.

The similarities in the *sharing experience* and *giving advice* genres mentioned above can also be seen in posts in which sharing experience dominates but which actually report on best-practice guidance for a certain procedure. By couching it in personal experience terms, advice is passed on in a very subtle way. Consider the underlined passage in the following example:

Example 140: Giving Advice IV – Best Practice

Burned bottom milk pudding – Kazan Dibi
>> Thursday, July 21, 2011
{A Turkish style milk pudding}
[...]
In the kitchen, after two litres of milk, a few burned pans, finally I have been able to recreate my favourite milk pudding!
[...]
The trick to make milk pudding, I found, is in the ratio of starch and rice flour. I first tried a 100% rice flour based pudding, and the result was a bit too heavy and grainy. Greg Malouf has a100% corn starch based recipe, but it lacked texture. A combination of these two flours produces much better pudding.

(*A Food Lover's Journey*, additional excerpt 21.7.2011, my emphasis, P. S.)

Such a subtle mixture of sharing experience and giving advice practices can also be found on *Blonde Girl Chronicles* (II.C) – also on cooking – and on *Bboy* (II.C), dealing with break dancing.

7.2.7 Interim Summary

Hybrids of several post genres such as Example 127 underline that there are numerous overlaps among the genres discussed so far and that the communicative reality is often more complex than the types presented here suggest. However, I would like to take the opportunity to summarise the features of the primarily informative post genres focussed on in this sub-chapter. Thereby, I would like to highlight both their distinctness but also their closeness regarding several aspects.[165]

Table 44: Primarily Informative Post Genres – Summary

		Filter	Update	Sharing Experience	Voicing Opinions	Review	Giving Advice
	alternative labels	*share / point to sources*	*news, minutiae, report*	*musing*	*expressing point of view, sharing opinions*	–	*tip, warning, guide*
Structure (language / image)	language	concision; matter-of-fact vs. author-centred vs. language play	concision, author-centred (1st person pronoun)	elaborate, author centred (1st person pronoun), cohesive devices	author-centred (1st person pronoun), rhetorical strategies	evaluative verbs (*prefer, feel like, like* etc.) and adjectives	imperatives, rhetorical questions
	Language – (moving) image	in period II extended to images / videos	mainly language-based	images often illustrative; language-image-chain	mainly language-based	(product) images mainly illustrative	mainly language-based
	Hyperlinks	key element: presentation, synopsis, evaluation	not present	sparingly used, providing background knowledge	starting point for argument; quotations as arguments	sparingly used, providing background knowledge	background knowledge, further sources for advice
Semantic structure	Topic(s)	sources, external content on various topics	*What's happened recently?*	Experiences (e.g., everyday life)	the author's opinion on X	the author's evaluation of X	best procedure to reach X / if X
	Sub-topics, structure	various, unconnected	various, unconnected	dual structure: reporting and reflecting	thesis, arguments, examples	dual structure: report and assessment	at times dual structure: report and advice
	topic treatment	descriptive		narrative and descriptive	argumentative	descriptive, argumentative, narrative	argumentative, at times narrative
	Stance	epistemic and evaluative		epistemic, evaluative, emotive	evaluative, motivational	evaluative	preferential
Context	audience concept	unspecific	at times friends/ family, audience as witness	varying, audience as witness/ therapist	unspecific, but at times directed at individuals	unspecific	unspecific, audience as advice seekers
	Additional features	growing WWW, the author's web travels	at times limited time frame	–	at times blog-conversations	at times sponsoring	expert-lay people constellation
Function	*Communica-tive* purpose	information, ap-peal (hyperlinks), entertainment	information, contact (friends/family)	information	information, seldom appeal (adopt opinion)	information	information, appeal (instruction)
	Writing process	–	–	making sense of experiences, release emotional tension	structure thoughts, becoming aware of opinions and reasoning	–	–

165 Cells that are marked with – in the following table indicate that my analysis did not yield any results on that aspect. Most likely, future studies (on the DIABLOC, an

7.3 Primarily Appellative Post Genres

While the primarily informative genres discussed above are very well attested and commented on in the discourse of the blogging community (and the DIABLOC), the picture is a bit different for appellative post genres. What follows is therefore less based on meta comments in the DIABLOC and relies more on the results of the studies summarised in Table 43, and textual analysis, of course.

7.3.1 *ACTIVISTA*: Appealing to the Audience

Generally, appeals to the imagined audience are frequently found on personal weblogs and can take a variety of different forms. A particularly salient group of appeals is represented by the following two excerpts:

Example 141: Asking for Active Support

ACTIVISTA!
activism is an extremely important responsibility of every global citizen and this weekend starts a very important period for activism in NYC. SO REPRESENT YALL. This weekend is going to be dope. Reproductive rights march on saturday (more) and then of course the united for peace march on sunday (more)
Its your call...either you are with the right wingers or you are against them. the time is now. regime change is needed.

(*angrybit* 4–5, II.A)

Volunteer Travel, Part 2: Navajo Nation, AZ November 22–29, 2008!
October 3rd, 2008 by Jenn
Join The Caravan of Support To Big Mountain Resistance Communities of Black Mesa, AZ. November 22–29, 2008!
Hug a sheep Today!
Here is an opportunity to travel to Black Mesa/ Big Mountain and **do the type of work I did back in 1998** - something that made a lasting impression on my life, as it allowed me to do something for others and to work for a cause I believe in with all my heart. A way to help preserve indigenous sovereignty in this country and to help protect our natural resources!
****

(*Jenn's Travel Close Up* 34–43, II.B)

---

extended version or entirely different corpora) might therefore supplement details my analysis has not been able to discover (not to mention the possibility of *qualifying* aspects mentioned here, of course). The dashes should therefore not be understood as a statement about a post genre being underspecified regarding a certain aspect.

In both excerpts, the readers are asked to get active and support a political (*angrybit*) or charitable (*Jenn's Travel Close Up*) project. In both excerpts, the appellative function is realised by exclamation marks (especially in the headlines) and imperatives. The key imperative in the first excerpt *REPRESENT YALL* is written in capital letters, probably as an attempt to imitate a loud verbal exclamation, as is the assimilation *you all* > *yall*. Both posts follow an argumentative pattern: The imperatives serve as theses, which are underpinned by arguments and, in the second excerpt, examples from experience. Hyperlinks either support the argument (for example, the reference to a post describing a similar experience in the second excerpt) or are already part of the activity asked for: for instance, following the *more* hyperlinks in the first excerpt to obtain more information about the event. Both authors obviously make use of the potential of the communication form to reach a mass audience, whom they address in an unspecific way by *you* (2nd person plural).

A second group of appeals asks the audience for spiritual support. Even though this is a fairly personal request, the following two excerpts address, again, an unspecific mass audience:

Example 142: Spiritual Support

Brezlon is now taking his entrance exam for admittance into Holy Cross Catholic School.
I registered him on Tuesday. [...]
Please pray that this school will be a positive experience for him.
(*Andrena's Ankh* 75–77, II.A)

Would really appreciate prayer for my CIM exams this week on Tuesday and Thursday (14:00–17:00). Thanks!
(*andy moore* 110, II.A)

The appeal is more indirect than in Example 141; only the first excerpt contains an imperative, which is weakened by the particle *please*. In the second excerpt (*andy moore*), the appeal is realised as an assertive speech act.

Similar strategies can often be found in a group of appeals in which the bloggers ask for some sort of help. Consequently, the following two excerpts also contain unspecific forms of address. It's likely that the authors build on the probability that at least one member of the potential mass audience might be able to solve their problem:

Example 143: Asking for Help

> I am now searching the Web for a copy of the poster. If you know where I can get one, please email me.
>
> (*Bump* 36, I)
>
> - banner font colour suggestions? anyone? schram? i'm looking ~~at you~~ in your direction.
>
> (*at last there is nothing left to say* 26, II.A)

In the second excerpt, the indefinite pronoun is corrected by turning towards a more specific addressee. This excerpt chooses the form of a question, whose appellative nature is underlined by the description imagined gaze at that particular person.

Another group of appeals can be summarised under the label *seeking others' opinion* (see Table 43):

Example 144: Seeking Others' Opinion

> I would really like to know people's opinion on THIS.
> Basically, this is a new proposal in the UK:
> Residential treatment centres should be opened for the most dangerous paedophiles, says the government ... [...]
> So what do you think?
> Do you think it makes sense??
> Do you think the public would seriously be **safer** if sex offenders live in such places?
> And where would they locate them? In cities? In the countryside?
> Would the location be kept secret to protect these monsters? or would the public have the right to know there is such a place near their homes?
> There are just so many questions...
>
> (*A la Coque Wonderland* 85–89, II.A)
>
> What your thoughts on aging gracefully? Would you go under the knife? Would you do cosmetics procedures like Botox or are you just gonna go au natutrale? Also are you attracted to people that age naturally? Or do you prefer the forever young?
>
> (*Chef's Widow* 10, II.B)

Again, the audience concept appears to be rather unspecific; the readers are addressed by the collective *people* in the first and by *you* (2nd person plural) in the second excerpt. In both cases, the appeal is realised by a succession of questions, opened by a request to voice opinions on a certain topic: *So what do you think* and *What your [sic!] thoughts on aging gracefully?* The author of the second excerpt actually asks a series of leading questions, giving away her own stance on the subject. This case, then, appears to exhibit overlaps with those instances of the genres *filter* (7.2.1) and *voicing opinions* (7.2.4) which use a filtered source as starting point of an argument (see Example 118 and Example 131).

Finally, I would like to consider a special case of appeal:

Example 145: To-Do List

November 2004 To Do List
1. Do not buy things on Ebay.
2. Pray for one person besides myself each day.
3. Read a Chapter of the Bible each day.
4. Change the flyers on my bulletin boards on time.
5. Go to bed before 2AM Sunday through Thursday.
6. Take my vitamin every day.
7. Write my 50,000 words for the month of November.

(*This is not a fairy tale* 142–150, II.A)

This to-do list is particularly interesting as it is aimed at multiple addressees, namely the audience *and* a future self of the author. For both addressees, the list fulfils an informative function. Additionally, an appellative function, valid only in relation to the author's future self, should be taken into account This function is illustrated by the fact that the list does not only contain items that have to be done but also things that should be avoided. In that sense, item 1 on the list can be interpreted as prohibition. The verbs on the list, too, can be read as imperatives in the direction of the author's future self; item 5, in particular is most likely also a prohibition of *not* going to bed later than 2am.

7.3.2 *free shit for me and free shit for you*: Advertising

There are several forms of advertising on blogs, including, for instance placing third-party ads in the sidebar and earning money depending on the number of clicks on these ads. As this chapter is about *post* genres, however, I will focus on advertising *posts* alone here.

Many advertising posts contain some appeal which is realised explicitly as an imperative. A closer look, however, reveals several advertising strategies. First of all, we have to distinguish between advertising of the blogger's own products and third-party advertising. The following excerpts represent the first category – own products:

Example 146: Advertising Own Products

I've started doing some t-shirts, so go and have a look and buy one. [...]
Buy my t-shirts

(*andrewf my life* 98–100, II.A, my emphasis, P. S.)

Check out my store, you might see something you like!
http://stores.ebay.com/AA-Discount-Domain_W0QQsspagenameZMEQ3aFQ3aSTQQtZkm

(*This is not a fairy tale* 232–235, II.A)

Doubling my audience
Just a quick post to announce that I've put all my books up for Smashwords read an ebook a day promotion. Since I've been spending almost all of my time promoting Kindle and Amazon, this opens up a whole new readership with Nook and many other ereader devices. I've got a great author site where you can get my books on these devices for 25% off during this week! Just use the coupon posted on the site.
http://www.smashwords.com/profile/view/storymaster

(*Always Writing* 92–94, II.C)

Andrewf my life advertises his product outright with a series of four imperatives. The author of *This is not a fairy tale* proceeds in a fairly similar fashion. The last excerpt, however, chooses a more subtle strategy: The first lines are rather informative and strongly resemble a sharing experience post (7.2.3). It's only in the second part that the advertising character of the post becomes apparent, namely when the author uses an exclamation announcing a *25% off* sale. Finally, an imperative asks the readers to follow a link and use a coupon.

It's only from II.B onwards that third-party advertising can be detected in DIABLOC posts:

Example 147: Advertising Third-Party Products

And don't forget to enter my contest to win these fantastic Stride Rite pink Gabby baby girl shoes!

(*Chef's Widow* 15, II.B,)

Just before the week ends let me give you an updated list of giveaways for you to enter over the weekend. [...]

- Silpada Designs Sterling Silver & Glass Drop Earrings – 3/17
- LeapFrog LeapPad – 3/17
- Up to $270 Cash – 3/17 [...]

(*Bay Area Mommy* 76–82, II.C)

The excerpt from *Chef's Widow* asks the audience to participate in a contest hosted by the author to win a sponsored product. The author has already published a review on that product and implements the hyperlink to remind her readers of that review. Both the contest and the review are indirect strategies employed by the sponsor to advertise their own product. The excerpt from *Bay Area Mommy* works along similar lines. The hyperlinks given in the list partly point to product reviews written by the author, which also contain links to the sponsor sites. The entry *Up to $270 Cash* leads to a site listing the sponsors of the contest. This list, in turn, is accompanied by the request to visit each of these sites and take part in other contests.

The inclusion of a list of hyperlinks makes the excerpt resemble a filter post (7.2.1) with the sole difference that the hyperlinks do not lead to external sources but mainly to reviews on the same blog. It can be assumed that the author consciously alludes to an established blogging practice here (filtering as non-profit source of information) and, thereby, modifies the established filter genre for advertising purposes.

Similarly, the author of *Baby Blackbird* (II.C) shares her experiences as a mother, accompanied by image series depicting her son dressed according to current fashion trends. Most interestingly, every image series is complemented by a list of all items of clothing and their respective brand, just like in a fashion magazine. Many of these brands are listed as sponsors of this blog in the sidebar. In this case, it's apparently the genre *sharing experience* (7.2.3) which is exploited for advertising purposes. Part of this strategy is also the principle of similarity (5.7.3): It's very likely that, predominantly, other mothers of toddlers will be interested in a mother's experience about the *coo-coo-crazy stage* (*Baby Blackbird*) around the fourth birthday. As it happens, these mothers are also the primary target group of the fashion labels advertised on the blog.

In many cases, it can only be speculated to what extent and in what ways the authors themselves actually profit from advertising. The issue is most straightforward for personal weblogs like *andrewf my life* (Example 146), *The EarthaKnittery* (II.A), *This is not a fairy tale* (II.A), *Always Crave Cute* (II.C) as the authors of these blogs advertise their own products. In the case of third-party advertising, however, there are apparently a number of reward mechanisms, with financial profit being only one:

Example 148: Reward for Reviews

> This blog is NOT a moneymaker. I have the ads. I don't make the dough. So I have started reviewing which means free shit for me and free shit for you.
>
> (*Chef's Widow* 23, II.B)

No matter what profits authors gain from advertising, *if* they use their blog in such a way, they are under pressure to confirm the authenticity of their content.

This is also connected to the code of authenticity discussed in 5.6.1 and 5.8.1. Recipients might get the impression that individual posts are not free from a conflict of interests.[166] It's probably for that reason that some personal weblogs in II.B and II.C contain a page entitled *Legal*, *Disclaimer* or *Terms of Use*, which the authors use to address this potential conflict and confirm the authenticity of their posts:

Example 149: Confirmation of Authenticity

This blog is a personal blog written and edited by me. This blog accepts forms of cash advertising, sponsorship, paid insertions or other forms of compensation. The compensation received may influence the advertising content, topics or posts made in this blog. That content, advertising space or post may not always be identified as paid or sponsored content.
The owner(s) of this blog is compensated to provide opinion on products, services, websites and various other topics. Even though the owner(s) of this blog receives compensation for our posts or advertisements, we always give our honest opinions, findings, beliefs, or experiences on those topics or products. The views and opinions expressed on this blog are purely the bloggers' own. Any product claim, statistic, quote or other representation about a product or service should be verified with the manufacturer, provider or party in question.
This blog does not contain any content which might present a conflict of interest.
(*Blonde Girl Chronicles*, II.C, additional excerpt *Legal*)

In the end, it's the recipients' task to decide to what extent they trust in the authenticity of the content.

7.3.3 Interim Summary

In this sub-chapter, I've discussed post genres with a primarily appellative function. One common denominator appears to be that authors intend to use their blog's affordance of reaching a potential mass audience. I've addressed two broad categories: On the one hand, authors issue appeals for help, mental support and even political and other activity, although the latter practice is not that common in DIABLOC posts. On the other hand, bloggers use their posts to advertise both their own and third-party products, implementing various interesting strategies. I've shown that some of these strategies create fascinating blends with established post genres such as filtering (7.2.1) and sharing experience (7.2.3).

---

166 See also Blood's (2002: 120) warning to make sure to prevent exactly these conflicting interests.

7.4 *My First Friday Five*: Getting and Keeping in Touch

Besides providing information and appealing to the readership, some blogging practices primarily focus on the communicative contact itself and, thereby, exhibit what Brinker (e.g., 2010) terms a *contact-oriented* textual function. A post genre that most obviously exhibits this purpose is the welcome note:

Example 150: Welcome Note

So to each and everyone of you hello! hope you enjoy the blog...**feel free to jump in and comment** on anything that you see here...after all it's good to have feedback! Also if you want to say hello back...this is the post to do it on...**let us know** who you are and a bit about yourself - what you do for a living etc. **Don't be shy now!**

(*Freya Bletsoe's Personal Blog* 12, II.B, my emphasis, P. S.)

In this excerpt, I've highlighted expressive speech acts which convey the author's psychological state and primarily serve the purpose of establishing communicative contact. Most interestingly, this welcome note also makes use of a number of directive speech acts (in bold), which also serve this purpose in that they encourage the audience to get in touch. The long-term purpose of posts such as Example 150 is most likely captured by the category *community building* mentioned in several ethnographic studies (Table 43) – establishing a growing and stable community around a specific personal weblog.

Another group of posts expresses recognition towards the audience, for instance, *thank-you* and *sign-off* notes as in the following two examples:

Example 151: Thank-you *and* Sign-off *Posts*

Goodbye

Guess this is a formal sign-off. Thought I could carry on posting ad-hoc, but that's just pussyfooting around, isn't it? [...]

Thanks for reading, and, to many of you, thanks for providing such **excellent** material in return.

Oh, and if anyone knows any major publishers with six-figure deals burning a hole in their pockets...

(*audi Olympics* 2, II.A, my emphasis, P. S.)

Thanks!

A quick note between posts (I am working on another entry), I would like to thank all those who have commented, you have my **appreciation**. :)

Keep the comments coming. ;p

(*A stranger here myself* 7–8, II.B, my emphasis, P. S.)

The author of *audi Olympics* is obviously interested in maintaining the communicative contact even after retreating from blogging: At the end of the post, he indirectly asks for projects as a freelance-author. The *audi Olympics* post, then, again illustrates the aim of establishing and keeping a stable community centred round a blog, even after the sign-off.

This strategic aim is also, most likely, the ultimate goal of posts which don't resemble the traditional examples given by Brinker (*thank- you notes* and *birthday cards*, for instance) and don't even feature any expressive speech acts at all. One quite illustrative example is quoted in Example 152 – the announcement of a competition staged by the author of *amy's little life*:

Example 152: Announcing a Competition

Amy's Saturday Competition
I think it's permanently gonna be on Saturday's now...
After last weeks competition when I had to decide between people's entries by imagination, I think I'm going for a question that is either right or wrong! It's hard to think of ones though! I can't ask a question about my Uni room cos some people have a rather large advantage and I can't ask questions about home cos other people have a rather large advantage.
Ok so this is how it's gonna work... I'm gonna ask 6 questions about me / my life... Some of the info will be somewhere on my website... and some won't. Submit your answers to the questions... After each person has submitted the answer, I will mark them (out of 6) in the comments [...]

(*amy's little life* 41–44, II.A)

As far as the overt textual function is concerned, the excerpt represents an informative text explaining the rules of the competition. At the same time, the post conveys the appeal to take part in the competition, signalled merely by the imperative *submit*. I would like to assume, though, that both information and appeal eventually serve the purpose of establishing and maintaining communicative contact. After all, the competition – planned to take place on a regular basis – consists mainly of questions about the author to be answered at least partly by reading her blog. Therefore, the appeal to take part in the competition is actually double-layered and expresses the author's striving for maintaining personal contact with her readers: *Read my posts and let me know you did!* From a strategic perspective, appointing a winner each week and commenting on the answers create a number of new opportunities for communication,[167] supporting the assumption of a contact-orientation for this post.

167 Both types of activity can, in fact, be detected on *amy's little life*.

Games like the one on *amy's little life* also take place on a larger scale, distributed over several personal weblogs. These practices are termed *meme*, *award*, *tag* etc. The common denominator of all these collective practices can be described as follows: These practices use the affordances of the blog communication form – particularly of comment function, permalink and trackback, 4.5 – very skilfully in order to acquaint authors of different personal weblogs with each other, strengthen their personal contact and build some sort of community spirit.

One of the earliest and most well-known games is *Friday Five*. Every Friday, the game leader asks five questions which other bloggers answer on their blogs. Finally, bloggers leave a link to their answers in the respective comment section on the *Friday Five* blog.

Example 153: Friday Five

My first Friday Five! (So what if it's Saturday?! I only just remembered to do this. ^_^)
1. List five things you'd like to accomplish by the end of the year.
* Finish updating and uploading all sections of my renovated website, to a decent & functional standard
* Move house!
* Reinstate our cats' happiness in their new home... I hate seeing them like this...
* Read The Return Of The King BEFORE the film, then enjoy the film
* Have a happy Xmas wif family (should be easy, heh heh) [...]

(*across a roaring hill* 18, II.A)

Apparently, the game was led by *fridayfive.org* until May 2004.[168] After this, the game spread to a number of similar domains adopting the same or a similar principle.[169]

The following example illustrates the different principle of tags:

168 The beginnings of the game cannot be dated properly due to archiving issues.
169 At the time of writing, the game is (probably among others) led by f.riday5.com.

Example 154: Tagging

I was Tagged a while back and I am finally ready to answer the questions, tag some other bloggers and wait to see what happens. If you aren't familiar with tagging then let's start from the beginning.
The Tag Rules:

1. Thank your tagger.
2. You must post the rules!
3. Answer the questions and then create eleven new questions for those that you've tagged.
4. Tag eleven people and link to them.
5. Let them know you've tagged them.

Thank you Barbara from March House Books for tagging me. It was fun to read your answers as well as those of your other tag-ees. I have posted the rules, so now on to answering Barbara's questions.

(*Always Crave Cute* 78, II.C)

The game is spread among bloggers according to a snowball system. By embedding a link to the *tagger* (*March House Books* in the example above) and the new players, members of the community get to know each other and connections among them are strengthened. In Example 154, there are also expressive speech acts (expressing thanks to *Barbara*) as well as recognition of other participants. This also supports the contact-orientation of the post or, more precisely, the series of posts which Example 154 is part of. This basic principle of exchanging *recognition* is reflected on in an ironic way by the author of *All back to mine*:

Example 155: Tagging – *Ironic Reflection*

So... the way it works is this. A very fine man mentioned me when he did this, so I have to mention three weblogs I enjoy reading, and we all mutually masturbate ourselves (metaphorically speaking, natch) into a nice warm fuzz of literary achievement...
(Sorry - that sounded way harsher than it was supposed to. I was just trying to give myself spurious ironic distance. I love it really.)

(*All back to mine* 35, II.A)

Most likely, this striving for recognition is one, if not *the* main motivation for the contact-oriented posts and post genres discussed in this sub-chapter, also showing that blogs have more to offer in this respect than thank-you notes, making innovative use of the affordances of the blog communication form.

7.5 *Getting it all out*: Posts Focussing on the Writing Process

In this section, I would like to cut across the categories established in the previous sub-chapters and shift the focus from the *communicative* purpose to process-oriented purposes (1.3.4). In particular, this section addresses phenomena from the fields of cognition, creativity and emotion in as far as they are aims of the writing process itself. A disclaimer at the beginning: This sub-section is by far the most speculative of the entire book. Only sporadically do bloggers reflect on these aspects of their writing or state them explicitly as the purpose; furthermore, the indicators are more ambiguous. Finally, the benefits of the writing process most likely comprise several interrelated processes, illustrated, among others, by the wealth of categories in this field suggested by ethnographic studies (see Table 43).

Despite these methodological problems, there are, indeed a number of DIABLOC posts worth discussing in this section. Additionally, *some* meta-reflections can also be found, both in the DIABLOC and the extended corpus:

Example 156: Reflecting Purposes of the Writing Process

Anyway the above is something I needed to get out. The truth of it is rather like a muddled puddle. In other words...writing it was more of the point then its truth.
I can't talk to anyone about how I feel, so when I write it here I'm going to be honest and real. I don't want pity or advice...I just want it out of me.

(...*Life of L...* 15, II.A)

Yes, this may seem as the perfect outlet for my thoughts. They only need some organization. [...] Put a piece of fabric in a frame. Blogging can make you more conscious not only on the streets, as well in the act of writing it. As the previous example can be made sense of as a putting a magnifying glass on everyday experiences, the act of writing can be seen as freezing the moment and crystallizing the experience into a yet to be shaped diamond. In the act of writing, you can pick one of countless angles to look at the event. Force your thoughts into shape. Harden it by submitting, and your page is done. Fairly fixed, quite like old media. We all know the rule, the more diamonds circulate, the less valuable they become. But that's not our priority.

(Heijman 2010)

The excerpt from ...*Life of L...* has already been discussed and interpreted as an indicator for releasing emotional tension through the writing process (Example 76). Most likely, the post is an instance of the sharing experience genre. In the second excerpt, a blogger reflects in an elaborate way on cognitive processes such as reflecting on experiences and establishing sense, which are also quite likely part of sharing experience posts (see Example 124).

Regarding this cognitive aspect, there are also posts whose writing process is aimed at reaching a decision (Example 128), finding a solution or reflecting on the own self. These posts are usually marked by a pronounced focus on the author (for example, high frequency of 1st person pronouns), often in connection to questions about the blogger's self or a juxtaposition of various trains of thought, alternatives etc. as in the following example:

Example 157: Cognitive and Emotional Benefits of the Writing Process

> I got some news a few hours ago. I'm not sure if it's good or bad. I guess a bit of both. Jack got a co-op job in New York for next term. I should be happy for him, right? But I can't help but want to cry. I don't know why. I mean...practially the first twelve months of our relationship was a long-distance one. And we survived through that. It was really hard at times, but it was worth it. I just don't know why I'm feeling this way. I feel like such a jerk for not being excited about it. It's just four months, right? No biggie. And depending on how much money I have, I might go visit him (highly unlikely though). Still...I can't help but wallow in my own self pity. Unless he got a job in Waterloo, I wouldn't be seeing him very much anyway. So it shouldn't be a shock that I won't get to see him for a while. I guess it is better than him getting a job in England or Germany. Man, I'm such a bitch. This is such a good opportunity for him and all I can think about is how much this will affect me. BAH! I want to kick myself right now. But I just can't shake this feeling. What's wrong with me?!! I'm retarded.
>
> (*AMS' Blog* 15, II.A)

Additionally, releasing emotional tension might also be part of this post's purposes.[170] On the language level, this is mirrored in exclamations such as *BAH!* and *What's wrong with me?!!*, which are also supported graphostylistically by capitalisations and reduplications (see 6.4.2). The high frequency of expressive and pejorative (in this case, auto-aggressive) lexis such as *bitch*, *kick myself*, *retarded* points in a similar direction. Other posts exhibit similar indicators:

170 A similar striving for catharsis is mirrored in the title of the personal weblog *Getting It All Out* (II.A), which was obviously initiated in an emotionally highly stressful situation. This blog contains only one post entitled *Feeling so low* in which the author reports on traumatic experiences with her bipolar husband.

Example 158: Releasing Emotional Tension

It seems to be one disappointment in my life after another. Every second of everyday I want to cry. Fuck. WHY AM I LIKE THIS? WHY? Why can't I just be like everyone else? Why can't making friends...making even petty conversation come easy to me? HOLY FUCK WHY WHY WHY?

(*...Life of L...* 15, II.A)

I hope you've liked my mini-rant about those COCK SUCKING SHIT EATING FUCK HEADS that are THE TURDS OF THE INTERNET, SPAMMERS.

(*Angry Pigeon* 16, II.A)

So hey Cosmo and ridiculous assumptions on what women should weigh, GO F*CK YOURSELF!

(*And at what place* 23, II.C)

Probably, the expressives used in both Example 157 and Example 158 are *negative emotion words*, which Pennebaker (1997: 165) lists as indicator for therapeutic writing.

The post from *Angry Pigeon* quoted partly in Example 158 is actually labelled as *rant*. This label is even present in some titles of personal weblogs such as *Harmless Ranting* (II.A) and *A mandatory Rant* (II.C). Reed (2005) describes this practice as follows:

> Weblogging is presented as a kind of therapy, a means of clearing the mind in order to move a subject's thought process along. Crucial to this action is what bloggers term the 'rant' – an unstructured outpouring of personal feeling or passing rage. These entries, which tend to be longer than other posts, provide an outlet for everyday frustrations. (Reed 2005: 228)

According to Reed, a central characteristic of this practice is a blend of cognitive and emotional process-oriented aspects. This is connected to a therapeutic effect,[171] which is, at least that's my assumption, part of many posts on personal weblogs, and not only of the *rant* genre.

That the writing process may also serve purposes of creatively generating new ideas becomes most apparent where authors try to fuse different, actually unrelated concepts in an innovative way. The personal weblog *ColorMe Livid* (2008), for instance, connects the typical post genre sharing experience with a lyrical form. Furthermore, all posts relate to the title of this personal weblog in that the topic of each of them is represented by one symbolic colour:

171 Most prominently, *confessions* can be assumed to serve this purpose, as well. However, posts of this genre are rather exceptional in the DIABLOC.

Example 159: Creative Fusion of Forms

> ColorMe (Your Deepest Darkest) Red
> Being happy is overrated
>
> It truly is
> at least now seems to be my reality
>
> But, if this is how i feel,
> perhaps it means happiness has gone away
> I wish you had let me keep it
> over something as mundane as this
> taking away my long sought prize possession [...]
>
> (*ColorMe Livid*, additional excerpt 04.09.2008)

This blending (1.5.3) of sharing experience posts with lyrical patterns throughout a personal weblog is unique in the DIABLOC. In other personal weblogs, for example *Bound and Gagged* (II.C), lyrical patterns are quoted at singular instances; quite often, not the whole but only part of the post makes use of the innovative form. Creative forms of expression also include *hint memoirs* and even collaborative *serials* as those introduced in the following example.

Example 160: Collaborative Serial

> The Friendly Pencil - A Short Collaborative Story
> This is a collaborative piece that was passed on to me from Jayne at Suburban Soliliquy. She is a lovely writer, fellow New Englander and I look forward to her "Friday Night Frolics" weekly. Here is how it works:
> Let's watch creativity happen right in front of our eyes! The first and final sentence of a short story have been provided, and the rest will be created by people in the blogosphere.
>
> (*Living authentically* 21, II.C)

Example 160 illustrates particularly well why Rebecca Blood (2002: 28–29) names *writing practice* as an important aim and benefit of writing blog posts of any genre and why other bloggers do so, too:

Example 161: Reflecting on Blogging as Writing Practice

How can I write? How can I not write? Collaborative blogging began for me in a joint fear and compulsion. Overwhelmed by a looming doctoral dissertation, I felt paralyzed, incapable of creating anything of the size and polish to meet my own expectations. I needed to break that monolithic document into parts, while staging each out not as a perfect culmination but as a series of drafts. At the same time I was trying to find a new writing practice I was feeling extremely isolated professionally, in a vacuum and cut off from the feedback of peers.

(*Writer Response Theory* in Benton 2006a)

Could I do it? Did I have it in me to write every day?
I met my self-imposed goal. Through that exercise I discovered that I most enjoy writing for my blog when I have something to say that has touched me.

(*Toggle Switch* in Benton 2006a)

I blog to keep honing my feminist critical skills.

(*The Feminist Spectator* in Benton 2006b)

In sum, the writing process itself can be considered an important aspect of many post genres discussed above. Therefore, the overall purpose of each of these genres, that is, their textual function (1.3.4), can only be grasped when a mixture of several functional components is taken into account.

7.6 From Repertoire to Frequency: A Quantitative Account of Posting Genres

In this sub-chapter, I'd like to take a bird's eye view of the post genres I've discussed in the last sections. First, I'll discuss the heterogeneity of blog-pages in terms of post genres. Second, I'll focus on the frequency of post genres both from a synchronic and a diachronic perspective.

7.6.1 Heterogeneity of the Blog-Page

It's likely that blog authors choose from the repertoire of post genres according to their current needs when composing a new post. However, there is no personal weblog in the DIABLOC which makes use of the *whole* repertoire. Table 45 is based on a survey of informative and appellative post genres and shows that, depending on the corpus period, between two and three of these post genres could be detected on the blog-pages:

Table 45: Post Genres per Blog-Page

Period	Post Genres per Blog-Page				N (of total)
	Min.	Max.	Mean	σ	
I	1.00	7.00	2.20	1.29	30 (30)
II.A	0.00	7.00	2.91	1.56	100 (100)
II.B	0.00	6.00	2.74	1.27	100 (100)
II.C	0.00	8.00	2.56	1.39	100 (100)

Even though the table shows a slight increase in II.A, followed by a decrease towards II.C, this is not statistically significant, according to t-test. The maximum value is also very interesting: On some personal weblogs, readers are obviously confronted with up to eight post genres.

In singular instances, bloggers choose *one* post genre and do not diverge from it. By contrast, it appears to be a rather common phenomenon that bloggers name a strictly delimited purpose in their first post or on their *about* site, but do not stick to it consistently. The author of *Blushes and Shimmy Shakes* (30, II.B), for instance, opens her blog by referring to the sharing experience genre: "So the point of this blog is to share my session by session experience of a 'Beginners Burlesque' course, embarrassing moments and all." Later, however, she also makes use of the *voicing opinions* genre. Most interestingly, the author reflects on this divergence from her original plan, thus underlining her awareness of communicative purposes and post genres: "My intention is never to make this a political blog, but I wanted to put in my humble 2 pence worth, so there you go:)" (21)

In this respect, the question arises as to whether there are particular affinities among the post genres. In other words: Do some genres tend to occur *together* on a blog-page?[172] However, only the genres *filter* and *voicing opinions* as well as *sharing experience* and *update* co-occur in a statistically significant way, in some corpus periods, at least:

- The relation between filter and voicing opinions is *not* significant for period I ($\varphi_c = 0.074$, $p = 0.685$). In the periods II.A to II.C, however, the relation is stronger and significant throughout.[173] Interestingly, the statistical relation results both from the two genres being present on a blog page (II.A, e.g., 33%) *and*, at the same time, being absent from other blog-pages (II.A, e.g., 38%).

172 This question at least scratches Luginbühl's (2014) aspect of *intertextual relations* among (post) genres (see 1.4).

173 II.A: $\varphi_c = 0.419$, $p < 0.0001$ | II.B: $\varphi_c = 0.369$, $p < 0.0001$ | II.C: $\varphi_c = 0.341$, $p=0.001$.

In other words: If bloggers do one thing, they also tend to do the other, or they don't subscribe to either practice. I'd like to assume that this observation supports what I have discussed above: Filter posts after period I tended to occur as a blend with the voicing opinions genre. Authors present and evaluate a hyperlink and then set out to argue for their stance on the content of the source. There is, then, a smooth transition from filtering to voicing opinions.

- Regarding update and sharing experience, a significant statistical relation can only be claimed for period II.C ($\varphi_c = 0.224$, $p = 0.025$). This relation most probably reflects an affinity of the update genre towards sharing experience posts: In only 3% of the cases, update posts were present on a blog-page *without* the simultaneous presence of sharing experience posts. Assumedly, updates only occurred in II.C if the respective personal weblog was already tuned in on the sharing experience practice and, therefore, on the author's everyday life anyway. Sharing experience posts, on the other hand, didn't show such an affinity towards the update genre as they occurred on 47% of the II.C personal weblogs without the update genre. I'll come back to this relation between update and sharing experience again in 7.6.2.

Diagram 3: Topic vs. Ego-Blogging (following Puschmann 2010: 41–42)

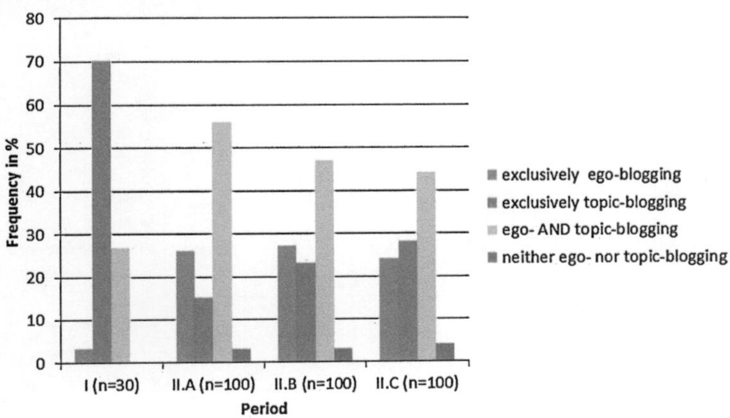

The affinities discussed above might be interpreted as pointing in the direction of a blog-typology of author-centred vs. topic-centred blogs as proposed, for instance, by Puschmann (2010: 41–42) as "basic dichotomy" for "private blogs". In order to test this hypothesis, I've subsumed the genres *update* and *sharing experience* under Puschmann's label *ego-blogging*, whereas filtering, giving advice, voicing opinions and review counted as instances of *topic-blogging*. Diagram 3 shows that, from this perspective, topic-blogging is dominant in period I. However, even in period I, and even more in later periods, *both* ego- and topic-blogging can be detected on a *single* blog-page. There is, admittedly, a slightly decreasing tendency from II.A (56%) to II.C (44%). Nevertheless, the *co-occurrence* of ego- and topic-blogging genres can count as *typical* of the personal weblog. Therefore, a classification into ego- and topic-blogging does not prove valid for personal weblogs – and does not entirely mirror the state of affairs for period I weblogs, either.[174] The data, then, supports the assumption that the blogging practices discussed in this chapter are genres on the *post* rather than on the blog level.

To sum up, personal weblogs picked and chose from the repertoire of post genres outlined in sections 7.2 to 7.4 and, mainly, cannot be sorted into categories of either ego- or topic-blogging. Statements about the co-occurrence of certain post genres can also hardly be made. Despite that, there are apparently core post genres which were more likely to be encountered on personal weblogs than others. This will be the focus of the next section.

7.6.2 Posting Genre Frequencies

Diagram 4: Repertoire and Frequency of Posting Genres (n: blog-pages)

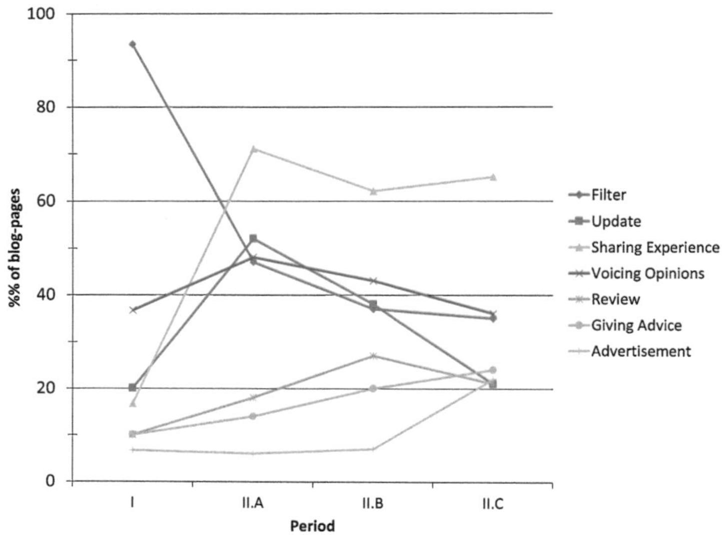

174 Apparently, Puschmann (2013) also distances himself from this dichotomy as "as a clear-cut system of categorization" (Puschmann 2013: 92).

Diagram 4 gives an overview of informative and appellative post genres. It becomes apparent that there is, indeed, a shift concerning *the* core post genre. While filtering was very dominant in period I, where it was found on 93.3% of the blog-pages, it decreased to 47% in II.A and even further to 38% in II.B and finally to 34% in II.C. However, even in II.C, the practice could be found on roughly one third of all blog-pages, showing that filtering remains an important part of personal weblogs even in later years. With values above 60% from II.A to II.C, sharing experience is *the* post genre on personal weblogs.[175]

In period I, the other post genres occupied rather marginal positions as compared to filtering. Despite that, I'd like to highlight that the whole repertoire of informative and appellative post genres was already present in that period. It is, therefore, in my opinion, legitimate to speak of function continuity. After period I, no further genres were added to the repertoire; rather the established repertoire continued with altered frequencies. This assumption doesn't exclude, of course, the possibility of changes *within* a post genre (see, for example, the shift to multimodal filtering discussed in 7.2.1).

Some post genres which occurred less frequently in period I showed pronounced tendencies of emancipation in later periods. This is not only true for the sharing experience genre. Particularly the genres *update*, *giving advice* and *advertisement* increased considerably. The advertisement exhibits a steep increase from II.B to II.C. In the last corpus period,[176] 22% – over one fifth – of the DIABLOC authors made use of this genre. This observation corresponds to what was said about the customer role of the audience in 5.7.4. These observations underline Rosenberg's (2009: 180–185) thesis that professional and hobby blogging were and will be blending more and more (see also 5.2).

Another interesting development is that of the update genre.[177] After a steep increase in II.A from 20% to 52%, updates declined again to 38% (II.B) and 21% (II.C). Possibly, influences from other communication forms and genres came into play here. As I've argued elsewhere in more detail (Schildhauer forthc.), we can assume that social network sites[178] play an important role in this respect. Status messages on Facebook, which Lee (2011) subsumes under *microblogging*, are highly

175 There is a significant statistical relation between filtering and period ($\varphi_c = 0.327$, $p < 0.0001$). With $\varphi_c = 0.302$ and $p < 0.0001$, the same holds for sharing experience.

176 With $\varphi_c = 0.226$, $p = 0.001$, the relation between the advertisement genre and the corpus periods is significant.

177 With $\varphi_c = 0.273$, $p < 0.0001$, there is a significant relation between the update genre and the corpus periods.

178 See boyd & Ellison (2007) for a definition and historical overview.

suitable for updates as they can quickly and conveniently reach all (Facebook-) friends or well-defined parts of the audience. In 2007 and 2008, Facebook's status message textbox prompted users with the question *What are you doing right now?*, which mirrors the topic of update posts very closely. Lee (2011) establishes eleven categories of status messages, four of which appear to reflect aspects of the update genre outlined above (7.2.2), namely *What are you doing right now?*, *everyday life*, *reporting mood* and *away message*. These four categories account for about 40% of the status messages in Lee's corpus (periods 2008–2009 and 2009–2010, Lee 2011: 117), which underlines the importance of the update practice for Facebook status messages. Facebook was opened to the public in several steps from 2005 to 2006 (boyd & Ellison 2007), which coincides with the transition from II.A to II.B. Consequently, we can assume a growing impact of Facebook and its update-focussed use in II.B and II.C.

Additionally, the launch of Twitter in 2006 and its successive exponential increase in popularity (Java et al. 2007; Carlson 2011) certainly played a part in the decrease of the update genre on personal weblogs. Java et al. draw the following conclusion:

> Most posts on Twitter talk about daily routine or what people are currently doing. This is the largest and most common user [sic!] of Twitter. (Java et al. 2007: 62)

Thereby, the authors actually name updates as the key purpose of tweets and also suggest possible reasons for the dominance of this practice:

> Compared to regular blogging, microblogging fulfills a need for an even faster mode of communication. By encouraging shorter posts, it lowers users' requirement of time and thought investment for content generation. This is also one of its main differentiating factors from blogging in general. The second important difference is the frequency of update. On average, a prolific blogger may update her blog once every few days; on the other hand a microblogger may post several updates in a single day. (Java et al. 2007: 57)

The interplay of concision addressed in the first part of the quote has also been discussed regarding the update post genre (7.2.2).[179] There appears to be a difference in quality regarding immediacy between personal weblogs and tweets. This is also underlined in, for instance, the personal weblog *evidently* (II.B), which contains a Twitter link in its sidebar with the author stating: *When you just can't wait for the blog entry.* In other words: Immediacy, the *here* and *now* of (micro)

---

179 See also my remarks on the multimodality of status messages (Schildhauer in press) concerning updating by quickly posting / tweeting photographs (e.g., taken with a mobile phone).

blogging are even more advanced on Twitter, as Java et al. stress in the second part of the quote above.[180]

Rosenberg (2010) additionally stresses that "Twitter is great at 'now.' But so far, it's lousy at 'then.' It offers no interface to the past. You can't easily navigate your way backwards in time." This shows that the blog communication form, offering archives by default, possesses a decisive advantage as compared to Twitter when it comes to recording – and reflecting on – the past. In sum, I think it is plausible to speak of a functional differentiation between personal weblogs (dominated by the sharing experience practice) and social network sites which are dominated by updates.[181]

7.7 Summary

This chapter focussed on the question of what bloggers actually did on personal weblogs. I approached this aspect with the help of Luginbühl's (2014) concept of genre profiles, assuming that blog posts can be related to certain post genres, which in turn are more delimited in a structural and functional way than the super-genre personal weblog (1.4, 7.1).

In 7.2 to 7.4, I provided detailed descriptions of primarily informative, appellative and contact-oriented post genres. My focus was strongly on the informative genres as they occurred most frequently and were often explicitly commented on by the bloggers themselves. In an additional, cross-cutting section (7.5), I showed that genres of blog posts do not, in most cases, only serve *communicative* purposes, but that the writing process itself also fulfils important functions for the authors; for example, structuring thoughts and reaching insights, releasing emotional tension and generating creative ideas.

This chapter also provided a quantitative perspective on post genres. I argued that bloggers picked and chose from the repertoire of these genres according to

---

180 Rosenberg (2010) also suggests a similar tendency for the filtering practice: "Today, the single-line post and the linklog aren't dead, but certainly, much of the energy of the people who like to post that way is now going into Twitter." This assumption is supported by Java et al., who categorise 13% of their tweets as "sharing information/URL" (Java et al. 2007: 63).

181 Smith's (2011) study addresses social network sites in general (not only Facebook and Twitter). The results of this study at least allow for the assumption that this process of functional differentiation holds between personal weblogs and social network sites in general.

their current needs. Usually, between two and three post genres could be encountered on a single blog-page. Bloggers appear to have been rather flexible in their choices and conclusions about co-occurrences of certain post genres are difficult to draw. Certain affinities were stated for filtering and voicing opinions as well as updating and sharing experiences (7.6.1). I also argued that blog-typologies based on dichotomies such as ego-blogging vs. topic-blogging do not hold for most of the personal weblogs of the DIABLOC.

The concluding bird's eye view revealed that we can speak of functional continuity between the early weblogs (period I) and personal weblogs (period II): The repertoire of post genres remained stable but the frequencies of individual post genres changed. The most considerable changes were described regarding filtering (the core genre in period I), sharing experience (the core genre in period II) as well as advertising, giving advice and updating. With regard to updates, I argued for a functional differentiation between social network sites (updates in status messages and tweets) and personal weblogs (focussing on sharing experience).

Part C: Conclusions

8 Summary: A Genre History of the Personal Weblog

In the previous chapters, I looked at each dimension of the genre model (1.3) in turn and provided detailed 'mini-histories' of the personal weblog. Here, I would like to present a synthesis of these discussions and give an overview of the history of the personal weblog, paying particular attention to its ancestor genres, most importantly, the weblog as an immediate online ancestor. I'll suggest four phases to structure this account; these phases arose as a result of reviewing what was discussed in the previous chapters. Wherever possible, I'll make reference to the genre change patterns outlined in 1.5.

8.1 The Beginnings: Emergence and Consolidation of the Weblog (1997–1999)

According to the genre concept developed in chapter 1, an important indicator for the emergence of a genre is the use of a genre label. The christening of the weblog has been traced back to late 1997 in 2.2.1, with Jorn Barger coining the term and others spreading it. However, the term lagged behind the launch of some websites for which it was soon used retrospectively. An important part was played by *Scripting News,* launched in January 1997 (Winer 2001). Its author Dave Winer was a leading figure of the mid-1990s IT-scene. His mailing list *DaveNet,* founded in 1994, and the *24 Hours of Democracy Project* (1996) helped to extent his influence (Rosenberg 2009: 58). *Scripting News* can therefore count as the beginning of the emergence of the weblog in the wider sense.

Period I weblogs were mainly characterised by the dominance of filter posts (7.2.1), meaning that they often featured a high number of external hyperlinks. Their authors usually worked in the fields of web design or other IT-related branches (5.5); this is also mirrored in typical IT-related topics and key words (6.3.4) as well as the fact that the majority of weblogs were coded by hand (4.2).

The weblog didn't emerge within a vacuum but in the context of several other established genres (Figure 14 below):

- A migration process (see the bold arrow in Figure 14) can be assumed for the offline genre logbook: The genre label *weblog* is an instance of the metaphor USING THE WWW IS A (MARITIME) VOYAGE, which is also mirrored in compounds such as *webtravel* or the browser name *Netscape Navigator.* With its "nautical air, a Star Trek echo" (Rosenberg 2009, p. 79) the compound *web + log(book)* neatly fits this conceptual realm. Thus, the genre label makes explicit reference to the logbook as its offline ancestor; a typical post in period I logged the author's *webtravels*.

- An important genre split (1.5.2) involves the personal website as an online ancestor of the weblog (thinly dotted arrow in Figure 14), which also served purposes of self-presentation on the WWW (Rosenberg 2009: 24–28; see also Chandler 1998). Period I bloggers explored ways of overcoming the static presentation of content on personal websites. The majority switched to the post-paradigm, presenting all posts on *one* page in reverse chronological order. Others adhered to the page-paradigm: *Need to Know* as well as *Linky & Dinky*, for instance, published one page per week (6.3.4). Both solutions allowed for the presentation of new content without losing readability or deleting older information. Regarding both the dynamics of contents and its presentation, the weblog diverged from the personal website, which continued to exist.
- Publishing one page per week with several topical sections, *Need to Know* and *Linky & Dinky* implemented e-zine patterns of publication. The newspage, rooted in Tim Berners-Lee's *What's New*-site, was a likely source for the reverse chronological order pattern (Rosenberg 2009: 59).

Figure 14: Emergence of the Weblog in the Context of other Genres (visualised by J. Pflaeging)

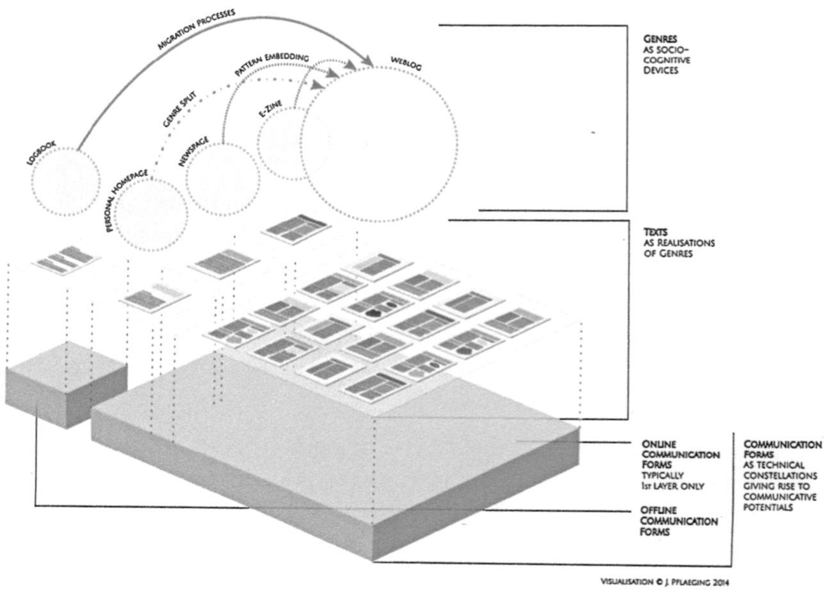

8.2 The Crisis of the Weblog and the Emergence of the Personal Weblog (1999–2000/2001)

At the beginning of 1999, more and more weblogs were created. As early as the first months of 1999, Brigitte Eaton, in compiling a catalogue of all weblogs, withdrew to the single criterion "that the site consist of dated entries" (Blood 2000). Debates about what could be considered a weblog spread, as illustrated by Cameron Barrett's essays (Barrett 1999a/b). In terms of genre description, the category *weblog* increasingly contained peripheral members. Consequently, the fuzziness of the category boundaries intensified.

These developments were apparently sped up by the increased availability of user-friendly blog-software; *Blogger*, for instance, was launched in August 1999. Selecting some structural variants of period I weblogs and setting them as standard (for example, 4.3), a specific blog communication form emerged, building on the WWW and designed by bloggers for bloggers' specific needs. The usability and accessibility of these new systems widened the range of potential blog-authors beyond the circle of web-programmers and IT-aficionados of period I (5.5). The new authors accentuated different blogging practices, most importantly sharing personal experience (7.2.3).

The spread of sharing experience posts fuelled the debate about what constitutes the weblog as a genre. Members of the first blogging community rejected the practices of the newcomers, as Blood recounted some years later: "These are diaries, not Weblogs. Weblogs are about links." (Blood 2004: 54; see also McNeill 2009: 153) This phase led to the establishment of the new genre label *personal weblog*, which stressed both the weblog-ancestry and the new quality of these texts. The emergence of the personal weblog thus involved a genre split, exceptionally well reflected in the community's discourse. Figure 15 below illustrates this process and also highlights the second layer of the communication form (1.3.1) which became relevant for personal weblogs as opposed to weblogs.

The end of this process cannot be dated with certainty due to a lack of data; the DIABLOC, for instance, does not cover the year 2001 (see 2.3.1). It is certain, however, that the genre category *personal weblog* was part of the blog directory *Globe of Blogs* launched in 2002. In other words, the genre had acquired a label by then, and this was even codified in a directory. Therefore, the emergence of the personal weblog can be considered completed by 2002 the latest.

The particular importance of the *diary* for the personal weblog has already been highlighted (see, e.g., Kitzmann 2003, 2004; Herring & Paollilo 2006; McNeill 2003, 2005, 2009; Karlsson 2006; Yus 2011). There are several reasons to assume a process of migration: Some corpus texts have been labelled *diary* or *journal* (e.g., *andrewf my life*, II.A and *SanityWarp*, II.B), and some blog-systems, such as *LiveJournal*, build on the diary-metaphor (boyd 2004). The influence of the diary is especially notable regarding the sharing experience genre (7.2.3), respective topics (6.3.4) and some benefits of the writing process such as releasing emotional tension or making sense from experience (7.5). Additionally, the fact that the personal weblog appears to be a mainly language-based genre, even in later corpus periods (6.3.4, Table 33), can be seen as a connection to (stereo)typical diary writing (see, e.g., Kitzmann 2004: 30; Serfaty 2004: 28). The standards of authenticity and truthfulness typical of the personal weblog (5.6.1; 5.8.1) can be compared to the "contract of autobiography" (Kitzmann 2004: 12) assumed for diary-writing. As "the diary may always have been a communicative genre" (Karlsson 2006: 8–9), the potential publicity of the WWW may not have constituted a radical caesura in this migration process (van Dijck 2004). However, extending the potential audience to utter strangers, which also had implications, for, for example, the intimacy of self-disclosure (5.6.3) transformed some features of the ancestor genre, giving the new genre a distinct quality.

The genre *online diary* can be assumed to constitute a possible intermediate stage in this migration process, also illustrated in Figure 15. Online Diaries date back to 1995 (Serfaty 2004: 19) and expressed an even stronger connection to their offline ancestor by their genre label. Apparently, they contrasted with personal weblogs in implementing the page-paradigm (Bausch et al. 2002: 89), that is, setting a new page for each post, and attaching less importance to readership numbers (Rosenberg 2009: 28; but see McNeill 2005 on the reader-author relation on online diaries). The online diary, which emerged long before (personal) weblogs, is therefore another plausible reference genre in addition to the 'traditional' diary, and a migration process from the online diary into the specific blog communication form can also well be imagined.

However, there is more to personal blogging than sharing experience, which the outline of the post genre repertoire has shown (7). For some other post genres, a number of additional offline ancestors can be assumed. Baron (2008: 106) suggests the ancestor *talk radio*, which could be connected to *voicing opinions*-posts. Puschmann (2010: 72) additionally assumes ancestors in journalistic genres. In the genre repertoire presented here, the review is the most plausible candidate for such journalistic ancestry. However, this genre might also have been influenced considerably by non-journalistic reviews (for example, on platforms such as Amazon).

Figure 15: The Personal Weblog in the Context of Other Genres (visualised by J. Pflaeging)

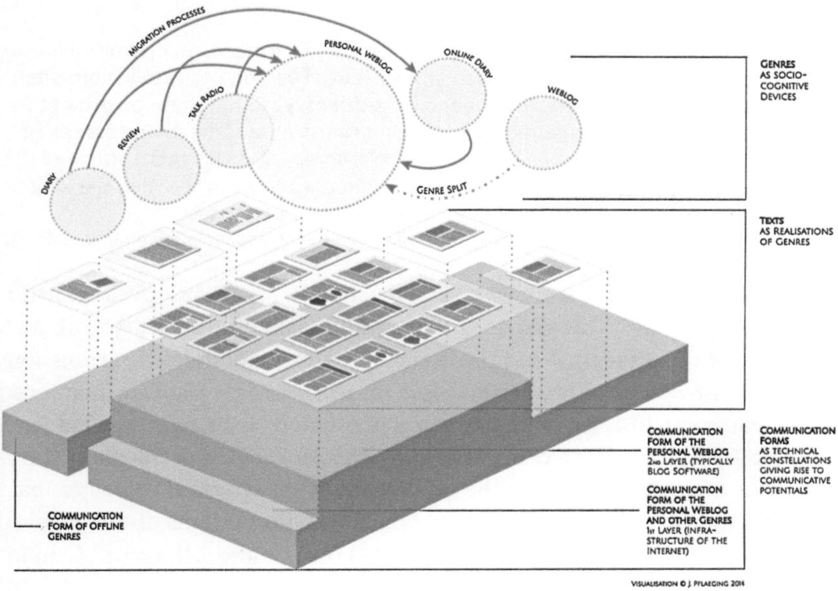

8.3 Consolidation of the Personal Weblog as a Genre and Development of Further Blog Genres (2001 to late 2000s)

The corpus periods II.A and II.B mirror a consolidation of the genre personal weblog. Most importantly, the genre was reflected in the category system of the *Globe of Blogs*-directory, which indicates its established status. Furthermore, a comparison of period II.A and II.B reveals only minor changes in the frequencies of post genres (7.6.2). The appearance of playful uses of the established genre can be interpreted as another sign of consolidation:[182]

182 This excerpt was also analysed in 5.8.1 when discussing the quality maxim (Example 77).

Example 162: Playful Uses of the Personal Weblog

An Offer of Optimism
I don't like to think I'm naive. I prefer to consider myself, instead, an optimist. I like to believe my eagerness to find the hidden answer is what sometimes (lately more often) results in my less than favorable situational hardships. Take my shitty apartment for example. There's barely any plumbing. It's beginning to freeze at night. And a week ago, I found a winged rat had chewed through my loaf of bread. [...] This said, I attended the wedding of Sam Hain over the weekend. Sam Hain the Scarecrow Master, the King of Halloween, the Exalted Patriarch of Pumpkins, His Haunted Holiness...
(*Dandy Darkly*, II.B, additional excerpt 02.11.2009)

At first glance, this post strongly resembles sharing experience posts in its focus on everyday life. This resemblance is additionally underlined by the high frequency of the pronoun *I* and the occurrence of temporal deictic expressions (*over the weekend*). It's only when *a winged rat* and later *Sam Hain* are mentioned that a reader might infer that, actually, a ghost story is being presented here. Example 162 is therefore a case of blending (1.5.3): Patterns of the ghost story-genre (for example, fictionality, the occurrence of supernatural characters etc.) are continuously embedded into a text which exhibits patterns of the personal weblog and which has been assigned this label by its author. The result is an interesting blend of fictional and non-fictional genre patterns.

While the personal weblog was being consolidated as a genre, other blog genres emerged by splitting off from it. The corporate blog, for instance, developed around 2003 (Puschmann 2010: 82–84) out of personal weblogs written by employees with a focus on their work or their company's products. These so-called employee blogs (Efimova & Grudin 2007), in turn, emerged around 2001, probably at the same time as science blogs (Fritz 2013: 547).[183] These (and other) blog-genres were embedded in their own communities (members/affiliates of the scientific community, company members etc.), which were part of the wider blogging community and probably overlapped with the community of personal weblog authors.

8.4 Competition, Variation, Commerce (end of 2000s to 2012)

In 7.6.2, I've shown that update-posts notably declined after period II.A, and that filter posts did so even earlier. The decline of filtering in II.A has been attributed to the demographic shifts in blogging around the millennium and to a growing

183 On science blogs also Fritz (2011), Mahrt & Puschmann (2012), Puschmann & Mahrt (2012), Mauranen (2013a, 2013b).

fuzziness of the weblog genre, which was underway even before 2000. The dramatic decrease of both filtering and updating after II.A, however, was most likely connected to the influence of social network sites such as Facebook and Twitter. Both status messages and tweets were commonly used for updating friends and sharing hyperlinks (Schildhauer forthc.). Most fittingly, the decrease of frequency in both post genres started in period II.B, shortly after Facebook opened to a global audience and the launch of Twitter (both: 2006, boyd & Ellison 2007: 212). Sharing experience didn't take part in this development but, rather, consolidated its position as the core category. It can be assumed that a functional differentiation took place in period II.B and II.C: Whereas social network sites were used for short update and filter posts, personal weblogs became the place for longer and elaborate reflections on single instances. From a structural perspective, I've connected these developments to the decreasing importance of (external) hyperlinks (6.4.1) and to an increase in post length (Table 33) as sharing experience posts tend to be longer than concise update and filter posts.

At the same time, some structural features showed an increased scope of variation. In 1.5.1, I have argued that this is a usual phenomenon in genre change as, often, not all members of a community immediately pick up new patterns. I've highlighted this aspect in connection to the use of images, for instance (6.4.4): Images were used more and more frequently, probably due to the widened affordances of the communication form. However, there were bloggers in each period who didn't exploit these potentials and composed their posts without images. The increasing use of widgets and plug-ins (4.9.3) was probably also the result of experimentation with new functionalities and striving for individualised self-expression.

Variation can also be observed in connection to commercialisation: In 7.6.2, I've highlighted that the post genre *advertisement* showed a considerable increase towards period II.C, with authors using their leisure activity to advertise their own or third-party products. The personal weblog *Baby Blackbird*, for instance, blended the genres *sharing experience* and *advertisement*: While reflecting on her experiences as a mother, an author advertised children's clothes and listed sponsors in the sidebar. Other personal weblogs in period II.C followed similar strategies (for example, *Bay Area Mommy*). Concerning these cases, and especially with some authors advertising their own products (*Always Crave Cute*, for instance), the boundary between the personal weblog and the corporate blog grew increasingly fuzzy.

Rosenberg (2010) states that in "2008 […], blogging was already declared dead." This final phase in the history of the personal weblog, however, points in a different direction. It shows that the personal weblog is alive and kicking. By sharpening its profile, it competed successfully with social network sites, took part in recent developments concerning multimodality (6.4.3; 6.4.4) and modularity (4.9.3) and even found its way into new spheres of life (e-commerce). This final phase supports Rosenberg's prediction from 2010 (no pag.): "And that is why [personal] blogging will continue to thrive, as more ephemeral schemes for Web domination and profit-eking come and go."

9 Theoretical Concerns

In this chapter, I'd like to re-visit several aspects discussed in this book and interpret them in the light of two theoretical concerns. First, I'll look at questions of *explaining* genre change. Referring to the mechanisms introduced in 1.5.5, regenerative cycle and Keller's *Invisible Hand Theory*, I'll try to explain selected aspects of the history of the personal weblog. I'll then broaden the view to include issues of stability and change in web-based genres in general.

9.1 The Invisible Hand in the History of the Personal Weblog

Let's reflect on the spread of the post genre *sharing experience* after the advent of accessible blog systems. This new blog communication offered a way of fulfilling two basic human needs: the need for social contact and for sharing subjectively-important events. Some of the new blog-systems were highly accessible and, therefore, relatively undemanding in terms of financial and cognitive effort (4.2). In that way, they met another basic human need: Economy.[184] Composing a sharing experience post is an individual communicative act, but of course, not only one but many authors used the new blog communication form in such a way in order to meet their need for contact and sharing in an economical way. Particularly in the beginning, we can assume that these individual authors acted *independently* from one another. These intentional individual acts cumulated in the following results:

- The new communication form was dominated by the *sharing experience* post genre from its very beginning.
- This dominance was perceived by period I authors as alienating. Striving to preserve their and the weblog genre identities, they started to label the 'new' blogs as something different (8.2).
- The label *personal weblog*, which had been used only marginally before, became the established term for these 'new' blogs, maybe also as result of an Invisible Hand process (2.2.3). Obviously, this label was not only used by period I weblog authors, but also by the authors of personal weblogs themselves.
- The personal weblog emerged as a genre in its own right, marked considerably by the post genre *sharing experience* as "frequently travelled path" (Schryer 1993: 207), fulfilling the needs of contact and sharing.

184 Keller's famous example of the emergence of beaten tracks is based on that principle of economy.

In later periods, this pattern continued in two ways. First, it was recognised by authors as typical personal weblog practice, taken up and reproduced. McNeill (2009: 157) argues convincingly (referring to Miller & Shepherd 2004) that a voyeuristic need for authentic self-disclosure on the part of the potential blog audience was a decisive factor in the success of the sharing experience practice. Bloggers realised that they had to write "more personal, if not confessional" (McNeill 2009: 157) as compared to, for instance, filtering (7.2.1), in order to gain the audience's attention. Consequently, we can assume that bloggers also reproduced the sharing experience genre because they perceived it as socially successful. Second, we can assume that some authors of personal weblogs composed their blog posts *independently* from established practices, that is, without knowing about what other bloggers did. This would then be similar to the initial phase of the personal weblog outlined above. Therefore, the *continuation* of the sharing experience practice can be explained by the regenerative cycle (first scenario) and the Invisible Hand theory in its narrow reading (authors acting independently from one another, second scenario).

Another example for the Invisible Hand in the history of the personal weblog is the process of commercialisation discussed above (8.4). Some authors realised that personal weblogs provide an easy way (economy!) to reach certain audiences according to the principle of similarity (5.7.3) and make use of that for advertising (5.7.4, 7.3.2). Of course, the intention of the individual author was to generate profit. The un-intended (Invisible Hand) effects were:

- Commercial practices became more central to the personal weblog than ever before
- A potential conflict of interest (for example, for reviews) may have led to restricted cooperation, at least in some cases
- Therefore, authors had to confirm the authenticity of their opinions on *disclaimer* and *legal* sites

It's entirely possible that this practice of advertising will spread further in the coming years, either through the regenerative cycle or according to the narrow reading of the Invisible Hand theory.

9.2 Stability and Change of Web-Based Genres

My final point will address genres and their change on the web from a meta-level. When I began my studies on this subject a couple of years ago, one of the first volumes I got hold of was Mehler et al. (2011). In their introductory article, the authors compare genre research on the WWW to the adventure of riding "rough waves" (Santini et al. 2011: 9). Santini et al. (2011: 9) voice their impression that web-based documents are "much more uncontrolled and unpredictable" as compared to print-based/'old media' genres. Similarly, Giltrow & Stein (2009b: 9) also refer to the "chameleon-like properties of Internet genres". Therefore, recent research on web-based genres frequently dwells on a central paradox: Genres are *recurrent* forms of communicative action (1.1), but *grasping the recurrent* – assuming that it exists – in a WWW which is in "a permanent state of transition" (Crystal 2006: 16) appears to be highly challenging. Crowston & Kwásnik, therefore, provide the following characterisation of genres and their change on the web:

> New document genres have emerged, while older ones have blended, changed, and been incorporated into different social endeavors. Print-document genres adapted to the web, and new electronic genres emerging frequently, appear to be shuffled, disassembled, and then put together again, in a seemingly *chaotic* manner. (Crowston & Kwásnik 2005: 79, my emphasis, P. S.)[185]

This image of the chaotic is, for instance, supported by Pfänder & Wagner (2008: 153), who describe "una communidad virtual que cada día parece de crearse de nuevo" – a virtual community which appears to invent itself anew every day.

In the light of such an extent of heterogeneity, dynamics and innovation, it's hard to imagine how users find their way through the WWW at all. However, the opposite seems to be the case; people communicate on the WWW successfully and – I'm speculating here – mainly intuitively every day:

> Regardless of its potential, the celebration of the internet as new and revolutionary marks a stark contrast to the habitual, mundane communications that dominate the internet habits and practices of many ordinary users. (Lomborg 2014: 6–7)

Reasonably, we should therefore assume a minimum degree of stability under the fluid surface of the "rough waves" of the WWW for the communication not to fail. This stability is provided by, among others, recurrent communicative patterns, that is, genres. This stability is supported by a number of studies in Giltrow & Stein (2009b), which rather stress the *stability* and even accentuate transmedial continuity of web-based genres with regard to online diaries (McNeill 2009) and genres of digital folklore (Heyd 2009), for instance.

Form a methodological point of view, a shift is needed. Instead of 'fishing' for genres on today's WWW, I'd like to argue for a diachronic approach which traces the development of a single genre over time. Such an approach has been

185 See also Fraas (2009: 373), who describes the mediality of the Internet in terms such as *flexibility, dynamics, volatility, individualisation, difference, decentrialisation, interactivity, de-historicisation, and de-contextualisation* (my translation).

exemplified in this book. It enables us to comprehend genres as complex entities which combine both stability and change. In other words: While features on one dimension might currently be changing, others remain stable and provide the recurrence necessary for the genre not to collapse and for communication not to fail.

Regarding the weblog and the personal weblog, I've highlighted several recurrent features that characterise both genres from the emergence of the first weblogs in the 1990s until the youngest personal weblogs in the DIABLOC from 2012. (Personal) weblogs were mainly kept by *one* author only (5.4) as leisure activity (5.2). Posts were often composed following an "ethos of immediacy" (Reed 2005: 237) and according to a code of authenticity and truthfulness (5.6.1; 5.8.1). In this regard, the quality maxim played an important role, but 5.8 has shown that blog posts were also oriented towards the other Gricean maxims. A decisive aspect in all periods was the recognition of the audience (5.7.2), often imagined, according to the principle of similarity (5.7.3), as a group of similar-minded people, or even as friends/family (5.7.1). From a structural perspective, reverse chronological order was *the* dominant principle in all periods (4.3, 6.3.4.) If images were used, typically from II.B onwards, they were most likely snapshots taken by the author (6.4.3) used in an illustrative way (6.4.4). Posts are usually related to a specific post genre. The repertoire of these genres remained stable from period I onwards; however, there were significant quantitative changes (7.6.2) and, of course, changes also concerning the quality of certain post genres (for example, filtering, 7.2.1).

In addition to these relatively stable features, I've pointed out a number of changes: for instance, concerning the potentials of the communication form and the implementation of widgets (4.9.3), the use of hyperlinks (6.4.1) and images (6.4.3, 6.4.4) as well as post length (6.3.4) and others.[186] All in all, this book is an account of the fact that Saussure was right in stating that "l'immobilité absolue n'existe pas" ([Saussure]Wunderli 2013: 226) – absolute stability doesn't exist – but that different features (on different dimensions) of a genre may change at a different pace. Both continuity and change can be observed in one genre at a time. Continuity, that is, *recurrence*, ensures that a genre can serve as a cognitive device for successful communication (1.2).

Stability is not only provided by genres alone. Another important factor is that genre change mainly occurs according to certain patterns (1.5) and less in "a chaotic manner" (Crowston & Kwásnik 2005: 79). At several points in this

186 For a comprehensive overview, see chapter 8.

book, I've highlighted features of the personal weblog developing along the lines of an evolutionary change. I've also focussed on genre splits such as personal homepage → weblog, weblog → personal weblog, personal weblog → corporate weblog, as well as migration processes (for example, diary and others → personal weblog) and pattern embedding (reverse chronology on news pages → weblog, for instance). What these patterns of change all have in common is that they establish continuities within the change as, usually, relations to other recurrent patterns are established.

Even though the diachronic approach exemplified in this book, and propagated in this chapter, has provided interesting insights into the birth and subsequent development of the personal weblog, of course much remains to be done. As Saussure wrote exactly 100 years ago: "Le fleuve de la langue coule sans interruption." ([Saussure]Wunderli 2013: 290) – The river of language flows incessantly.

10 Summary and Outlook

"Long live the Weblog." With these words, Rebecca Blood (2004) closes her article on how *Blogging Software Reshapes the Blogging Community*. Blood's words are an expression of nostalgia, looking back to how blogging began with hand-coded weblogs which typically filtered the new and exciting World Wide Web. More than ten years later, in this book, I've attempted to provide a comprehensive linguistic account of the history of the personal weblog including its immediate ancestor, the weblog. Of course, this linguistic history had something to say about the decisive impact of blog software but also broadened its view to include genre birth and genre split (rather than genre death), and a whole network of other genres contributing to a vivid and interesting genre history, which is far from over with the end of this book.

At the beginning, I set the theoretical frame for this genre history by drawing on several schools of text and media linguistics. I introduced a dynamic genre model (1.1 to 1.3) and discussed several patterns of genre change (1.5). The various dimensions of the genre model – communication form, situation, multimodal structure and function – provided several lenses through which the personal weblog could be studied. I showed that a bundle of different methods from social sciences and linguistics was needed to do so (3.1) and provided an outline of the DIABLOC – the research corpus this study is based on (2.3). The main part of this book, then, approached the personal weblog and its immediate ancestor, the weblog, from various angles and gave an account of various phenomena, for example:

- The development of reverse chronological order, *the* structural feature of blogs in general (4.3, 6.3.4)
- The development of a complex blog communication form and various interrelations between the potentials provided by the communication form, and their specific use in personal weblogs (4.10.2)
- Who the bloggers actually were, how they imagined their audiences and what communicative guidelines they apparently followed (5.5 to 5.8)
- Changes (and continuities!) in what personal weblogs looked like (6.3), what kind of language bloggers used (6.4.2) as well as to what extent and how they relied on images (6.4.3; 6.4.4)
- *Purposes* of blogging via reconstruction of the genre profile of the personal weblog, including a repertoire of post genres (7.2 to 7.5), their frequencies (7.6.2) and intertextual relations (7.6.1).

The final chapters have provided a synthesis of these spotlights in various ways. Chapter 8 attempted to present a coherent history of the personal weblog in several phases and chapter 9 addressed theoretical questions about genre change concerning the personal weblog (9.1) as well as stability and change of web-based genres (9.2).

At the end of this book, much still remains to be done. For instance, the study I've presented here is highly dependent on the research corpus DIABLOC, whose period II was, in turn, compiled relying on *one* blog directory only. The results reported on here should certainly be qualified against blogs from other directories. Additionally, the Internet Archive only provides access to websites linked to by other sites. Therefore, I can't claim to be able to make any statements about personal weblogs that exist in isolation, without any other website pointing to them and also leave that to future research.

Furthermore, the categories and methods I used here should be developed further, possibly qualified but most certainly differentiated more, by comparative research on other web-based genres. Are there, for instance, sub-types of migration (1.5.4), as for instance Brock (2013) suggests? Comparative research is also needed to make more grounded statements about the influence of the communication form on the shape of genres. A diachronic corpus of web-based genres, annotated on several levels (including multimodal elements), might provide the basis for sound research in that direction.

As far as the personal weblog is concerned, this book has shown how Dave Winer's vision has become reality to a certain extent (see chapter 0):

> Imagine being able to find out what's *really* going on in anyone's life. What if everyone wrote about their issues. We could all learn from each other. Friendship would mean a lot more. We could grow more quickly, accomplish more in our lives, live more richly, have more fun. (Dave Winer 1995 in Rosenberg 2009: 53)

And even though Blood's nostalgia after a phase of profound genre change is more than understandable, the wealth and vividness of the history of the personal weblog are rather an incentive to rephrase Blood's nostalgic words into an exclamation:

Long live the Personal Weblog!

:-)

Part D: Appendix

11 Corpus and Citation

11.1 How the DIABLOC is Cited in this Book

Throughout this book, I have used the following way of citing corpus excerpts (DIABLOC and extended corpus):

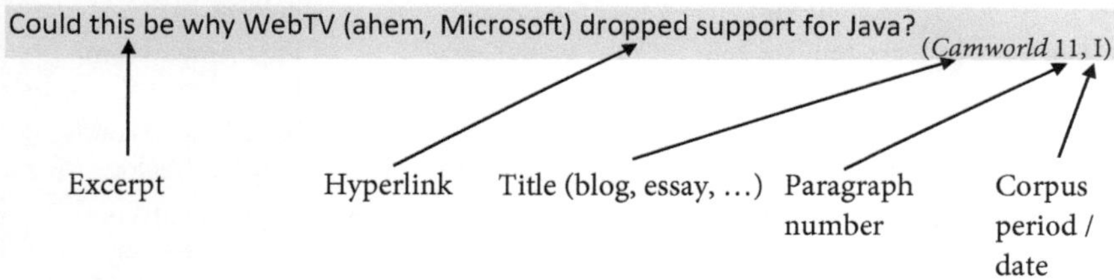

Excerpts were reproduced with as few changes as possible in order to preserve peculiarities in spelling, graphostylistics etc. I only modified font type and size in order to provide a more legible text.

Paragraph numbers refer to the automatic numbering attached by the coding software MaxQDA 10. The texts and coded passages published on the website www.pschildhauer.com follow the same numbering algorithm.

Additionally to the metadata illustrated above, some excerpts are labelled as *additional excerpt* – usually followed by some additional date or page title. On the one hand, these additional excerpts cite information contained on *about*-sites, *disclaimer*-sites etc. (Example 149). On the other hand, additional excerpts were used to present (parts of) blog posts which are not part of the blog-page of a personal weblog contained in the DIABLOC but on a page with earlier entries of the respective blog. In this case, I gave the exact date of the respective post.

The personal weblogs *A Food Lover's Journey*, *Alumimnum Lunch*, *Brookston Family Blog*, *Color Me Livid* and *Pop Goes the Artist* are cases for which the validity regarding a certain corpus period could not be proven (see 2.3.2). However, these personal weblogs provide interesting insights and neatly illustrate some points I made in this book (based on period-valid corpus texts); therefore I decided to cite them and mark the quotes as *additional excerpt* without a corpus period.

Texts of the extended corpus were cited by giving the most exact date possible. Blogging guides, essays, articles etc. that are part of the extended corpus (for example, Rebecca Blood's writings) are cited in the manner of excerpts, but using the common (year: page number) stylesheet.

11.2 URLs of DIABLOC Blog-Pages

Period I			
Bump	http://tinyurl.com/bump-weblog	memepool	http://tinyurl.com/memepool
Camworld	http://tinyurl.com/camworld-weblog	metacontent	http://tinyurl.com/metacontent-weblog
Cosmodrome	http://tinyurl.com/cosmodrome	linkwatcher metalog	http://tinyurl.com/linkwatcher
DanDot	http://tinyurl.com/dandot-weblog	Need to Know	http://tinyurl.com/ntk-weblog
EatonWeb	http://tinyurl.com/eatonweb	NowThis	http://tinyurl.com/nowthis-weblog
Flutterby	http://tinyurl.com/flutterby-weblog	The Obscure Store and Reading Room	http://tinyurl.com/obscure-weblog
Genehack	http://tinyurl.com/genehack-weblog	Perfect	http://tinyurl.com/perfect-weblog
GeoffsGems	http://tinyurl.com/geoffsgems	Peterme	http://tinyurl.com/peterme
Gulker	http://tinyurl.com/gulker-weblog	PigDog	http://tinyurl.com/pig-weblog
Hack the Planet	http://tinyurl.com/hack-weblog	rc3.org	http://tinyurl.com/rc3-weblog
Honeyguide	http://tinyurl.com/honey-weblog	ResearchBuzz	http://tinyurl.com/buzz-weblog
Infoshift	http://tinyurl.com/infoshift	RobotWisdom	http://tinyurl.com/robot-weblog
Linky & Dinky	http://tinyurl.com/linkydinky	Scripting News	http://tinyurl.com/scripting-weblog
LtSeek	http://tinyurl.com/ltseek-weblog	whump	http://tinyurl.com/whump-weblog
MacRonin	http://tinyurl.com/macronin	Windowseat	http://tinyurl.com/window-weblog

Period II.A			
&she travels onward	http://tinyurl.com/travels-pb	Andrew's Weblog	http://tinyurl.com/andrewblog-pb
(sometimes) cynical nature	http://tinyurl.com/cynical-pb	Andy Carvin's Waste of Bandwidth	http://tinyurl.com/carvin-pb
…Life of L…	http://tinyurl.com/life-l-pb	andy moore	http://tinyurl.com/moore-pb
Andy Merrett	http://tinyurl.com/merrett-pb	Angels dwell in ancient places	http://tinyurl.com/angels-pb
A la Coque Wonderland	http://tinyurl.com/wonder-pb	Angry Biker Chronicles	http://tinyurl.com/angrybiker-pb
at last there is nothing left to say	http://tinyurl.com/at-last-pb	Angry Pigeon	http://tinyurl.com/pigeon-pb
Anela Palekaiko	http://tinyurl.com/anela-pb	Ash says	http://tinyurl.com/ashsays-pb
1 Ideal Life	http://tinyurl.com/1ideal-pb	asiknewher	http://tinyurl.com/knewher-pb
2bitstudios	http://tinyurl.com/2bit-pb	Ask!	http://tinyurl.com/askblog-pb
3 Blind Mice	http://tinyurl.com/3blindmice-pb	Askingforthirds	http://tinyurl.com/askingfor-pb
4 moons	http://tinyurl.com/4moons-pb	Ask Jewels	http://tinyurl.com/jewels-pb
4.5% acidic	http://tinyurl.com/acidic-pb	Asleep in the City	http://tinyurl.com/asleep-pb
22 over 7	http://tinyurl.com/22over7-pb	aspirasi	http://tinyurl.com/aspirasi-pb
24 Hours To Live	http://tinyurl.com/24hours-pb	Astrology of Markets and Current Affairs	http://tinyurl.com/astrology-pb
a from l	http://tinyurl.com/afroml-pb	Astronaut Ambition	http://tinyurl.com/astronaut-pb
August Dreams	http://tinyurl.com/august-pb	At her master's feet	http://tinyurl.com/master-pb
A Whirlpool of Dimensional Thought	http://tinyurl.com/whirlpool-pb	at loggerheads	http://tinyurl.com/loggerheads-pb
abracapocus	http://tinyurl.com/abracapocus-pb	Atomic Raygun	http://tinyurl.com/raygun-pb
Absoblogging-lutely	http://tinyurl.com/abso-pb	AtomicPup's Blog	http://tinyurl.com/atompup-pb

Period II.A			
abuddhas memes	http://tinyurl.com/buddha-pb	attention whore	http://tinyurl.com/attention-pb
Ache	http://tinyurl.com/ache-pb	audi Olympics	http://tinyurl.com/audi-pb
ACME baseball	http://tinyurl.com/acme-pb	Auguries of Innocence	http://tinyurl.com/auguries-pb
across a roaring hill	http://tinyurl.com/hill-pb	Aunti Craker	http://tinyurl.com/craker-pb
Across the Brooklyn Bridge	http://tinyurl.com/bridge-pb	Bound and Gagged	http://tinyurl.com/gagged-pb
Across, Beyond, Through	http://tinyurl.com/across-pb	Botton Your Lip	http://tinyurl.com/botton-pb
AC's Blog	http://tinyurl.com/acblog-pb	Bottled Poetry	http://tinyurl.com/bottled-pb
Adambox	http://tinyurl.com/adambox-pb	Bosquet's Land	http://tinyurl.com/bosquet-pb
Adam's Weblog	http://tinyurl.com/adam-pb	boredwithporn	http://tinyurl.com/boredporn-pb
All back to mine	http://tinyurl.com/allback-pb	Boonville Blog	http://tinyurl.com/boonville-pb
all my tediousness upon thee	http://tinyurl.com/tedious-pb	Bourbon Rocks	http://tinyurl.com/bourbon-pb
All of this and Nothing	http://tinyurl.com/allnothing-pb	coffeestoned	http://tinyurl.com/coffee-pb
all the grrls hate her	http://tinyurl.com/hateher-pb	danny don't go	http://tinyurl.com/danny-pb
all about eve	http://tinyurl.com/allabouteve-pb	Getting it all out	http://tinyurl.com/getting-pb
Alliekat	http://tinyurl.com/alliekat-pb	Harmless Ranting	http://tinyurl.com/ranting-pb
AllJoneses	http://tinyurl.com/joneses-pb	Interalia	http://tinyurl.com/inter-pb
AllThings Heather	http://tinyurl.com/heather-pb	Lovin' Spoonfuls	http://tinyurl.com/spoon-pb
Alvaro Pascotto	http://tinyurl.com/alvaro-pb	ModBlog	http://tinyurl.com/modblog-pb
Always Almost Summer	http://tinyurl.com/summer-pb	My Life	http://tinyurl.com/mylife-pb

Period II.A			
AMR blog	http://tinyurl.com/amrblog-pb	Mysteries of M	http://tinyurl.com/mysteries-pb
AMS' Blog	http://tinyurl.com/amsblog-pb	'N' is for Neville	http://tinyurl.com/neville-pb
Amy L. Marr	http://tinyurl.com/amymarr-pb	angrybit	http://tinyurl.com/angry-pb
Amyo is a Geek	http://tinyurl.com/amyo-pb	AskmyPaul	http://tinyurl.com/askpaul-pb
amy's little life	http://tinyurl.com/amy-life-pb	random and odd	http://tinyurl.com/randomodd-pb
An Arsenal Fan View	http://tinyurl.com/arsenal-pb	reborn by design	http://tinyurl.com/reborndes-pb
an insider's view of life	http://tinyurl.com/insider-pb	tc123	http://tinyurl.com/tc123-pb
An Oasis	http://tinyurl.com/oasis-pb	The Allure of the Cheshire Cat	http://tinyurl.com/catblog-pb
Analogous Member	http://tinyurl.com/member-pb	the asylum	http://tinyurl.com/asylum-pb
And on that note…	http://tinyurl.com/onthatnote-pb	The EarthaKnittery	http://tinyurl.com/knittery-pb
Andrena's Ankh	http://tinyurl.com/ankhblog-pb	The Almighty Guru	http://tinyurl.com/guru-pb
andrewf my life	http://tinyurl.com/andrewf-pb	This is not a fairy tale	http://tinyurl.com/fairy-pb

Period II.B			
A Girl Worth Saving	http://tinyurl.com/saving-pb	Eat Train Sleep	http://tinyurl.com/train-pb
a stranger here myself	http://tinyurl.com/stranger-pb	Edibles and Economics	http://tinyurl.com/edible-pb
Alone in Tacoma	http://tinyurl.com/tacoma-pb	Electric Car Blogging	http://tinyurl.com/ecar-pb
alone with all my wrongs	http://tinyurl.com/wrongs-pb	Emerge	http://tinyurl.com/emerge-pb
Also But Only Not	http://tinyurl.com/alsoonlynot-pb	Ephemerist	http://tinyurl.com/ephemerist-pb
amiething goes	http://tinyurl.com/amiething-pb	esyLife	http://tinyurl.com/esylife-pb
aquababie's world	http://tinyurl.com/aqua-pb	Evan4sh	http://tinyurl.com/evan-pb
Armchair Literati	http://tinyurl.com/armchair-pb	evidently	http://tinyurl.com/evid-pb
ars scribendi	http://tinyurl.com/scribendi-pb	Excessively Diverted	http://tinyurl.com/divert-pb
Art by Serena	http://tinyurl.com/serena-pb	Experiencing the Journey	http://tinyurl.com/journ-pb
art of arguing in a phone box	http://tinyurl.com/phone-pb	Feed my Tummy	http://tinyurl.com/tummy-pb
art of living and dying	http://tinyurl.com/living-pb	Finance and Funnies	http://tinyurl.com/finan-pb
Asilive	http://tinyurl.com/asilive-pb	Firefighter Spot	http://tinyurl.com/fifispo-pb
Bert Gilbert and Carol Jones	http://tinyurl.com/bert-pb	First Person Irregular	http://tinyurl.com/firstpers-pb
brit blogger	http://tinyurl.com/britblogger-pb	Flying Confessions	http://tinyurl.com/confe-pb
Cheek and Bluster	http://tinyurl.com/cheekbluster-pb	Food and Wine 100	http://tinyurl.com/foodwine-pb
Chef's Widow	http://tinyurl.com/widow-pb	Freak Parade	http://tinyurl.com/freak-pb
Cheré takes on the world	http://tinyurl.com/chere-pb	Freya Bletsoe's Personal Blog	http://tinyurl.com/freya-pb
Choc's Corner	http://tinyurl.com/chocscorner-pb	Funny Brew	http://tinyurl.com/fubrew-pb

Period II.B			
Chris Loyd	http://tinyurl.com/chrisloyd-pb	Getting Hitched	http://tinyurl.com/hitch-pb
Civin.org	http://tinyurl.com/civin-pb	Good Pancreas	http://tinyurl.com/panc-pb
class (of something)	http://tinyurl.com/classsomething-pb	Head in Knots	http://tinyurl.com/headknots-pb
Clog Almanac	http://tinyurl.com/clogalmanac-pb	Heaven nose	http://tinyurl.com/heavnos-pb
cocktail nerd	http://tinyurl.com/cocktail-pb	Hello Stranger	http://tinyurl.com/strang-pb
Comedy Writer	http://tinyurl.com/comedy-pb	Her Heart my Hands	http://tinyurl.com/herheart-pb
Compassionate Council	http://tinyurl.com/council-pb	Here on Columbia Ave	http://tinyurl.com/colave-pb
CT Fishing Reports	http://tinyurl.com/fishing-pb	herzeleid knits	http://tinyurl.com/herzknit-pb
Cult of Qelqoth	http://tinyurl.com/qelqoth-pb	House renovation on a budget	http://tinyurl.com/renov-pb
Cupcake Pajamas	http://tinyurl.com/cupcake-pb	I love the smoke	http://tinyurl.com/smoke-pb
Da Boss and BryGuy	http://tinyurl.com/boss-pb	I love you too much	http://tinyurl.com/toolove-pb
Daily Home Renovation Tips	http://tinyurl.com/renovation-pb	It's ok to cry here	http://tinyurl.com/oktocry-pb
Dale Hay	http://tinyurl.com/dalehay-pb	Jenn's Travel Close Up	http://tinyurl.com/jenn-pb
Dandy Darkly	http://tinyurl.com/dandy-pb	Lace & Stars	http://tinyurl.com/lacestar-pb
Darlene Wrecker's	http://tinyurl.com/darlene-pb	Life passed by	http://tinyurl.com/lifeby-pb
Darnell Clayton	http://tinyurl.com/clayton-pb	Lil Miss Vee Vee's Thoughts	http://tinyurl.com/vee-pb
David McFarlane	http://tinyurl.com/farlane-pb	London Hotel News	http://tinyurl.com/londhot-pb
David Parkinson	http://tinyurl.com/parki-pb	Overbloated	http://tinyurl.com/overbl-pb
Dead Rooster	http://tinyurl.com/rooster-pb	politics is applesauce	http://tinyurl.com/applesauce-pb

Period II.B			
Deglazed	http://tinyurl.com/deglazed-pb	princess portal	http://tinyurl.com/princess-pb
Delaney's World	http://tinyurl.com/delaney-pb	Ria	http://tinyurl.com/riablog-pb
Dementia Thoughts	http://tinyurl.com/dementia-pb	Scrapbooking with Words	http://tinyurl.com/scrap-pb
Die Bergziege	http://tinyurl.com/berg-pb	Sanitywarp	http://tinyurl.com/sanity-pb
Dig your own hole	http://tinyurl.com/hole-pb	Scott Janz	http://tinyurl.com/scott-pb
Double Edged Sword	http://tinyurl.com/double-pb	sEmi	http://tinyurl.com/semi-pb
Dressed in Style	http://tinyurl.com/dress-pb	Sentinent Wannabe	http://tinyurl.com/sentinent-pb
Drink this Blog	http://tinyurl.com/drink-pb	September 10th	http://tinyurl.com/sept10-pb
dysfunctional playground	http://tinyurl.com/playground-pb	The Core	http://tinyurl.com/thecore-pb
E-Housewife	http://tinyurl.com/ehouse-pb	The Far Corner	http://tinyurl.com/corner-pb
East Village	http://tinyurl.com/east-pb	The Honeymoon Phase	http://tinyurl.com/honeymoon-pb
Eat my Yard	http://tinyurl.com/yard-pb	The Undomestic Princess	http://tinyurl.com/princ-pb

Period II.C			
…i digress	http://tinyurl.com/digress-pb	Blonde Girl Chronicles	http://tinyurl.com/blonde-pb
100 Miles	http://tinyurl.com/miles-pb	Blonde Nonbeliever	http://tinyurl.com/nonbeliever-pb
100 Ways to Coupon	http://tinyurl.com/coupon-pb	bLTravels	http://tinyurl.com/bltravels-pb
365+ photo	http://tinyurl.com/365photo-pb	Blushes and Shimmy Shakes	http://tinyurl.com/blushes-pb
50 years of Angst	http://tinyurl.com/angst-pb	Boston Knuckle Head	http://tinyurl.com/knuckle-pb
A Blog about what	http://tinyurl.com/what-pb	Confusion and Frustration	http://tinyurl.com/confusion-pb
A Blog in the Rough	http://tinyurl.com/rough-pb	David's Musings	http://tinyurl.com/david-pb
A Mandatory Rant	http://tinyurl.com/rant-pb	dogBoi	http://tinyurl.com/dogboi-pb
Almost Somewhat positive	http://tinyurl.com/positive-pb	Gadget Blurb	http://tinyurl.com/gadget-pb
Always Crave Cute	http://tinyurl.com/cravecute-pb	Gardening to Distraction	http://tinyurl.com/gardening-pb
Always Writing	http://tinyurl.com/writing-pb	Geeker's Heaven	http://tinyurl.com/geeker-pb
Amanda Clarison	http://tinyurl.com/clarison-pb	Gentle Apocalypse	http://tinyurl.com/gentle-pb
American Debt	http://tinyurl.com/amdebt-pb	Gently Said	http://tinyurl.com/gently-pb
An Ongoing Effort	http://tinyurl.com/effort-pb	Girlfriends are like shoes	http://tinyurl.com/girlfriends-pb
And at what place	http://tinyurl.com/place-pb	Gluten Free Betsy	http://tinyurl.com/gluten-pb
Andy hmmm	http://tinyurl.com/hmmm-pb	Graceful Glutton	http://tinyurl.com/glutton-pb
Angel eyes	http://tinyurl.com/angeleyes-pb	Grandma's Briefs	http://tinyurl.com/briefs-pb
Anita's notebook	http://tinyurl.com/anita-pb	Great Moments with Mister Lincoln	http://tinyurl.com/lincoln-pb
Anything at Anytime	http://tinyurl.com/anything-pb	Greedy Rosie	http://tinyurl.com/rosie-pb

Period II.C			
Are we nearly there yet	http://tinyurl.com/thereyet-pb	Greg Kendall Ball	http://tinyurl.com/greg-pb
Army Mom	http://tinyurl.com/army-pb	Hands, House, and Heart Full	http://tinyurl.com/housefull-pb
around my kitchen table	http://tinyurl.com/kitchen-pb	Happy Booker	http://tinyurl.com/booker-pb
Damn You Technology	http://tinyurl.com/damn-pb	Heart that burns	http://tinyurl.com/heartburns-pb
Artist Obscure	http://tinyurl.com/artist-pb	Hello Interloper	http://tinyurl.com/helloint-pb
ArtLove	http://tinyurl.com/artlove-pb	Hey it's Pat Ryan's Blog	http://tinyurl.com/patryan-pb
As a Star	http://tinyurl.com/star-pb	Historical Digression	http://tinyurl.com/histdig-pb
Asian Polyglot	http://tinyurl.com/asian-pb	Horses & Heels	http://tinyurl.com/horses-pb
Ask Temptress	http://tinyurl.com/temptress-pb	I am the Man letters	http://tinyurl.com/letters-pb
Baby Blackbird	http://tinyurl.com/baby-pb	In a Silent Way	http://tinyurl.com/silent-pb
Back2Brooklyn	http://tinyurl.com/back2brooklyn-pb	In this hectic life	http://tinyurl.com/hectic-pb
Bankrupt Dad	http://tinyurl.com/bankdad-pb	John P. Logsdon	http://tinyurl.com/logsdon-pb
Barefoot Travelers	http://tinyurl.com/barefoot-pb	Just another crazy day	http://tinyurl.com/crazyday-pb
Bay Area Mommy	http://tinyurl.com/baymum-pb	Lime Green Movie Girl	http://tinyurl.com/limegr-pb
Bboy	http://tinyurl.com/bboy-pb	Living authentically	http://tinyurl.com/authent-pb
Beautiful Dreamer	http://tinyurl.com/dreamer-pb	Living the Dream	http://tinyurl.com/dream-pb
Beautifully Brainy Music	http://tinyurl.com/music-pb	Love and Literature	http://tinyurl.com/lovlit-pb
Before Charlee's 30	http://tinyurl.com/charlee-pb	Maternal Experiment	http://tinyurl.com/matexp-pb
Being Alexus	http://tinyurl.com/alexus-pb	Meanbean	http://tinyurl.com/meanbean-pb

Period II.C			
Bella Vida	http://tinyurl.com/bella-pb	Melanie's Blog	http://tinyurl.com/melblog-pb
Beloved Parrot	http://tinyurl.com/parrot-pb	Mind The Gap	http://tinyurl.com/mindgap-pb
Ben Acheson	http://tinyurl.com/acheson-pb	Musings from the Slush Pile	http://tinyurl.com/slush-pb
Beneath the glass	http://tinyurl.com/glass-pb	My Right Hip	http://tinyurl.com/righthip-pb
Better at ev.	http://tinyurl.com/betterat-pb	Of Interest to Me	http://tinyurl.com/ofinttome-pb
Bhutan Diary	http://tinyurl.com/bhutan-pb	Pomgranate Tutu	http://tinyurl.com/tutu-pb
Bill Bennett	http://tinyurl.com/bill-pb	Pukeko Flat	http://tinyurl.com/flat-pb
Biscuits and Buns	http://tinyurl.com/biscuits-pb	Put it to bed	http://tinyurl.com/tobed-pb
Bizzie Mommy	http://tinyurl.com/bizzie-pb	Random Feet	http://tinyurl.com/feet-pb
Blah blah Blog	http://tinyurl.com/blahblah-pb	Rants of the Uninformed	http://tinyurl.com/unrants-pb
Blog to great	http://tinyurl.com/great-pb	Ravenwood Ranch	http://tinyurl.com/ranch-pb
Blogs are for Losers	http://tinyurl.com/loser-pb	Rebelle Fleur	http://tinyurl.com/fleur-pb

Personal Weblogs Cited Additionally			
A Food Lover's Journey	http://tinyurl.com/foodlov-pb	Alumimnum Lunch	http://tinyurl.com/lunch-pb
ColorMe Livid	http://tinyurl.com/colorme-pb	Pop goes the Artist	http://tinyurl.com/popartist-pb
The Brookston Family Blog	http://tinyurl.com/brookston-pb		

11.3 Extended Corpus

11.3.1 Blogging Guides

Period I	-
Period II.A	Bausch, P. et al. (2002). *We blog: Publishing Online with Weblogs.* Indianapolis, IN: Wiley Pub. Blood, R. (2002). *The Weblog Handbook: Practical Advice on Creating and Maintaining Your Blog*. Cambridge (MA): Perseus. Stauffer, T. (2002). *Blog On: The Essential Guide to Building Dynamic Weblogs*. Berkeley, Calif.: Osborne.
Period II.B	Hayder, H. (2006). *WordPress Complete: A Comprehensive, Step-By-Step Guide on How to Set Up, Customize, and Market Your Blog Using WordPress*. Birmingham, UK: Packt Publ. Lee, W. M. (2006). *The Rational Guide to Google Blogger*. Rollinsfold, NH: Rational Press. Stauffer, T. (2008). *How to Do Everything with your Web 2.0 Blog*. New York: McGraw-Hill. Yang, J. (2006). *The Rough Guide to Blogging*. London: Penguin.
Period II.C	Cole, A. (2010). *Build Your Own Wicked WordPress Themes.* Collingwood: SitePoint. Hussey, T. (2011). *Using WordPress*. Indianapolis, Ind: Que. Frankemölle, G. (2010). *Weblog mit WordPress 3: Das grosse Buch.* Düsseldorf: Data-Becker. White, C.& Biggs, J. (2011). *Bloggers Boot Camp: Learning How to Build, Write, and Run a Successful Blog*. Waltham, MA: Focal Press. Wright-Porto, H. (2010). *Beginning Google Blogger*. New York: Springer. Wright-Porto, H. (2011). *Creative blogging: Your first Steps to a Successful Blog*. [Berkeley, Calif.], New York: Springer.

11.3.2 FAQ-Sites and Tutorials

PyraLabs (2002). How To. http://tinyurl.com/pyra02 (28.12.2015).

Coggins, S. A. M. (2004). Web Logs How Tos Index. http://tinyurl.com/coggins04 (28.12.2015).

Improbulus (2005). Display links to your posts via Blogger Backlinks, Icerocket Link Tracker etc. http://tinyurl.com/improb05 (28.12.2015).

LiveJournal (2012). State of the Goat 2012. http://tinyurl.com/ljrel12 (28.12.2015).

WordPress Codex (2005). WordPress Features. http://tinyurl.com/wpcod05 (28.12.2015).

SixApart (2003a). MovableType: Features. http://tinyurl.com/sixap03a (28.12.2015).

Six Apart (2003b). TypePad Personal Weblogging Service: Features and Pricing. http://tinyurl.com/sixap03b (28.12.2015).

Tumblr, Inc. (2009). Tumblr is the easiest way to express yourself. http://tinyurl.com/tumbab09 (28.12.2015).

Tumblr, Inc. (2010). About us. http://tinyurl.com/tumab2010 (28.12.2015).

11.3.3 Bloggers' Reflections

Barrett, C. (1999a). Anatomy of a Weblog. http://tinyurl.com/barrett99a (28.12.2015).

Barrett, C. (1999b). More About Weblogs. http://tinyurl.com/barrett99b (28.12.2015).

Benton, M. (2006a). Why I Blog: Part 1. In: Reconstruction 6 (4). http://tinyurl.com/benton06a (28.12.2015).

Benton, M. (2006b). Why I Blog: Part 2. In: Reconstruction 6 (4). http://tinyurl.com/benton06b (28.12.2015).

Blood, R. (2000). Weblogs: A History and Perspective. http://tinyurl.com/blood2000 (28.12.2015).

Blood, R. (2004). How Blogging Software Reshapes the Online Community. In: Communications of the ACM 47 (12), 53–55.

Brook, D. (2002). Why I Fucking Hate Weblogs! http://tinyurl.com/hateweblg (28.12.2015).

Coates, T. (2003). On Permalinks and Paradigms… http://tinyurl.com/coates03 (28.12.2015).

Heijman, Marline (2010). Blogging and IKEA. http://tinyurl.com/blogIKEA (28.12.2015).

Hourihan, M. (2002). What We're Doing When We Blog. http://tinyurl.com/megnut2002 (28.12.2015).

Mullenweg, M. (2003). The Blogging Software Dilemma. http://tinyurl.com/matt003 (28.12.2015).

Winer, D. (2001). The history of weblogs. http://tinyurl.com/winer01 (28.12.2015).

Winer, D. (2003a). RSS 2.0 Specification. http://tinyurl.com/winer03 (28.12.2015).

Winer, D. (2003b). What Makes a Weblog a Weblog? http://tinyurl.com/winer03b (28.12.2015).

Winer, D. (2004). RSS History. http://tinyurl.com/winer04 (28.12.2015).

List of Illustrations

Diagrams

Examples

Figures

Tables

References

Adamzik, K. (1995). *Textsorten – Texttypologie: Eine kommentierte Bibliographie.* Münster: Nodus-Publikationen.

Adamzik, K. (2004). *Textlinguistik: Eine einführende Darstellung.* Tübingen: M. Niemeyer.

Adamzik, K. (2011). Textsortennetze. In S. Habscheid (ed.): *Textsorten, Handlungsmuster, Oberflächen: Linguistische Typologien der Kommunikation.* Berlin, New York: de Gruyter, 367–385.

Adolphs, S. (2006). *Introducing Electronic Text Analysis: A Practical Guide for Language and Literary Studies.* London: Routledge.

Androutsopoulos, J. (2010). Multimodal – intertextuell – heteroglossisch: Sprach-Gestalten in "Web 2.0"-Umgebungen. In A. Deppermann & A. Linke (eds.): *Sprache intermedial: Stimme und Schrift, Bild und Ton.* Berlin: Walter de Gruyter, 419–446.

Anonymous (1998). To Reveal or not to Reveal: A Theoretical Model of Anonymous Communication. *Communication Theory* 8 (4), 381–407. http://onlinelibrary.wiley.com/doi/10.1111/j.1468-2885.1998.tb00226.x/pdf.

Askehave, I. (1999). Communicative Purpose as Genre Determinant. *Hermes* 23, 13–23. http://download2.hermes.asb.dk/archive/FreeH/H23_02.pdf (28.12.2015).

Askehave, I. & A. E. Nielsen (2005). Digital Genres: A Challenge to Traditional Genre Theory. *Information Technology & People* 18 (2), 120–141.

Askehave, I. & J. M. Swales (2001). Genre Identification and Communicative Purpose: A Problem and a Possible Solution. *Applied Linguistics* 22 (2), 195–212. http://tinyurl.com/askehaveswales (28.12.2015).

Baikie, K. & K. Wilhelm (2005). Emotional and Physical Health Benefits of Expressive Writing. *Advances in Psychiatric Treatment* 11 (5), 338–346. http://tinyurl.com/baikie05 (28.12.2015).

Balakina, J. (2011). *Anglicisms in Russian and German Blogs: A Comparative Analysis.* Frankfurt am Main: Peter Lang.

Baldry, A. & P. J. Thibault (2006). *Multimodal Transcription and Text Analysis.* London: Equinox Pub.

Baron, N. S. (2008). *Always on: Language in an Online and Mobile World.* Oxford: OUP.

Barrett, C. (1999a). Anatomy of a Weblog. http://tinyurl.com/barrett99a (28.12.2015).

Barrett, C. (1999b). More About Weblogs. http://tinyurl.com/barrett99b (28.12.2015).

Bateman, J. A. (2011). *Multimodality and Genre: A Foundation for the Systematic Analysis of Multimodal Documents*. Basingstoke: Palgrave Macmillan.

Baumer, E. et al. (2008). Exploring the Role of the Reader in the Activity of Blogging. In M. Burnett (ed.): *CHI 2008: The 26th Annual CHI Conference on Human Factors in Computing Systems*. New York: Association for Computing Machinery, 1111–1120.

Bausch, P. et al. (2002). *We Blog: Publishing Online with Weblogs*. Indianapolis, IN: Wiley Pub.

Bazerman, C. (1994). Systems of Genre and the Enactment of Social Intentions. In A. Freedman & P. Medway (eds.): *Genre and the New Rhetoric*. London, Bristol, PA: Taylor & Francis, 79–101.

Beißwenger, M. (2002). Das interaktive Lesespiel: Chat-Kommunikation als mediale Inszenierung. In M. Beißwenger (ed.): *Chat-Kommunikation: Sprache, Interaktion, Sozialität und Identität in synchroner computervermittelter Kommunikation*. Stuttgart: ibidem, 79–138.

Benninghaus, H. (2007). *Deskriptive Statistik: Eine Einführung für Sozialwissenschaftler*. Wiesbaden: VS.

Bergs, A. (2005). *Social Networks and Historical Sociolinguistics: Studies in Morphosyntactic Variation in the Paston letters (1421–1503)*. Berlin, New York: Mouton de Gruyter.

Bergs, A. (2006). Analyzing Online Communication from a Social Network Point of View: Questions, Problems, Perspectives. *Language@Internet*. http://www.languageatinternet.org/articles/2006/371 (28.12.2015).

Berkenkotter, C. & T. N. Huckin (1993). Rethinking Genre from a Sociocognitive Perspective. *Written Communication* 10 (4), 475–509.

Berkenkotter, C. & T. N. Huckin (1995). *Genre Knowledge in Disciplinary Communication: Cognition/Culture/Power*. Hillsdale, N.J: Erlbaum.

Biber, D. (1988). *Variation Across Speech and Writing*. Cambridge: CUP.

Bittner, J. (2003). *Digitalität, Sprache, Kommunikation: Eine Untersuchung zur Medialität von digitalen Kommunikationsformen und Textsorten und deren varietätenlinguistischer Modellierung*. Berlin: E. Schmidt.

Blood, R. (2000). Weblogs: A History and Perspective. http://www.rebeccablood.net/essays/weblog_history.html (28.12.2015).

Blood, R. (2002). *The Weblog Handbook: Practical Advice on Creating and Maintaining your Blog*. Cambridge (MA): Perseus.

Blood, R. (2004). How Blogging Software Reshapes the Online Community. *Communications of the ACM* 47 (12), 53–55. http://tinyurl.com/btg2yps (15.12.2011).

Bolter, J. D. & R. Grusin (2001). *Remediation*. Cambridge, Mass: MIT Press.

boyd, d. (2004). Broken Metaphors: Blogging as Liminal Practice. http://tinyurl.com/boyd2004 (28.12.2015).

boyd, d. et al. (2010). Tweet, Tweet, Retweet: Conversational Aspects of Retweeting on Twitter. http://tinyurl.com/boydetal2010 (28.12.2015).

boyd, d. & N. Ellison (2007). Social Network Sites: Definition, History, and Scholarship. *Journal of Computer-Mediated Communication* 13 (1), 210–230. http://jcmc.indiana.edu/vol13/issue1/boyd.ellison.html (28.12.2015).

Brake, D. (2007). Personal Webloggers and their Audiences: Who do They Think They are Talking to. http://tinyurl.com/brake2007 (28.12.2015).

Brandt, M. & I. Rosengren (1992). Zur Illokutionsstruktur von Texten. *Zeitschrift für Literaturwissenschaft und Linguistik* 22 (86), 9–51. http://pao.chadwyck.co.uk/PDF/1350905773281.pdf (28.12.2015).

Brinker, K. (2000a). Textfunktionale Analyse. In K. Brinker et al. (eds.): *Linguistics of Text and Conversation: An International Handbook of Contemporary Research:* Mouton de Gruyter, 175–186.

Brinker, K. (2000b). Textstrukturanalyse. In K. Brinker et al. (eds.): *Linguistics of Text and Conversation: An International Handbook of Contemporary Research:* Mouton de Gruyter, 164–175.

Brinker, K. (2010). *Linguistische Textanalyse: Eine Einführung in Grundbegriffe und Methoden*. Berlin: E. Schmidt.

Brock, A. (2004). *Blackadder, Monty Python und Red Dwarf: Eine linguistische Untersuchung britischer Fernsehkomödien*. Tübingen: Stauffenburg Verlag.

Brock, A. (2009). Zur Variation komischer Textsorten – der Fall britischer Fernsehcomedies. In F. Lenz (ed.): *Schlüsselqualifikation Sprache.: Anforderungen – Standards – Vermittlung*. Frankfurt am Main: Peter Lang, 235–253.

Brock, A. (2013). On the Corruption of Text Types: The Cases of Comedy and Readers' Commentaries in Online Newspapers. In A. Ammermann et al. (eds.): *Facets of Linguistics*. Frankfurt am Main: Peter Lang, 63–74.

Bruns, A. & J. Jacobs (2006). Introduction. In A. Bruns & J. Jacobs (eds.): *Uses of Blogs*. New York: Peter Lang, 1–7.

Brüsemeister, T. (2000). *Qualitative Forschung: Ein Überblick*. Wiesbaden: Westdeutscher Verlag.

Buckingham, D. (2008). Introducing Identity. In D. Buckingham (ed.): *Youth, Identity, and Digital Media*. Cambridge, Mass.: MIT Press, 1–24.

Bündgens-Kosten, J. (forthc.). Das Tagebuch im Internet? Wie Lehrerinnen und Lehrer Blogs im Unterricht einführen. In E. M. Eckkrammer et al. (eds.): *Medienlinguistik 3.0: Formen und Wirkung von Textsorten im Zeitalter des Social Web*. Berlin: Frank & Thimme.

Burger, H. & M. Luginbühl (2014). *Mediensprache: Eine Einführung in Sprache und Kommunikationsformen der Massenmedien*. Berlin [u.a.]: de Gruyter.

Carlson, N. (2011). The Real History of Twitter. http://tinyurl.com/carlson2011 (25.07.2014).

Chesher, C. (2005). Blogs and the Crisis of Authorship. http://incsub.org/blogtalk/?page_id=40 (25.07.2014).

Claridge, C. (2011). *Hyperbole in English: A Corpus-based Study of Exaggeration*. Cambridge: CUP.

Croft, W. (2000). *Explaining Language Change: An Evolutionary Approach*. Harlow: Longman.

Crowston, K. & B. Kwásnik (2005). Introduction to the Special Issue: Genres of Digital Documents. *Information Technology & People* 18 (2), 76–88 (12.10.2011).

Crystal, D. (2006). *Language and the Internet*. Cambridge: CUP.

Crystal, D. (2011). *Internet Linguistics: A Student Guide*. Abingdon: Routledge.

Dang-Anh, M. & J. O. Rüdiger (2015). From Frequency to Sequence: How Quantitative Methods can Inform Qualitative Analysis of Digital Media Discourse. *10plus1: Living Linguistics* 1 (1), 57–73. http://tinyurl.com/danganhruediger (28.12.2015).

Devitt, A. J. (2009). Re-fusing Form in Genre Study. In J. Giltrow & D. Stein (eds.): *Genres in the Internet: Issues in the Theory of Genre*. Amsterdam, Philadelphia: Benjamins, 27–47.

Dittmann, M. (2001). *Sprachverwendung im Internet: Untersuchungen zu Sprache und Nutzung des Internet Relay Chat (IRC) in Deutschland und Frankreich*. Sarlat: Éditions Indoles.

Dunning, T. (1993). Accurate Methods for the Statistics of Surprise and Coincidence. *Computational Linguistics* 19 (1), 61–74.

Dürscheid, C. (2005). Medien, Kommunikationsformen, kommunikative Gattungen. *Linguistik online* 22 (1), 1–16. http://www.linguistik-online.de/22_05/duerscheid.pdf (28.12.2015).

Eckkrammer, E. M. (2002). Brauchen wir einen neuen Textbegriff?. In U. Fix et al. (eds.): *Brauchen wir einen neuen Textbegriff? Antworten auf eine Preisfrage*. Frankfurt am Main: Peter Lang, 31–57.

Eckkrammer, E. M. & M. E. Eder (2000). *(Cyber)Diskurs zwischen Konvention und Revolution. Eine multilinguale textlinguistische Analyse von Gebrauchstextsorten im realen und virtuellen Raum*. Frankfurt am Main: Peter Lang.

Efimova, L. (2009). *Passion at Work: Blogging Practices of Knowledge Workers*. Dissertation. Universiteit Utrecht, Enschede.

Efimova, L. & J. Grudin (2007). Crossing Boundaries: A Case Study of Employee Blogging: *Proceedings of the 40th Annual Hawaii International Conference on System Sciences*. Los Alamitos, Calif: IEEE Computer Society Press.

Efimova, L. & A. de Moor (2005). Beyond Personal Webpublishing: An Exploratory Study of Conversational Blogging Practices. http://tinyurl.com/efi2005 (28.12.2015).

Erickson, T. (2000). Making Sense of Computer-Mediated Communication (CMC): Conversations as Genres, CMC Systems as Genre Ecologies. http://tinyurl.com/erikson2000 (28.12.2015).

Ermert, K. (1979). *Briefsorten: Untersuchung zu Theorie und Empirie der Textklassifikation*. Tübingen: Niemeyer.

Ess, C. & AoIR ethics working committee (2002). Ethical Decision-Making and Internet Research: Recommendations from the AoIR Ethics Working Committee. http://tinyurl.com/87swmuj (28.12.2015).

Feistel, K. (2013). *Weiterbildungsfinanzierung in kommunalen Unternehmen: Eine explorative Studie vor dem Hintergrund bildungsökonomischer Theorien*. Hamburg: Kovač.

Fraas, C. (2009). Online-Diskurse: Neue Impulse für die Diskursforschung. In O. Stenschke & S. Wichter (eds.): *Wissenstransfer und Diskurs*. Frankfurt am Main [u.a.]: Lang, 363–379.

Fritz, G. (2011). Texttypen in wissenschaftlichen Blogs: Eine exemplarische Analyse am Beispiel des Language Log. In G. Fritz & T. Gloning (eds.): *Digitale Wissenschaftskommunikation – Formate und ihre Nutzung*. Gießen: Gießener Elektronische Bibliothek, 205–287.

Fritz, G. (2013). *Dynamische Texttheorie*. Gießen: Gießener Elektronische Bibliothek.

Fritz, G. & A. Bader (2010). Digitale Formate in der Wissenschaftskommunikation: Konstellationen und Konvergenzen. In H.-J. Bucher (ed.): *Neue Medien – neue Formate: Ausdifferenzierung und Konvergenz in der Medienkommunikation*. Frankfurt am Main [u.a.]: Campus-Verl, 337–355.

Gallery, H. (2000). "bin ich-klick ich" – Variable Anonymität im Chat. In Caja Thimm (ed.): *Soziales im Netz: Sprache, Beziehungen und Kommunikationskulturen im Internet*. Wiesbaden: Opladen, 71–87.

Gansel, C. (2011). *Textsortenlinguistik*. Stuttgart: UTB.

Garcia, A. u. J. J. (1999). The Eyes of the Beholder: Understanding the Turn-Taking System in Quasi-Synchronous Computer-Mediated Communication. *Research on Language and Social Interaction* 32 (4), 337–367.

Gerdes, M. de (2005). Textual and Linguistic Attributes of American English Weblogs. In P. Schlobinski & T. Siever (eds.): *Sprachliche und textuelle Merkmale in Weblogs: Ein internationales Projekt*. Hannover: networx, 86–130.

Giltrow, J. (1994). Genre and the Pragmatic Concept of Background Knowledge. In A. Freedman & P. Medway (eds.): *Genre and the New Rhetoric*. London, Bristol, PA: Taylor & Francis, 155–178.

Giltrow, J. (2013). Genre and Computer-Mediated Communication. In S. Herring et al. (eds.): *Pragmatics of Computer-mediated Communication*. Berlin: De Gruyter Mouton, 717–737.

Giltrow, J. & D. Stein (2009a). Genres in the Internet: Innovation, Evolution, and Genre Theory. In J. Giltrow & D. Stein (eds.): *Genres in the Internet: Issues in the Theory of Genre*. Amsterdam: Benjamins, 1–25.

Giltrow, J. & D. Stein (eds.) (2009b). *Genres in the Internet: Issues in the Theory of Genre*. Amsterdam, Philadelphia: Benjamins.

Giora, R. (1997). Discourse Coherence and Theory of Relevance: Stumbling Blocks in Search of a Unified Theory. *Journal of Pragmatics* 27, 17–34.

Glaser, B. G. & J. Holton (2004). Remodeling Grounded Theory. *Forum: Qualitative Social Research* 5 (2). http://www.qualitative-research.net/index.php/fqs/article/view/607/1316 (21.01.2014).

Goffman, E. (1983). *Forms of Talk*. Philadelphia: University of Pennsylvania Press.

Grice, H. P. (1975). Logic and Conversation. In P. Cole & J. Morgan (eds.): *Speech Acts*. New York: Academic Press, 41–58.

Gries, S. T. (2009). *Statistics for Linguistics with R: A Practical Introduction*. Berlin, New York: Mouton de Gruyter.

Grieve, J. et al. (2011). Variation Among Blogs: A Multi-Dimensional Analysis. In A. Mehler et al. (eds.): *Genres on the Web: Computational Models and Empirical Studies*. Dordrecht: Springer, 303–322.

Grube, P. (2011). *Chatten im Fremdsprachenunterricht: Möglichkeiten und Grenzen webchat-basierter Methoden auf dem Weg zum mündlichen Sprachgebrauch am Beispiel der Zielsprache Englisch*. Wissenschaftliche Hausarbeit zur Ersten Staatsprüfung für das Lehramt an Gymnasien. Universität Halle-Wittenberg, Halle. Institut für Anglistik / Amerikanistik.

Grube, P. (2013). Anything goes – everything done? Personal Weblogs unter diachroner Perspektive. Tagungsvortrag auf der Tagung der DGPuK-FG "Mediensprache und Mediendiskurse" 2013 in Trier. http://roughwaves.files.

wordpress.com/2013/03/anything-goes-everything-done-manuskript.pdf (28.12.2015).

Gumbrecht, M. (2004). Blogs as "Protected Space". http://www.blogpulse.com/papers/www2004gumbrecht.pdf (25.07.2014, no longer available).

Hauser, S. et al. (eds.) (2014). *Musterwandel – Sortenwandel: Aktuelle Tendenzen der diachronen Text(sorten)linguistik*: Peter Lang.

Hauser, S. (2014). Netze im Wandel – Wandel in Netzen: Diachrone Perspektiven auf die Vernetztheit von Textsorten. In S. Hauser et al. (eds.): *Musterwandel – Sortenwandel: Aktuelle Tendenzen der diachronen Text(sorten)linguistik:* Peter Lang, 275–312.

Heinemann, M. & W. Heinemann (2002). *Grundlagen der Textlinguistik: Interaktion – Text – Diskurs*. Tübingen: Max Niemeyer Verlag.

Heinemann, W. (2000a). Aspekte der Textsortendifferenzierung. In K. Brinker et al. (eds.): *Linguistics of Text and Conversation: An International Handbook of Contemporary Research:* Mouton de Gruyter, 523–546.

Heinemann, W. (2000b). Textsorte – Textmuster – Texttyp. In K. Brinker et al. (eds.): *Linguistics of Text and Conversation: An International Handbook of Contemporary Research:* Mouton de Gruyter, 507–523.

Heinemann, W. & D. Viehweger (1991). *Textlinguistik: Eine Einführung*. Tübingen: Max Niemeyer.

Hendrick, S. & L. Efimova (2004). In Search for a Virtual Settlement: An Exploration of Weblog Community Boundaries. http://tinyurl.com/hendrick2004 (28.12.2015).

Henn-Memmesheimer, B. & E. Eggers (2010). Inszenierung, Etablierung und Auflösung: Karriere einer grammatischen Konstruktion im Chat zwischen 2000 und 2010. http://www.mediensprache.net/networx/networx-57.pdf (28.12.2015).

Herring, S. (2003). Past, Present, and Future of Weblogs. vw.indiana.edu/talks04/herring.ppt (28.12.2015).

Herring, S. et al. (2004). Bridging the Gap: A Genre Analysis of Weblogs. http://tinyurl.com/herrscheidt04 (28.12.2015).

Herring, S. et al. (2006). A Longitudinal Content Analysis of Weblogs: 2003–2004. http://tinyurl.com/herring2006 (28.12.2015).

Herring, S. (2007). A Faceted Classification Scheme for Computer-Mediated Discourse. *Language@Internet* 4. http://www.languageatinternet.org/articles/2007/761/ (28.12.2015).

Herring, S. & J. C. Paolillo (2006). Gender and Genre Variation in Weblogs. *Journal of Sociolinguistics* 10 (4), 439–459. http://ella.slis.indiana.edu/~herring/jslx.pdf (28.12.2015).

Herring, S. C. et al. (2005). Weblogs as a Bridging Genre. *Information Technology & People* 18 (2), 142–171.

Heyd, T. (2008). *Email Hoaxes: Form, Function, Genre Ecology*. Amsterdam, Philadelphia: Benjamins.

Heyd, T. (2009). A Model for Describing 'New' and 'Old' Properties of CMC Genres: The Case of Digital Folklore. In J. Giltrow & D. Stein (eds.): *Genres in the Internet: Issues in the Theory of Genre*. Amsterdam: Benjamins, 239–262.

Hodkinson, P. (2006). Subcultural Blogging? Online Journals and Group Involvement among U. K. Goths. In A. Bruns & J. Jacobs (eds.): *Uses of Blogs*. New York: Peter Lang, 187–195.

Hoffmann, C. R. (2010). *From Monologue to Dialogue? Cohesive Interaction in Personal Weblogs*. Dissertation. Universität Augsburg, Augsburg.

Hollenbaugh, E. E. (2008). *Journaling for the World (Wide Web) to See: A Conceptual Model of Disclosure in Blogs*. Dissertation. Kent State University, Kent.

Hollenbaugh, E. E. (2010). Personal Journal Bloggers: Profiles of Disclosiveness. *Computers in Human Behavior* 26, 1657–1666.

Hollenbaugh, E. E. & M. K. Everett (2013). The Effects of Anonymity on Self-Disclosure in Blogs: An Application of the Online Disinhibition Effect. *Journal of Computer-Mediated Communication* 18 (3), 283–302.

Holly, W. (2006). Mit Worten sehen: Audiovisuelle Bedeutungskonstitution und Muster transkriptiver Logik in der Fernsehberichterstattung. *Deutsche Sprache* 34, 135–150.

Holly, W. (2009). Der Wort-Bild-Reißverschluss: Über die perfomative Dynamik audiovisueller Transkriptivität. In A. Linke & A. Deppermann (eds.): *Oberfläche und Performanz: Untersuchungen zur Sprache als dynamischer Gestalt*. Tübingen: Niemeyer, 389–406.

Holly, W. (2010). Besprochene Bilder – bebildertes Sprechen: Audiovisuelle Transkriptivität in Nachrichtenfilmen und Polit-Talkshows. In A. Deppermann & A. Linke (eds.): *Sprache intermedial: Stimme und Schrift, Bild und Ton*. Berlin: Walter de Gruyter, 359–382.

Holly, W. (2011a). Bildüberschreibungen: Wie Sprechtexte Nachrichtenfilme lesbar machen (und umgekehrt). In H. Diekmannshenke et al. (eds.): *Bildlinguistik: Theorien – Methoden – Fallbeispiele*. Berlin: E. Schmidt, 233–253.

Holly, W. (2011b). Medien, Kommunikationsformen, Textsortenfamilien. In S. Habscheid (ed.): *Textsorten, Handlungsmuster, Oberflächen: Linguistische Typologien der Kommunikation*. Berlin, New York: de Gruyter, 144–163.

Honneth, A. (1994). *Kampf um Anerkennung: Zur moralischen Grammatik sozialer Konflikte*. Frankfurt am Main: Suhrkamp.

Huffaker, D. A. & S. L. Calvert (2005). Gender, Identity, and Language Use in Teenage Blogs. *Journal of Computer-Mediated Communication* 10 (2). http://jcmc.indiana.edu/vol10/issue2/huffaker.html (28.12.2015).

Jäger, L. (2002). Transkriptivität: Zur medialen Logik der kulturellen Semantik. In L. Jäger & G. Stanitzek (eds.): *Transkribieren: Medien-Lektüre*. München: Fink, 19–41.

Java, A. et al. (2007). Why We Twitter: Understanding Microblogging Usage and Communities. http://tinyurl.com/javaetal2007 (28.12.2015).

Karlgren, J. (2011). Conventions and Mutual Expectations: Understanding Sources for Web Genres. In A. Mehler et al. (eds.): *Genres on the Web: Computational Models and Empirical Studies*. Dordrecht: Springer, 33–46.

Karlsson, L. (2006). Acts of Reading Diary Weblogs. *Human IT* 8 (2), 1–59. http://etjanst.hb.se/bhs/ith/2-8/lk.pdf (28.12.2015).

Keller, R. (1990). *Sprachwandel: Von der unsichtbaren Hand in der Sprache*. Tübingen: Francke.

Kendall, L. (2007). "Shout Into the Wind, and It Shouts Back": Identity and interactional tensions on LiveJournal. *First Monday* 12 (9). http://tinyurl.com/cfgj4yd (28.12.2015).

Kitzmann, A. (2003). That Different Place: Documenting the Self within Online Environments. *Biography* 26 (1), 48–65.

Kitzmann, A. (2004). *Saved from Oblivion: Documenting the Daily from Diaries to Web Cams*. New York: P. Lang.

Klemm, M. (2002). Wie hältst Du's mit dem Textbegriff? Pragmatische Antworten auf eine Gretchenfrage der (Text-)Linguistik. In U. Fix et al. (eds.): *Brauchen wir einen neuen Textbegriff? Antworten auf eine Preisfrage*. Frankfurt am Main: Peter Lang, 143–161.

Klemm, M. & S. Michel (2015). MediaCultureLinguistic Perspectives on Social TV: Questions and Desiderata of Analysing TV-Appropriation in Social Media. *10plus1: Living Linguistics* 1 (1), 49–56. http://tinyurl.com/klemmmichel2014 (28.12.2015).

Klemm, M. & H. Stöckl (2011). "Bildlinguistik": Standortbestimmung, Überblick, Forschungsdesiderate. In H. Diekmannshenke et al. (eds.): *Bildlinguistik: Theorien – Methoden – Fallbeispiele*. Berlin: E. Schmidt, 7–18.

Koch, P. & W. Oesterreicher (1985). Sprache der Nähe – Sprache der Distanz: Mündlichkeit und Schriftlichkeit im Spannungsfeld von Sprachtheorie und Sprachgeschichte. *Romanisches Jahrbuch* 36, 15–43.

Koch, P. & W. Oesterreicher (1994). Schriftlichkeit und Sprache. In H. Günther & O. Ludwig (eds.): *Schrift und Schriftlichkeit*. Berlin, New York: de Gruyter, 587–604.

Kohanyi, A. (2009). "The more I write, the better I write, and the better I feel about myself": Mood Variability and Mood Regulation in Student Journalists and Creative Writers. In S. B. Kaufman & J. C. Kaufman (eds.): *The Psychology of Creative Writing*. New York: CUP, 41–56.

Kress, G. R. (1998). Visual and Verbal Modes of Representation in Electronically Mediated Communication: The Potentials of New Forms of Text. In I. Snyder (ed.): *Page to Screen: Taking literacy into the electronic media*. London, New York: Routledge, 53–79.

Kress, G. R. & T. van Leeuwen (2001). *Reading Images: The Grammar of Visual Design*. London: Routledge.

Kumar, R. et al. (2004). On the Bursty Evolution of Blogspace. http://tinyurl.com/kumaretal04 (28.12.2015).

Lee, Carmen K. M. (2011). Micro-Blogging and Status Updates on Facebook: Texts and Practices. In C. Thurlow & K. R. Mroczek (eds.): *Digital Discourse: Language in the New Media*. Oxford: OUP, 110–128.

Lemke, J. L. (1999). Typology, Topology, Topography: Genre Semantics. http://tinyurl.com/lemke99 (28.12.2015).

Lenhart, A. & S. Fox (2006). Bloggers: A Portrait of the Internet's New Storytellers. http://tinyurl.com/cz9pclf (28.12.2015).

Levinson, S. C. (1988). Putting Linguistics on a Proper Footing: Explorations in Goffman's Concepts of Participation. In P. Drew & A. J. Wootton (eds.): *Erving Goffman: Exploring the Interaction Order*. Cambridge: Polity, 161–227.

Löbner, S. (2002). *Understanding Semantics*. London: OUP.

Lomborg, S. (2009). Navigating the Blogosphere: Towards a Genre-based Typlogoy of Weblogs. *First Monday* 14 (5). http://tinyurl.com/lomborg2009 (28.12.2015).

Lomborg, S. (2014). *Social Media, Social Genres: Making Sense of the Ordinary*. New York: Routledge.

Luginbühl, M. (2014a). Genre Profiles and Genre Change: The Case of TV News. In J. Androutsopoulos (ed.): *Mediatization and Sociolinguistic Change*. Berlin, Bostin: de Gruyter, 305–330.

Luginbühl, M. (2014b). *Medienkultur und Medienlinguistik: Komparative Textsortengeschichte(n) der amerikanischen „CBS Evening News" und der Schweizer „Tagesschau"*. Bern: Lang.

Luginbühl, M. (2015). Media Linguistics: On Mediality and Culturality. *10plus1: Living Linguistics* 1.

Lumsden, D. (2008). Kinds of Conversational Cooperation. *Journal of Pragmatics* 40, 1896–1908. http://tinyurl.com/lumsden2008 (28.12.2015).

Mahrt, M. & C. Puschmann (2012). Schnittstelle zur Öffentlichkeit oder virtueller Elfenbeinturm? Inhaltsanalytische Befunde zur Leserschaft von Wissenschaftsblogs. http://files.ynada.com/papers/schnittstelle.pdf, no longer available (28.12.2015).

Mangasser-Wahl, M. (2000). Roschs Prototypentheorie: Eine Entwicklung in drei Phasen. In M. Mangasser-Wahl (ed.): *Prototypentheorie in der Linguistik: Anwendungsbeispiele – Methodenreflexion – Perspektiven*. Tübingen: Stauffenburg Verlag, 15–31.

Marlow, C. (2004). Audience, structure and authority in the weblog community. Vortrag zur International Communication Association Conference. http://cameronmarlow.com/papers/audience-structure-and (28.12.2015).

Marx, K. & G. Weidacher (2014). *Internetlinguistik: Ein Lehr- und Arbeitsbuch*. Tübingen: Narr Francke Attempto.

Mauranen, A. (2013a). Hybridism, Edutainment, and Doubt: Science Blogging Finding Its Feet. *Nordic Journal of English Studies* 13 (1), 7–36 (28.12.2015).

Mauranen, A. (2013b). Why Take an Interest in Research Blogging? *The European English Messenger* 22 (1), 53–58.

Mayring, P. (2010). *Qualitative Inhaltsanalyse: Grundlagen und Techniken*. Weinheim: Beltz.

McNeill, L. (2003). Teaching an Old Genre New Tricks: The Diary on the Internet. *Biography* 26 (1), 24–47.

McNeill, L. (2005). Genre Under Construction: The Diary on the Internet. *Language@Internet* 2. http://www.languageatinternet.org/articles/2005/120 (28.12.2015).

McNeill, L. (2009). Brave New Genre, or Generic Colonialism? Debates over Ancestry in Internet Diaries. In J. Giltrow & D. Stein (eds.): *Genres in the Internet: Issues in the Theory of Genre*. Amsterdam, Philadelphia: Benjamins, 143–161.

Mehler, A. et al. (eds.) (2011). *Genres on the Web: Computational Models and Empirical Studies*. Dordrecht: Springer.

Meier, J. (2002). Zwischen Textphilologie, Literaturwissenschaft, Kulturwissenschaft und "neuen Medien": Interdisziplinäre Anmerkungen und Fragestellungen zum Textbegriff. In U. Fix et al. (eds.): *Brauchen wir einen neuen Textbegriff? Antworten auf eine Preisfrage*. Frankfurt am Main: Peter Lang, 83–92.

Meiler, M. (2013). Kommunikationsformenadressen oder: Prozeduren des Situationsvollzugs am Beispiel von Weblogs. *Zeitschrift für Angewandte Linguistik* 59 (2), 51–106.

Meindl, C. (2011). *Methodik für Linguisten: Eine Einführung in Statistik und Versuchsplanung*. Tübingen: Narr Francke Attempto.

Miller, C. (1984). Genre as Social Action. *Quarterly Journal of Speech* 70, 151–167. http://www4.ncsu.edu/~crmiller/Publications/MillerQJS84.pdf (28.12.2015).

Miller, C. (1994). Rhetorical Community: The Cultural Basis of Genre. In A. Freedman & P. Medway (eds.): *Genre and the New Rhetoric*. London, Bristol, PA: Taylor & Francis, 67–78.

Miller, C. & D. Shepherd (2004). Blogging as Social Action: A Genre Analysis of the Weblog. http://tinyurl.com/miller04 (28.12.2015).

Miller, C. & D. Shepherd (2009). Questions for genre theory from the blogosphere. In J. Giltrow & D. Stein (eds.): *Genres in the Internet: Issues in the Theory of Genre*. Amsterdam: Benjamins, 263–290.

Miller, H. (1995). The Presentation of Self in Electronic Life: Goffman on the Internet. http://www.dourish.com/classes/ics234cw04/miller2.pdf (28.12.2015).

Milroy, L. (1987). *Language and Social Networks*. Oxford: B. Blackwell.

Motsch, W. (2000). Handlungsstrukturen von Texten. In K. Brinker et al. (eds.): *Linguistics of Text and Conversation: An International Handbook of Contemporary Research:* Mouton de Gruyter, 414–422.

Myers, G. (2010). *The Discourse of Blogs and Wikis*. London: Continuum.

Nardi, B. et al. (2004a). Blogging as Social Activity, or, Would You Let 900 Million People Read Your Diary?. In J. Herbsleb & G. Olson (eds.): *Proceedings of the 2004 ACM conference on Computer-supported Cooperative Work*. New York: ACM, 222–231.

Nardi, B. et al. (2004b). Why We Blog. http://tinyurl.com/nardietal2004 (25.07.2014).

Newitz, A. (1995). Surplus Identity Online. *Bad Subjects* 18. http://bad.eserver.org/issues/1995/18/newitz.html (28.12.2015).

Nilsson [Hendrick], S. (2002). A Brief Overview of the Linguistic Attributes of the Blogosphere. http://tinyurl.com/hendrick2003 (28.12.2015, no longer available).

Nilsson [Hendrick], S. (2003). *The Function of Language to Facilitate and Maintain Social Networks in Research Weblogs*. Umeå Universitet.

Nöth, W. (2000a). Der Zusammenhang von Text und Bild. In K. Brinker et al. (eds.): *Linguistics of Text and Conversation: An International Handbook of Contemporary Research:* Mouton de Gruyter, 489–496.

Nöth, W. (2000b). *Handbuch der Semiotik*. Stuttgart: Metzler.

Paccagnella, L. (1997). Getting the Seat of Your Pants Dirty: Strategies for Ethnographic Research on Virtual Communities. *Journal of Computer-Mediated*

Communication 3 (1). http://jcmc.indiana.edu/vol3/issue1/paccagnella.html#s4 (28.12.2015).

Pennebaker, J. (1997). Writing about Emotional Experiences as a Therapeutic Process. *Psychological Science* 8 (3), 162–166. http://pss.sagepub.com/content/8/3/162.full.pdf+html (28.12.2015).

Pennebaker, J. & M. E. Francis (1996). Cognitive, Emotional, and Language Processes in Disclosure. *Cognition and Emotion* 10 (6), 601–626. http://tinyurl.com/penebakerfrancis (28.12.2015).

Pentrel, M. (2013). Usage, Status, and Function of Stand-Alone Ish. In A. Ammermann et al. (eds.): *Facets of Linguistics*. Frankfurt am Main: Peter Lang, 47–59.

Pentzold, C. et al. (2013). Online-mediale Texte: Kommunikationsformen, Affordancen, Interfaces. *Zeitschrift für germanistische Linguistik* 41 (1), 81–101.

Pfänder, S. & J. Wagner (2008). *La des/comunicacion y sus re/medios*. Buenos Aires: La Crujia.

Pflaeging, J. (2013). *On Visulalising Linguistic Theories: Potentials and Constraints of Transmodal Shifting from the Verbal to the Visual Mode*. Wissenschaftliche Hausarbeit zur Ersten Staatsprüfung für das Lehramt an Gymnasien. Martin-Luther-Universität, Halle-Wittenberg.

Pflaeging, J. (2015). "Things that Matter, Pass them on": 'ListSite' as Viral Online Genre. *10plus1: Living Linguistics* 1 (1), 156–181. http://tinyurl.com/pflaeging15 (28.12.2015).

Preece, J. et al. (2004). The Top Five Reasons for Lurking: Improving Community Experiences for Everyone. *Computers in Human Behavior* 20, 201–223.

Presch, G. (1991). Widersprüche zwischen Textfunktionen als Ausgangspunkt sozialgeschichtlicher Pragmalinguistik. In D. Busse (ed.): *Diachrone Semantik und Pragmatik: Untersuchungen zur Erklärung und Beschreibung des Sprachwandels*. Tübingen: M. Niemeyer, 83–100.

Püschel, U. (1997). "Puzzle-Texte" – Bemerkungen zum Textbegriff. In G. Antos et al. (eds.): *Die Zukunft der Textlinguistik: Traditionen, Transformationen, Trends*. Tübingen: Niemeyer, 27–41.

Puschmann, C. (2009). Diary or Megaphone? The Pragmatic Mode of Weblogs. http://ynada.com/pubs/diarymegaphone.pdf (28.12.2015, no longer available).

Puschmann, C. (2010). *The Corporate Blog as an Emerging Genre of Computer-mediated Communication: Features, Constraints, Discourse Situation*. Göttingen: Universitätsverlag Göttingen.

Puschmann, C. (2013). Blogging. In S. Herring et al. (eds.): *Pragmatics of Computer-mediated Communication*. Berlin: De Gruyter Mouton, 75–100.

Puschmann, C. & M. Mahrt (2012). Scholarly Blogging: A New Form of Publishing Online or Science Journalism 2.0?. In A. Tokar et al. (eds.): *Science and the Internet*. Düsseldorf: Düsseldorf University Press, 171–181.

Qian, H. & C. R. Scott (2007). Anonymity and Self-Disclosure on Weblogs. *Journal of Computer-Mediated Communication* 12 (4), 1428–1451. http://jcmc.indiana.edu/vol12/issue4/qian.html (28.12.2015).

Raible, W. (1996). Wie soll man Texte typisieren?. In S. Michaelis & D. Tophinke (eds.): *Texte - Konstitution, Verarbeitung, Typik*. München: LINCOM Europa, 59–72.

Raithel, J. (2008). *Quantitative Forschung: Ein Praxiskurs*. Wiesbaden: VS.

Reed, A. (2005). 'My Blog is Me': Texts and Persons in UK Online Journal Culture (and Anthropology). *Ethnos* 70 (2), 220–242.

Rehm, G. (2006). *Hypertextsorten: Definition – Struktur – Klassifikation*. Justus-Liebig-Universität Gießen, Gießen.

Rissanen, M. (1993). Preface. In M. Rissanen et al. (eds.): *Early English in the Computer Age: Explorations through the Helsinki Corpus*. Berlin, New York: Mouton de Gruyter, v-vii.

Rogers, E. M. (2003). *Diffusion of Innovations*. New York: Free Press.

Rolf, E. (2000). Textuelle Grundfunktionen. In K. Brinker et al. (eds.): *Linguistics of Text and Conversation: An International Handbook of Contemporary Research:* Mouton de Gruyter, 422–435.

Rosenberg, S. (2009). *Say Everything: How Blogging Began, What it's Becoming, and Why it Matters*. New York: Three Rivers Press.

Rosenberg, S. (2010). Postcript: Four Cases for the Persistence of Blogging. http://tinyurl.com/23ccksb (28.12.2015).

Runco, M. A. (2009). Writing as an Interaction with Ideas. In S. B. Kaufman & J. C. Kaufman (eds.): *The Psychology of Creative Writing*. New York: CUP, 180–209.

Sandig, B. (2000). Text als prototypisches Konzept. In M. Mangasser-Wahl (ed.): *Prototypentheorie in der Linguistik: Anwendungsbeispiele – Methodenreflexion – Perspektiven*. Tübingen: Stauffenburg Verlag, 93–112.

Sandig, B. (2006). *Textstilistik des Deutschen*. Berlin, New York: W. de Gruyter.

Santini, M. et al. (2011). Riding the Rough Waves of Genre on the Web: Concepts and Research Questions. In A. Mehler et al. (eds.): *Genres on the Web: Computational Models and Empirical Studies*. Dordrecht: Springer, 3–30.

Scheidt, L. A. (2006). Adolescent Diary Weblogs and the Unseen Audience. In D. Buckingham & R. Willet (eds.): *Digital Generations: Children, Young People, and New Media*. Mahwah, N.J: Lawrence Erlbaum Associates, 193–210.

Schiano, D. et al. (2004). Blogging by the Rest of Us. http://tinyurl.com/schiano04 (28.12.2015, no longer available).

Schildhauer, P. (forthc.). Blogs in der Krise? Zum Einfluss Sozialer Netzwerkseiten auf die Textsorte Personal Weblog. In E. M. Eckkrammer et al. (eds.): *Medienlinguistik 3.0: Formen und Wirkung von Textsorten im Zeitalter des Social Web*. Berlin: Frank & Thimme.

Schildhauer, P. (2013). The Textual Functions of Personal Weblogs: Stability, Diversity, and Change. In A. Ammermann et al. (eds.): *Facets of Linguistics*. Frankfurt am Main: Peter Lang, 117–130.

Schildhauer, P. (2014). *Textsorten im Internet zwischen Wandel und Konstanz: Eine diachrone Untersuchung der Textsorte Personal Weblog*. Dissertation. Martin-Luther-Universität, Halle-Wittenberg.

Schildhauer, P. (2015). Blogging Our Way to Digital Literacies? A Critical View on Blogging in Foreign Language Classrooms. *10plus1: Living Linguistics* 1 (1), 182–195. http://tinyurl.com/schildhauer15 (28.12.2015).

Schlobinski, P. (2001). *knuddel - zurueckknuddel - dich ganzdollknuddel*: Inflektive und Inflektivkonstruktionen im Deutschen. *Zeitschrift für germanistische Linguistik* 29 (2), 192–218.

Schlobinski, P. & T. Siever (2005a). Editorial zum Projekt "Sprachliche und textuelle Aspekte in Weblogs". In P. Schlobinski & T. Siever (eds.): *Sprachliche und textuelle Merkmale in Weblogs: Ein internationales Projekt*. Hannover: networx, 8–29.

Schlobinski, P. & T. Siever (2005b). Sprachliche und textuelle Merkmale in deutschen Weblogs. In P. Schlobinski & T. Siever (eds.): *Sprachliche und textuelle Merkmale in Weblogs: Ein internationales Projekt*. Hannover: networx, 52–85.

Schlobinski, P. & T. Siever (eds.) (2005c). *Sprachliche und textuelle Merkmale in Weblogs: Ein internationales Projekt*. Hannover: networx.

Schmidt, J. (2009). Weblogs: Formen und Konsequenzen ihrer Nutzung. In S. Moraldo (ed.): *Internet.kom: Neue Sprach- und Kommunikationsformen im World Wide Web*. Rom: ARACNE, 157–180.

Schmitz, U. (2010). Schrift an Bild im World Wide Web. Articulirte Pixel und die schweifende Unbestimmtheit des Vorstellens. In A. Deppermann & A. Linke (eds.): *Sprache intermedial: Stimme und Schrift, Bild und Ton*. Berlin: Walter de Gruyter, 383–418.

Schmitz, U. (2011). Sehflächenforschung: Eine Einführung. In H. Diekmannshenke et al. (eds.): *Bildlinguistik: Theorien – Methoden – Fallbeispiele*. Berlin: E. Schmidt, 23–42.

Schryer, C. (1993). Records as Genre. *Written Communication* 10, 200–234. http://wcx.sagepub.com/content/10/2/200.full.pdf (28.12.2015).

Schwartz-Shea, P. (2006). Judging Quality: Evaluative Criteria and Epistemic Communities. In D. Yanow & P. Schwartz-Shea (eds.): *Interpretation and Method: Empirical Research Methods and the Interpretive Turn*. Armonk, N.Y: M. E. Sharpe, 89–113.

Searle, J. R. (1982). *Ausdruck und Bedeutung: Untersuchungen zur Sprechakttheorie*. Frankfurt am Main: Suhrkamp.

Searle, J. R. (1999). *Mind, Language and Society: Philosophy in the Real World*. New York: Basic Books.

Serfaty, V. (2004). *The Mirror and the Veil: An Overview of American Online Diaries and Blogs*. Amsterdam: Rodopi.

Sexton, J. D. & J. Pennebaker (2009). The Healing Powers of Expressive Writing. In S. B. Kaufman & J. C. Kaufman (eds.): *The Psychology of Creative Writing*. New York: CUP, 264–273.

Siefkes, M. (2015). How Semiotic Modes Work Together in Multimodal Texts: Defining and Representing Intermodal Relations. *10plus1: Living Linguistics* 1 (1), 113–131. http://tinyurl.com/siefkes15 (28.12.2015).

Sinclair, J. (2004). Corpus and Text: Basic Principles. http://tinyurl.com/7j5u9rb (28.12.2015).

Sollie, D. L. & J. L. Fischer (1985). Sex-Role Orientation, Intimacy of Topic, and Target Person Differences in Self-Disclosure Among Women. *Sex Roles* 12 (9/10), 917–929. http://tinyurl.com/solliefischer (28.12.2015).

Stefanone, M. A. & C.-Y. Jang (2008). Writing for Friends and Family: The Interpersonal Nature of Blogs. *Journal of Computer-Mediated Communication* 13 (1), 123–140. http://jcmc.indiana.edu/vol13/issue1/stefanone.html (28.12.2015).

Stegbauer, C. (2000). Begrenzungen und Strukturen internetbasierter Kommunikationsgruppen. In Caja Thimm (ed.): *Soziales im Netz: Sprache, Beziehungen und Kommunikationskulturen im Internet*. Wiesbaden: Opladen, 18–38.

Steinseifer, M. (2011). Die Typologisierung multimodaler Kommunikationsangebote: Am Beispiel der visuellen Aspekte seitenbasierter Dokumente. In S. Habscheid (ed.): *Textsorten, Handlungsmuster, Oberflächen: Linguistische Typologien der Kommunikation*. Berlin, New York: de Gruyter, 164–189.

Stöckl, H. (2004a). *Die Sprache im Bild – das Bild in der Sprache: Zur Verknüpfung von Sprache und Bild im massenmedialen Text*. Berlin, New York: de Gruyter.

Stöckl, H. (2004b). In Between Modes: Language and Image in Printed Media. In E. Eija Ventola et al. (eds.): *Perspectives on Multimodality*. Amsterdam: Benjamins, 9–30.

Stöckl, H. (2006). Zeichen, Text und Sinn: Theorie und Praxis der multimodalen Textanalyse. In E. M. Eckkrammer & G. Held (eds.): *Textsemiotik: Studien zu multimodalen Texten*. Frankfurt am Main: Peter Lang, 11–36.

Stöckl, H. (2010). Textsortenentwicklung und Textverstehen als Metamporphosen – Am Beispiel der Werbung. In H. Stöckl & C. Grösslinger (eds.): *Mediale Transkodierungen: Metamorphosen zwischen Sprache, Bild und Ton*. Heidelberg: Winter, 145–172.

Storrer, A. (2001). Getippte Gespräche oder dialogische Texte? Zur kommunikationstheoretischen Einordnung der Chat-Kommunikation. In Andrea Lehr et al. (ed.): *Sprache im Alltag: Beiträge zu neuen Perspektiven in der Linguistik*. Berlin, New York: Walter de Gruyter, 439–465.

Swales, J. M. (1990). *Genre analysis: English in Academic and Research Settings*. Cambridge: CUP.

Thaler, V. (2007). Mündlichkeit, Schriftlichkeit, Synchronität: Eine Analyse alter und neuer Konzepte zur Klassifizierung neuer Kommunikationsformen. *Zeitschrift für germanistische Linguistik* 35 (1–2), 146–181.

The Internet Archive (2011). Frequently Asked Questions: The Wayback Machine. http://tinyurl.com/bffthy (28.12.2015).

van Dijck, J. (2004). Composing the Self: Of Diaries and Lifelogs. *fibreculture* 3. http://tinyurl.com/vandijck (28.12.2015).

Viégas, F. B. (2005). Bloggers' Expectations of Privacy and Accountability: An Initial Survey. *Journal of Computer-Mediated Communication* 10 (3). http://jcmc.indiana.edu/vol10/issue3/viegas.html (28.12.2015).

Winer, D. (2001). The history of weblogs. http://www.userland.com/theHistoryOfWeblogs (28.12.2015).

Winer, D. (2003a). RSS 2.0 Specification. http://cyber.law.harvard.edu/rss/rss.html (28.12.2015).

Winer, D. (2003b). What makes a weblog a weblog? http://tinyurl.com/winer03b (28.12.2015).

Winer, D. (2004). RSS History. http://tinyurl.com/winer04 (28.12.2015).

Yang, J. (2006). *The Rough Guide to Blogging*. London: Penguin.

Yus, F. (2011). *Cyberpragmatics: Internet-mediated Communication in Context*. Amsterdam: Benjamins.

Żebrowska, E. (2013). *Text – Bild – Hypertext*. Frankfurt am Main: Peter Lang.

Zimbardo, P. G. & R. J. Gerrig (2008). *Psychologie*. München: Pearson Studium.

Hallesche Sprach- und Textforschung
Language and Text Studies
Recherches linguistiques et textuelles

Herausgegeben von / Edited by / Dirigée par Alexander Brock und Annette Schiller

Band 1 Annette Schiller: Die présentatifs im heutigen Französisch. Eine funktionale Studie ihrer Vielfalt. 1992.

Band 2 Gertrud Bense (Hrsg.): Diachronie – Kontinuität – Impulse. Sprachwissenschaftliches Kolloquium Halle 1992. 1994.

Band 3 Wolfgang Boeck (Hrsg.): Sprache, Literatur und Landeskunde slavischer Völker. Funktionale Aspekte in der Beschreibung und Didaktik. 1994.

Band 4 Gertrud Bense (Hrsg.): Kommunikation und Grammatik. 1996.

Band 5 Gisela Hermann-Brennecke / Dietmar Schneider (Hrsg.): Dona Anglica. 120 Jahre Anglistik in Halle. 1997.

Band 6 Max Hans-Jürgen Mattusch: Vielsprachigkeit: Fluch oder Segen für die Menschheit? Zu Fragen einer europäischen und globalen Fremdsprachenpolitik. 1999.

Band 7 Christiane Schiller: Bilinguismus. Zur Darstellung eines soziolinguistischen Phänomens in der Literatur. Dargestellt an Beispielen der regionalen Literatur Preußisch-Litauens: Hermann Sudermann *Litauische Geschichten*, Ieva Simonaityte *Vilius Karalius*. 2000.

Band 8 Gertrud Bense: „Giedojam taw – Wir singen dir". Zur Textgeschichte der preußisch-litauischen Gesangbücher im 18. Jahrhundert. Mit besonderer Berücksichtigung der Liedersammlung von Fabian Ulrich Glaser (1688–1747) und ihrem Umfeld. 2001.

Band 9 Gertrud Bense / Gerhard Meiser / Edeltraud Werner (Hrsg.): August Friedrich Pott. Beiträge der Halleschen Tagung anlässlich des zweihundertsten Geburtstages von August Friedrich Pott (1802–1887). 2005.

Band 10 Julia Balakina: Anglicisms in Russian and German Blogs. A Comparative Analysis. 2011.

Band 11 Thomas Bremer /Annette Schiller (Hrsg.): Dialekt und Standardsprache in Italien und Europa. Edeltraud Werner zum 60. Geburtstag. 2012.

Band 12 Anne Ammermann / Alexander Brock / Jana Pflaeging / Peter Schildhauer (eds.): Facets of Linguistics. Proceedings of the 14th Norddeutsches Linguistisches Kolloquium 2013 in Halle an der Saale. 2013.

Band 13 Anja Neuber: Perspektiven des Friaulischen. Eine soziolinguistische Untersuchung am Beispiel junger Erwachsener. 2015.

Band 14 Peter Schildhauer: The Personal Weblog. A Linguistic History. 2016.

www.peterlang.com

www.ingramcontent.com/pod-product-compliance
Ingram Content Group UK Ltd.
Pitfield, Milton Keynes, MK11 3LW, UK
UKHW041825100926
8556IPUK00002B/35

9 783631 662748